THE
FIRST INDUSTRIAL
REVOLUTION

$$\frac{257}{233} \text{ inspect}$$

279 edjo... ...

child labor

1461

THE
FIRST INDUSTRIAL
REVOLUTION

PHYLLIS DEANE

PROFESSOR OF ECONOMIC HISTORY IN THE UNIVERSITY OF CAMBRIDGE
AND FELLOW OF NEWNHAM COLLEGE

SECOND EDITION

The right of the
University of Cambridge
to print and sell
all manner of books
was granted by
Henry VIII in 1534.
The University has printed
and published continuously
since 1584.

CAMBRIDGE UNIVERSITY PRESS

CAMBRIDGE

NEW YORK   NEW ROCHELLE

MELBOURNE   SYDNEY

Published by the Press Syndicate of the University of Cambridge
The Pitt Building, Trumpington Street, Cambridge CB2 1RP
32 East 57th Street, New York, NY 10022, USA
10 Stamford Road, Oakleigh, Melbourne 3166, Australia

First published 1965
Second edition 1979
Reprinted 1982, 1983, 1984, 1986, 1987

Printed in Great Britain at the
University Press, Cambridge

Library of Congress Cataloguing in Publication Data
Deane, Phyllis.
The first industrial revolution.

Bibliography: p.
Includes indexes.
1. Great Britain—Industries. 2. Great Britain—
Economic conditions—1760–1860. I. Title.
HC254.5.D3 1979 338′.0941 78–26388

ISBN 0 521 22667 8 hard covers
ISBN 0 521 29609 9 paperback
(First edition ISBN 0 521 04802 8 hard covers
ISBN 0 521 09863 5 paperback)

CONTENTS

PREFACE TO THE FIRST
EDITION

In recent years economists and policy makers have become increasingly concerned with questions of economic growth, and in particular with the problem of identifying the route by which today's poor countries might reach the high standards of living presently enjoyed by the industrial societies. Historians too have been impelled by the urgent contemporary problem to analyse their material in a new way, to apply the concepts of the economic-growth theorists and to seek the explanations underlying the relatively few cases of successful industrialization.

This book, which originated in a course of lectures given for undergraduates reading for Part I of the Cambridge Economics Tripos, is a product of the current interest in economic development. It is a study of the development of the British economy over the period 1750–1850 when the first industrial revolution took place and modern economic growth effectively began. The fact that the crucial break-through was achieved spontaneously and without the advantages of either planning or foresight seems to give it a special relevance to the problems of countries which are currently finding it difficult to begin or to sustain a process of industrialization. This is an attempt to apply the concepts and techniques of development economics to a vital section of the historical record.

Except in so far as it embodies some of the results of an inquiry into British economic growth which Dr W. A. Cole and I carried out at the Department of Applied Economics some years ago, it is not the product of original research. It draws heavily on the work of the now numerous economic and social historians who have been looking at the past through development spectacles, as well as on the classic histories of the industrial revolution; so much so indeed that this book is little more than a synthesis of their ideas and researches and the debt which it owes to them is inadequately reflected in the many direct quotations and footnote references.

There are four individuals to whom I should like to take this opportunity of expressing my gratitude more specifically, however. They are Professor Simon Kuznets, who first aroused my interest in the historical analysis of economic development; Professor T. S. Ashton, whose insight into this period of British history has coloured my own thinking to an immeasurable extent; Professor David Joslin, who read and commented on a very early draft; and Miss Edith Whetham, who put me right on some matters of agricultural history. It goes without saying that they are all innocent of any errors of fact, interpretation or analysis that I have committed here.

Cambridge, June 1965   P.M.D.

PREFACE TO THE SECOND EDITION

My aim in revising this book has been to take account of the major new knowledge and ideas on the industrial revolution emerging from the research results which have been published in the (roughly) fifteen years since the first edition went to press. The new knowledge has made it possible to write with more confidence or precision on a number of issues where paucity of evidence had led me to tentative, vague or misconceived conclusions. Lively recent debates in the journals and the criticisms I have got from reviews, colleagues and students (not only my own, but also from students who have been good enough to write to me on points of detail) have stimulated me to alter, or to put a different slant on, judgments which now seem to me to have been ill formulated. Apart from such rewritten passages, the major changes involved in the revision have taken the form of expanding the text in areas where we now know more, or where other questions have become of interest, and of incorporating references to recent publications. Those who are familiar with the first edition will find that the section which has been most extensively altered is the updated guide to future reading. In an effort to keep this deliberately introductory bibliography to a reasonable length, I have made way for new references by omitting some of the seminal items recorded in the first edition, knowing that they are fully referred to in the more recent sources, and I have generally omitted references to articles reprinted in books of readings on controversial topics already included.

Cambridge, July 1978   P.M.D.

CHAPTER I

THE STARTING POINT

It is now almost an axiom of the theory of economic development that the route to affluence lies by way of an industrial revolution. A continuous—some would say 'self-sustaining'—process of economic growth, whereby (wars and natural disasters apart) each generation can confidently expect to enjoy higher levels of production and consumption than its predecessors, is open only to those nations which industrialize. The striking disparity between the standards of living of the inhabitants of the so-called developed or advanced countries of the mid twentieth century and the standards prevailing in today's underdeveloped or backward countries is essentially due to the fact that the former have industrialized and the latter have not.

This does not imply that there is some definite process or event called an industrial revolution which takes the same form in all countries in which it occurs. But it does imply that there are certain identifiable changes in the methods and characteristics of economic organization which, taken together, constitute a development of the kind which we would describe as an industrial revolution. These include the following related changes: (1) widespread and systematic application of modern science and empirical knowledge to the process of production for the market; (2) specialization of economic activity directed towards production for national and international markets rather than for family or parochial use; (3) movement of population from rural to urban communities; (4) enlargement and depersonalization of the typical unit of production so that it comes to be based less on the family or the tribe and more on the corporate or public enterprise; (5) movement of labour from activities concerned with the production of primary products to the production of manufactured goods and services; (6) intensive and extensive use of capital resources as a substitute for and complement to human effort; (7) emergence of new social and occupational classes determined by ownership of or relationship to the means of production other than land, namely capital.

These interrelated changes, if they develop together and to a sufficient degree, constitute an industrial revolution. They have always been associated with a growth of population and with an increase in the annual volume of goods and services produced.

The first industrial revolution occurred in Great Britain and is of particular interest in that it occurred spontaneously, without the government assistance which has been characteristic of most succeeding industrial revolutions. Exactly when it took place is a matter of controversy. The first economic historian to discuss the British experience of industrialization in terms of this concept of a specific revolution was Arnold Toynbee, who delivered a course of lectures on the subject in the University of Oxford in the year 1880/1.[1] He took his starting-point as 1760 and for about half a century this view of the matter went unchallenged, until Professor Nef, the American historian, questioned the significance of the historical boundary it implied. He stressed the essential continuity of history and traced the beginnings of large-scale industry and technological change back to the sixteenth and early seventeenth centuries. According to Nef: 'The rise of industrialism in Great Britain can be more properly regarded as a long process stretching back to the middle of the sixteenth century and coming down to the final triumph of the industrial state towards the end of the nineteenth, than as a sudden phenomenon associated with the late eighteenth and early nineteenth centuries.'[2]

More recently, new interpretations have emerged from the work of economic historians, who have begun to explore and depend more heavily on the statistical evidence bearing upon the rate of economic growth. Because the overseas trade records constitute the best and most comprehensive set of statistical series covering the whole of the eighteenth century, the movements in foreign trade have largely conditioned the statistical interpretation of the industrial revolution. Paul Mantoux,

[1] Toynbee died in 1883 at the age of thirty but his lectures had made a tremendous impact on his pupils and in 1884 they published his *Lectures on the Industrial Revolution in England* on the basis of his and their notes of the lectures he gave in Oxford in 1880/1.

[2] J. U. Nef, *Economic History Review* (1934), reprinted in E. M. Carus-Wilson, *Essays in Economic History* (1954), vol. I, p. 105.

writing in the 1920's, had already pointed out that the curves of imports and exports and tonnage cleared from British ports 'rise almost vertically towards the end' of the eighteenth century, that is, following the slump of 1781 occasioned by the American War.[1] Professor Ashton has developed this theme:

After 1782 almost every available statistical series of industrial output reveals a sharp upward turn. More than half the growth in the shipments of coal and the mining of copper, more than three-quarters of the increase of broad cloths, four-fifths of that of printed cloth and nine-tenths of the exports of cotton goods were concentrated in the last eighteen years of the century.[2]

Professor Hoffmann, the German economist who compiled an index of industrial output for Britain, concluded that 'the year 1780 is the approximate date at which the annual percentage rate of industrial growth was first greater than two, a level at which it remained for more than a century'.[3]

The current convention then is to date the first industrial revolution from the 1780's when the statistics of British international trade show a significant upward movement. Following this convention, Professor W. Rostow has suggested an even more precise historical boundary and has developed the theory that the period 1783–1802 was 'the great watershed in the life of modern societies'. This is the period which he defined as the 'take-off into sustained growth' for the British economy, the interval when the forces of modernization made their decisive breakthrough and set up an automatic and irreversible process of economic growth.[4]

At one extreme then we have Professor Nef tracing the beginnings of the industrial revolution back to the middle of the sixteenth century, to the new capitalistic industries of Elizabethan times: at the other extreme we have Professor Rostow's dramatic compression of the essential transformation into a couple of decades at the end of the eighteenth century. The debate goes on. But fundamentally the differences between the

---

[1] Paul Mantoux, *The Industrial Revolution in the Eighteenth Century*, 12th ed. (1961), with introduction by T. S. Ashton.

[2] T. S. Ashton, *The Eighteenth Century* (1955), p. 125; see also Asa Briggs, *The Age of Improvement* (1959), p. 18.

[3] W. Hoffmann, *British Industry 1700–1950* (1955), p. 30.

[4] W. W. Rostow, *The Stages of Economic Growth* (1960). But see Rostow's later study, *The World Economy* (1978), where the British take-off is dated 1783–1830 and the 1783–1802 phase is characterized as an 'initial surge'.

protagonists in the debate are differences of emphasis rather than substance. No one would deny that the period which began around the middle of the eighteenth century was a period in which important and far-reaching changes took place in the characteristic tempo of economic life in Britain, and that these constituted a transformation that was, in a sense, the prototype of the transition from pre-industrial to industrial forms of economic organization which is everywhere a necessary condition of modern economic development. Those who, like Nef, choose to emphasize the underlying continuity of history will trace the origins of the process of industrialization back to earlier centuries. Those who, like Rostow, prefer to focus on the significant discontinuities of history will stress the revolutionary character of the changes taking place in relatively short periods of time and will look for the crucial watersheds, the irreversible upturns in the statistical series. These are differences in methods of historical analysis and interpretation rather than disputes about what actually happened in history. To understand the process of economic change one needs to take both approaches into account, and to recognize the significant discontinuities in the 'seamless web' of history.

If we take our starting-point as the middle of the eighteenth century, then, we begin with pre-industrial Britain, though it is evident that the process of industrialization had already begun. Within the following century a revolution took place in the social and economic life of Britain which transformed the physical appearance of the land and established a totally different way of living and working for the mass of its people. This first industrial revolution is of special interest not only to historians but also to students of modern economic development. For it represented the spontaneous beginnings of the process which created the affluent societies of today, a way of escape from poverty which roughly two-thirds of the inhabitants of the modern world, the people of the underdeveloped countries, are now desperately trying to discover for themselves.

What kind of economy, then, was the pre-industrial English economy of the mid eighteenth century? How like was it to the pre-industrial countries of the present day in, say, Asia, or Africa or South America? Can we assess the characteristics which distinguished it from its own developed form or from the industrialized countries of the mid nineteenth century? A list

of the characteristics of twentieth-century pre-industrial economies would stress their extreme poverty, their slow rate of
economic development, their unskilled, unspecialized labour
force and their regional disparities—that is, the wide differences
in standards of living or of economic development as between
one region and the next. How far were these factors—poverty,
stagnation, dependence on agriculture, lack of specialization
or of regional integration—characteristic of eighteenth-
century England?

I. POVERTY

First, then, how poor were the people of eighteenth-century
England?

One way of measuring poverty on a national scale is to
express it in terms of national-income data. The national
income of a country represents the sum total of the goods and
services bought by or produced by its people during a given
year. Since a community's income depends on the value of what
it produces and its purchasing power depends on its income,
there are in effect three ways of calculating the national income:
(1) by aggregating all the incomes earned by its residents, (2)
by valuing all the goods and services produced by them, and
(3) by summing their expenditures. In principle, after making
the kind of adjustments required to eliminate double counting
(e.g. counting only once the goods that are embodied in the
production of other goods produced within the same year), these
three ways of calculating the national income must lead to the
same result, which is a convenient measure of the total value
of a nation's economic activity. If we divide the national income,
thus calculated, by the population sharing in it, we get an
average which can be regarded as an index of the prevailing
level of productivity or of living standards.

Clearly any calculation of this kind which is based on
eighteenth-century statistics must be very rough indeed. But if
we are prepared to rely on the national-income calculations
made by reputable observers living at the periods in which we
are interested we can establish some benchmarks which may at
any rate indicate the orders of magnitude involved. One of the
earliest estimates of national income made for England and
Wales was that compiled by Gregory King at the end of the
seventeenth century to illustrate the economic strength of the

TABLE 1. *A Scheme of the Income & Expence of the several Families of England Calculated for the Year 1688*

Number of Families	Ranks Degrees Titles and Qualifications	Heads per Family	Number of Persons	Yearly Income per Family (£ s.)		Totall of the Estates or Income (£)	Yearly Income per Head (£ s.)		Expence per Head (£ s. d.)			Increase per Head (£ s. d.)			Totall Increase per annum (£)
160	Temporall Lords	40	6,400	2800	0	448,000	70	0	60	0	0	10	0	0	64,000
26	Spirituall Lords	20	520	1300	0	33,800	65	0	55	0	0	10	0	0	5,200
800	Baronets	16	12,800	880	0	704,000	55	0	51	0	0	4	0	0	51,200
600	Knights	13	7,800	650	0	390,000	50	0	46	0	0	4	0	0	31,200
3,000	Esquires	10	30,000	450	0	1,200,000	45	0	42	0	0	3	0	0	90,000
12,000	Gentlemen	8	96,000	280	0	2,880,000	35	0	32	10	0	2	10	0	240,000
5,000	Persons in offices	8	40,000	240	0	1,200,000	30	0	27	0	0	3	0	0	120,000
5,000	Persons in offices	6	30,000	120	0	600,000	20	0	18	0	0	2	0	0	60,000
2,000	Merchants & Traders by Sea	8	16,000	400	0	800,000	50	0	40	0	0	10	0	0	160,000
8,000	Merchants & Traders by Sea	6	48,000	200	0	1,600,000	33	0	28	0	0	5	0	0	240,000
10,000	Persons in the Law	7	70,000	140	0	1,400,000	20	0	17	0	0	3	0	0	210,000
2,000	Clergy Men	6	12,000	60	0	120,000	10	0	9	0	0	1	0	0	12,000
8,000	Clergy Men	5	40,000	45	0	360,000	9	0	8	0	0	1	0	0	40,000
40,000	Freeholders	7	280,000	84	0	3,360,000	12	0	11	0	0	1	0	0	280,000
140,000	Freeholders	5	700,000	50	0	7,000,000	10	0	9	10	0		10	0	350,000
150,000	Farmers	5	750,000	44	0	6,600,000	8	15	8	10	0		5	0	187,000
16,000	Persons in Sciences & Lib. arts	5	80,000	60	0	960,000	12	0	11	10	0		10	0	40,000
40,000	Shopkeepers & Tradesmen	4½	180,000	45	0	1,800,000	10	0	9	10	0		10	0	90,000
60,000	Artizans & handycrafts	4	240,000	40	0	2,400,000	10	0	9	10	0		10	0	120,000
5,000	Naval officers	4	20,000	80	0	400,000	20	0	18	0	0	2	0	0	40,000
4,000	Military officers	4	16,000	60	0	240,000	15	0	14	0	0	1	0	0	16,000
511,586		5¼	2,675,520	67	0	34,495,800	12	18	12	0	0		18	0	2,447,100

									Decrease
50,000	Common Seamen...	3	150,000	20 0	7 0	7 10 0	10 0	1,000,000	75,000
364,000	Labouring People & outservants	3½	1,275,000	15 0	4 10	4 12 0	2 0	5,460,000	127,500
400,000	Cottagers & Paupers	3¼	1,300,000	6 10	2 0	2 5 0	5 0	2,000,000	325,000
35,000	Common Souldiers	2	70,000	14 0	7 0	7 10 0	10 0	490,000	35,000
849,000		3¼	2,795,000	10 10	3 5	3 9 0	4 0	8,950,000	562,000
30,000	Vagrants		30,000		2 0	3 0 0	0 0 1	60,000	60,000
849,000		3¼	2,825,000	10 10	3 3	3 7 6	4 6	9,010,000	622,000
	So the General Account is			£ s.	£ s.	£ s. d.	£ s. d.	£	£
511,586	Increasing the wealth of the Kingdom...	5¼	2,675,520	67 0	12 18	12 0 0	18 0	34,495,800	2,447,100
849,000	Decreasing the wealth of the Kingdom...	3¼	2,825,000	10 10	3 3	3 7 6	4 6	9,010,000	622,000
360,586	Neat Totalls	4 4/20	5,500,520	£32 0	£7 18	£7 11 3	£0 6 9	£43,505,800	£1,825,100

SOURCE: Gregory King, *Natural and Political Observations and Conclusions upon the State and Condition of England*, reprinted in *Two Tracts by Gregory King*, ed. George E. Barnett (Baltimore, 1936).

economy at the time of the Glorious Revolution:[1] it is repro-
duced as Table 1. The next systematic attempt of this kind, so
far as we know, was Joseph Massie's list of the numbers and
earnings of different classes of the community, constructed for
a more limited purpose—that of showing how the burden of a
tax on sugar was distributed over the nation.[2] Finally, at the
end of the eighteenth century and at the beginning of the
nineteenth century, Pitt's income tax stimulated a number of
similar calculations of national income designed to assess the
taxable capacity of the country.[3]

If we take these estimates of contemporaries as our data, and
adjust them to fit modern concepts of what is contained in the
national income, we may deduce that the national income of
England and Wales at the end of the seventeenth century
amounted to a total which suggests an average of between £8
and £9 per annum per head of the population: in the 1750's
it was probably between £12 and £13, again per head of the
total population: at the end of the eighteenth century the
corresponding average was about £22. Of course it is difficult
to understand what the money incomes mean in real terms
without knowing what they would buy. Prices change and the
value of money alters. If we could measure the extent to which
prices have changed over the past two to three hundred years
we ought to be able to see eighteenth-century incomes in terms
of today's money values. Unfortunately, the persistent inflation
of prices since the Second World War and the accelerated
inflation which set in at the end of the 1960's has made of today's
values a highly ephemeral notion. An attempt to trace the
course of the price indices for the period between say, 1754 and
1954 indicates that the general level of prices multiplied roughly
six times in two centuries: but between 1956 and 1976 U.K.
prices more than trebled in just two decades while in some

[1] King's careful table of the income and expenditure of each social group in England
and Wales in 1688 is deservedly famous and has been reprinted many times. The
original tract from which it is extracted appears in full in *Two Tracts by Gregory King*,
edited with an introduction by George E. Barnett, Baltimore (1936). It is reclassified
in modern form as a set of social accounts in Phyllis Deane and W. A. Cole, *British
Economic Growth 1688–1959* (1962).
[2] P. Mathias, 'The Social Structure in the Eighteenth Century: a Calculation by
Joseph Massie', *Economic History Review*, vol. x (August 1957).
[3] Phyllis Deane, 'The Implications of Early National Income Estimates for the
Measurement of Long-term Economic Growth in the United Kingdom', *Economic
Development and Cultural Change* (1955).

contemporary newly developing countries the price rise was even more spectacular.

It may nevertheless be interesting to draw a rough comparison between estimates of the English national income level on the eve of the first industrial revolution and the corresponding levels for today's third-world countries beginning their first great spurt of industrialization. Applying the evidence of the price indices we might conclude that an average of £12 per head per annum for the early 1750's should be inflated to a level of about £90 to give an order of magnitude for the early 1960's. It would appear then that this represents a relatively high national income level by comparison with mid-twentieth-century newly-developing countries: the average for Nigeria in the early 1960's has been put at about a third of this figure and that for India lower still. Probably the average calculated for some of today's Central and South American countries came closer to the estimated level for mid eighteenth-century England: the average for Brazil in 1961, for example, has been put at about £95 and for Mexico £105.[1]

These rough calculations involving imprecise comparisons across wide distances of time and space are obviously crude and impressionistic. They certainly do not provide useful *measures* of relative living standards. All that we can reasonably deduce from them is that the level of economic development reached by England on the threshold of the first industrial revolution was distinctly higher than that prevailing in the developing countries of South Asia and Africa when they began to industrialize rapidly. This deduction is supported by other sorts of evidence for the view that pre-industrial England was more favourably situated than most mid twentieth-century under-developed economies. There is, for example, the evidence that the English economy was producing a substantial surplus of the nation's staple food. In 1750 the corn export was equivalent to the subsistence requirements of roughly a quarter of the total population of England. If India had a food surplus of this relative magnitude her foreign exchange problems would surely shrink. In 1751, to take another example, more than 7 million gallons of British spirits were charged to duty in England: indeed at the peak of the gin-drinking boom in England the

[1] P. Rosenstein-Rodan, 'International Aid for Underdeveloped Countries'. *Review of Economics and Statistics* (1961).

figure exceeded 8 million gallons and consumption averaged nearly $1\frac{1}{2}$ gallons per head of the total population (men, women and children)—which is a very high rate of consumption of hard liquor by any standards. Statistics such as these do not suggest a high standard of material well-being but they do indicate the existence of an economic surplus, even if this was distributed through socially undesirable channels.

The seasonal rise in the death rate in winter, the periodic food riots and the squalor and disease of the overcrowded townships give evidence of a level of living for the mass of the people that was exceedingly vulnerable to temporary hardship. But in the ordinary course of events and in the average country parish in which the majority of people lived, the paupers could rely on being relieved from complete destitution by the Poor Law in childhood, sickness and old age. It has even been argued that the labouring poor enjoyed higher standards of living in the immediately pre-industrial era than in the decades of economic and social revolution which followed. The Hammonds, for example, claimed that 'in comparison with the dishevelled century that follows, the eighteenth century was neat, well dressed and nicely appointed'.[1] We shall come back to this view when we come to discuss the famous controversy concerning the workers' standard of living in the industrial revolution, but at this stage the point to notice is that although the standard of life was simple, and sometimes disastrously vulnerable to climatic extremes in the mid eighteenth century, there was some economic surplus, some slack in the economy.

In all this, it may be noted, the English were better off than most of their contemporaries in other countries. In the eighteenth century it was obvious to contemporaries that the three richest countries in the world were Holland, England and France. This was the view of Gregory King writing in the 1690's and Adam Smith ranked them similarly in the 1770's. Probably there was little difference between the standards of living of English and Dutch by the middle of the eighteenth century, but there seems little doubt that the average Englishman was appreciably better off than his French counterpart. Foreign observers travelling in England remarked on the fact that 'the English labourer is better cloathed, better fed and better lodged

---

[1] J. L. and B. Hammond, *The Village Labourer 1760–1832* (1911), p. 129.

than the French'.[1] Arthur Young travelling in France on the
eve of the French revolution (i.e. in the 1780's) calculated that
the French labouring classes 'are 76 per cent less at their ease:
worse fed, worse clothed and worse supported than the same
classes in England'.[2] Unlike today's poverty-stricken millions
whose lot is worsened by the visible affluence of neighbouring
countries, eighteenth-century Englishmen were relatively well-
off compared with most foreigners. Perhaps this is why a
historian looking at the condition of the English people in the
eighteenth century found 'little evidence to show that the
average member of the labouring poor was filled with bitter
resentment or economic despair'.[3]

2. STAGNATION

Another characteristic of a pre-industrial community which
distinguishes it from an industrialized one is that its level of
living and of productivity is relatively stagnant. This is not to
say that there is no economic change, no economic growth even,
in a pre-industrial economy, but that such growth as does occur
is either painfully slow or spasmodic, or is readily reversible.

It is fair to say that before the second half of the eighteenth
century people had no reason to *expect* growth. Pamphleteers
writing in the 1740's, for example, used Sir William Petty's or
Gregory King's estimates, made half a century or more before,
to illustrate their assessments of the current economic situation.
So little evidence did they see for economic growth that they
were prepared to adopt calculations made in the 1670's or the
1690's to reflect the conditions of the 1740's. Population, prices
and productivity could, they judged, fluctuate upwards as
readily as downwards and there was no reason to expect them
to go in one direction rather than the other.

So far as we can judge they were broadly right in their
assumptions. Population, for example, fluctuated between about
5·8 and 6·0 millions in the first four or five decades of the
eighteenth century and was only about 5·9 million in 1741.[4]
Recent attempts to measure the rate of growth in output per

[1] J. H. Meister, *Letters written during a residence in England* (1799), p. 9.
[2] Arthur Young, *Travels in France*, ed. Maxwell (1929), p. 315.
[3] Dorothy Marshall, *English People in the Eighteenth Century* (1956), p. 193.
[4] These are Brownlee's estimates: See B. R. Mitchell, *Abstract of British Historical Statistics* (1926), p. 5, for a comparison with other estimates, and below pp. 23–4, for a discussion of the reliability of eighteenth-century population estimates.

head suggest that there was some improvement in the first half
of the century but it was so slow that it would have taken about
a century and a half to double the standard of living.[1] The
ordinary man saw little evidence of economic growth within his
own lifetime and no improvement that could not be eliminated
within a single year by the incidence of a bad harvest or a war
or an epidemic. Thus in pre-industrial England, as in many of
today's pre-industrial societies,[2] the normal long-term rate of
growth in real incomes per head was under half of one per cent
per annum, and it was almost as common for the economy to
slide into decline as it was for it to grow. Indeed there is some
evidence to suggest that the standard of living of the eighteenth-
century Englishman may actually have been lower than that
of his counterpart at the end of the fifteenth century. Professor
Phelps Brown, for example, has examined the figures of building-
craftsmen's wages and the prices of the goods that these would
buy, and has concluded that there was 'an advance in productivity deserving the title of a revolution that about doubled the
commodity equivalent [of builders' wages] between the Black
Death (1349) and Agincourt (1415)'. This plateau of prosperity
was apparently maintained for nearly a century and was
followed by a great decline—so great that by 1630 the builder's
real wage was perhaps 'as little as two-fifths of what it had been
through much of the fifteenth century'.[3]

   In effect, the levels of living in pre-industrial communities are
not static in the sense of never changing, but are stagnant in
the sense that the forces working for an improvement in output
or productivity are no stronger over the long run than the forces
working for a decline. An economy of this kind tends to be
characterized by long secular swings in incomes per head, in
which the significant variable is not so much the rate of growth
of output as the rate of growth of population. When population
rose in pre-industrial England, product per head fell: and if, for
some reason (a new technique of production or the discovery
of a new resource, for example, or the opening up of a new
market), output rose, population was not slow in following and

[1] Deane and Cole, *British Economic Growth*.
[2] Phyllis Deane, 'The Long Term Trends in World Economic Growth', *Malayan
     Economic Review*, vol. VI (1961).
[3] E. H. Phelps Brown and Sheila V. Hopkins, 'Builders' Wage-rates, Prices and
     Population: Some Further Evidence', *Economica* (1956), p. 306.

eventually levelling out the original gain in incomes per head. Alternately raised by prosperity and depressed by disease, population was ultimately contained within relatively narrow limits by static or slowly growing food supplies.

This essentially stagnant character of the pre-industrial community was reflected in its social and institutional framework. Social structure and place within the hierarchy of incomes were still closely linked with land rights: density of population was largely determined by the fertility of the soil and its distribution was frozen by institutional rigidities. Labour mobility, for example, was restricted by the 1662 Law of Settlement, which placed the burden of poor relief fairly and squarely on the parish. Families living near the margin of subsistence, and the majority were in this state, were imprisoned within their own parishes by the knowledge that there alone could they qualify for poor relief when overtaken by economic misfortune: and while agriculture remained the basic source of livelihood there were few families that did not live under the constant threat of climatic disaster.

3. DEPENDENCE ON AGRICULTURE

It goes without saying that a pre-industrial economy is one in which the principal economic activity is agricultural production. To quote a modern writer on economic development: 'An underdeveloped country may be defined as a country with 80 per cent of its people in agriculture and a developed country as one with 15 per cent of its employment in agriculture, in both cases giving or taking a little according to foreign trade.'[1] How underdeveloped was mid-eighteenth-century England according to this criterion?

We cannot say precisely how many people were engaged in agriculture, for there was no reliable census of occupations taken in England until 1841—by which time the industrial revolution was certainly more than half a century old. On the other hand we can get some idea of the situation at the end of the seventeenth century, say, by examining Gregory King's famous 'Scheme of the income and expence of the several families of England' (Table 1, p. 6). If we look at that part of his list which deals with families who were 'increasing the wealth of the

---

[1] H. Singer, 'The Concept of Economic Growth in Economic development', in *Economic Growth*, ed. Eastin Nelson (1960), p. 73.

nation', that is the families who were taking the most important economic decisions (which excludes the labourers, the cottagers, and the paupers, and the soldiers and seamen), and if we deduct those who were *not* mainly dependent on agriculture for their livelihood (civil servants, officers in the armed forces, merchants, shopkeepers, persons in the professions, and artisans and craftsmen) we are left with a group of *primarily* agricultural families who account for about 68 per cent of the total. By 1750 the proportion had almost certainly fallen somewhat, if only because there had been a greater degree of urbanization and some expansion of industry and overseas trade, but probably it still lay between about 60 and 70 per cent.

It is evident that the economy was predominantly agricultural, the population predominantly rural, and that the characteristic unit of production was the family. The principal industries—the textile trades in particular—were organized on a domestic basis and were subordinate to agriculture. Most of those who were engaged in making either woollen or cotton goods were working in their own homes. In the cotton industry, for example, women and children picked, cleaned and spun the raw cotton, and the men wove it. Nailmakers and other metal workers generally worked in sheds attached to their cottages. When a writer in the early eighteenth century calculated that nearly a million people were employed in the British woollen industry, for example, he may not have been exaggerating as wildly as is sometimes supposed. If every man who eked out his agricultural earnings by weaving in the farmers' slack seasons, if every woman who occasionally took in wool to spin and every child which helped its parents by carding wool was included in the total, it is not difficult to accept the possibility that one in ten of the population was concerned in the woollen industry. As late as 1841, official census returns for Ireland (then still at a pre-industrial stage) recorded a proportion of nearly one in eight occupied persons engaged in the textile industries.

Most of the inhabitants of eighteenth-century England lived in rural areas, though the towns were already beginning to expand. In 1695, again according to Gregory King, about a quarter of the population of England and Wales lived in the cities and market-towns, but most of these market-towns were barely more than large villages. Outside London (with about half a million inhabitants) there were only three towns in

England with more than 10,000 inhabitants—Norwich (with about 29,000), Bristol (with about 25,000) and Birmingham (with perhaps 12,000). By the middle of the eighteenth century the proportion of the population living in concentrations of 5,000 or more probably did not exceed 16 per cent. Most of them still lived in London, but Liverpool and Birmingham had joined Norwich and Bristol among the towns of over 25,000 and Manchester was rapidly growing towards this kind of size. Only one Englishman out of every five lived in a large town.

4. LACK OF OCCUPATIONAL SPECIALIZATION

A fourth respect in which a pre-industrial economy can generally be distinguished from an industrialized economy is that the latter is relatively specialized. It is rare for the industrial worker to make a complete article. He generally plays his part in the production process by performing a particular kind of task (sometimes a single distinct operation) in the lengthy chain of operations whereby a raw material is converted into a purchase by a final consumer. By contrast the worker in a pre-industrial economy is generally engaged in a variety of occupations and even in a variety of industries. He is typically a 'jack of all trades'.

There are plenty of illustrations of the unspecialized character of the labour force in eighteenth-century England. The major industries were domestic industries subordinate to agriculture: many of the labourers, even in capitalistic industries like mining, building or iron-working, moved from industrial to agricultural occupations at times of harvest or planting: and domestic servants were generally as occupied with their master's trade or industry as with his household. Peter Stubs, the industrialist whose career in the second half of eighteenth century has been described by Ashton, was innkeeper, maltster, brewer and filemaker at one and the same time.[1]

On the other hand, eighteenth-century England was not as unspecialized as some of today's underdeveloped regions of Asia or Africa where so much of economic activity is subsistence activity, that is concerned with the production of goods and services which never enter into the process of exchange but are consumed by the producer and his immediate family. The

[1] T. S. Ashton, *An Eighteenth Century Industrialist* (1939).

subsistence sector seems to have dwindled to minor importance in England even by the seventeenth century. If there were any producers who got the greater part of their incomes from untraded production they must have fallen within the category of 'cottagers and paupers' when Gregory King was drawing up his table of families at the end of the seventeenth century. Yet these accounted for under 6 per cent of national income and less than a quarter of the total population. A century or so later, when Patrick Colquhoun drew up a comparable list for 1803 of families and incomes in England and Wales, the subsistence producer seems to have faded into insignificance, for Colquhoun distinguishes no cottager class as such.[1]

In effect, the degree of specialization of the labour force is one index of the degree of economic development achieved by a community, and by the end of the eighteenth century Britain had already developed a fairly complex market economy. The income of the typical producer depended heavily on the production of goods and services for exchange in the market, often for exchange on an international market. There were already the beginnings of a proletariat in eighteenth-century England; that is, a working-class population without property which depended for its livelihood on employment by a proper-tied or capitalist group. By the time Adam Smith was writing in the 1770's there were factories which carried the division of labour to a considerable extent. His description of a pin factory in which the manufacture of a pin required eighteen distinct operations, each of which could be performed by a separate man, is the classic illustration of the advantages of the division of labour.[2] It was not yet true, of course, that the typical producer was an employee. In a modern industrialized economy the share of the national income going to employees is usually more than two-thirds—certainly more than half: whereas in today's underdeveloped areas (as in present-day Nigeria) the proportion may be less than 20 per cent. In early eighteenth-century England, if we may judge from Gregory King's tables, roughly a third of the national income was distributed in the form of wages and salaries: and in the light of the increased urbanization and the reduction of the subsistence sector which had certainly taken place by 1750 we

[1] P. Colquhoun, *Treatise on Indigence* (1806).
[2] Adam Smith, *The Wealth of Nations*, Cannan ed. (1950), pp. 6–7.

may reasonably deduce that it had risen above a third by mid-century.

More significant, however, than the disappearance of the subsistence sector or the growth of a proletarian labour force, were the specialized economic institutions which had been developed in eighteenth-century England. Trade with North America, Africa, India and the Levant was organized by chartered companies who got much of their capital from non-participant shareholders. The risks of overseas trade were covered by specialist underwriters and insurance brokers. The Bank of England had been set up in 1694 and by the middle of the eighteenth century the British banking system was providing extensive and complex financial services to the British government and to British and foreign merchants. The banking system had to develop a good deal more before it became as efficient in supplying currency and credit as it did in the nineteenth century. But it was nevertheless a *system* and as such it was superior to the indigenous monetary framework of most present-day underdeveloped countries.

5. THE LOW DEGREE OF GEOGRAPHICAL INTEGRATION

Finally, a fifth characteristic of a pre-industrial economy, which arises in part out of its dependence on agriculture and in part out of its low level of specialization, is the lack of integration among its regions. This is the result of a poor system of communications. The consequence is that for mid-eighteenth-century England the national economy is not always the most convenient unit of economic analysis. Most economic decisions were taken in relation to the conditions of the regional market, and as between one region and another the quality and levels of economic activity and the character and direction of economic change varied substantially. Regional differences in soils and climate, for example, associated with differences in purchasing power and local taste, led to different patterns of local consumption. The staple foodstuff might be wheat or oats or barley or rye. Money wages varied widely in level and trend; Mrs Gilboy found in her investigation of eighteenth-century wages no general tendency common to the three regions she considered (London, Lancashire and the South West): 'Not only the movement but the levels of wages differed.'[1] Commodity price

[1] E. Gilboy, *Wages in Eighteenth Century England* (1934), p. 219.

and output data show similar regional differences. When iron output was declining in most regions it was expanding in Shropshire and Staffordshire. The rise in the Yorkshire woollen industry was accompanied by the decline in East Anglian industry.

The effect of these regional variations in economic conditions is that statistics relating to a particular area may give no indication of the comparable movements for the nation as a whole and that the national aggregates may obscure the trends for regions in which the significant changes are taking place. An attempt to assess the quality and rate of economic change at the national level may not lead to meaningful results whether we are looking for the significant continuities or for the significant discontinuities of history.

In sum, therefore, it is evident that the British economy of the mid eighteenth century displayed (though to a limited extent) a number of the features which we now recognize as characteristic of a pre-industrial economy. It was poor, though not without some economic surplus; it was relatively stagnant, though not completely static; it was based on agriculture as its main economic activity, though commerce and industry—there was even some factory industry—were important sectors. The mass of the people lived close to economic disaster and, unless they were unusually lucky or hardworking, they had little prospect of enjoying an appreciably higher standard of living within their lifetime. Most of the community's economic decisions were taken by family-based units of production, whose output per member of the work force depended largely on the extent of their holdings in land, ships or stocks of consumer goods. It might be described as a 'traditional society' in the sense defined by Rostow as the first of his stages of economic growth. That is to say it was an economy in which something like 'a ceiling existed on the level of attainable output per head'.[1] Unlike an industrialized economy in which the regular and systematic application of modern science and technology ensures a continuous improvement in methods of production, its productive possibilities were contained within narrow and relatively predictable limits, though by the eighteenth century these limits were already being pushed outwards.

[1] Rostow, *Stages of Economic Growth*, p. 4.

The beginnings of industrialization and growth and structural change were clearly apparent by the middle of the eighteenth century. Population had begun to grow continuously in the 1740's. Pamphleteers writing in the early 1740's had written as though population, prices and incomes were much the same as they had been half a century ago. Adam Smith and Arthur Young, writing in the 1770's *before* the introduction of the innovations in textiles, steam and iron which symbolized the beginnings of the industrial revolution, were able to look back on an expansion in real incomes which was large enough to be obvious to contemporaries. In 1774, for example, Young wrote:

Let any person consider the progress of everything in Britain during the last twenty years. the great improvements we have seen in this period, superior to those of any other, are not owing to the constitution, to moderate taxation or to other circumstances of equal efficacy ever since the Revolution, as the existence of these circumstances did not before produce equal effects—the superiority has been owing to the quantity of wealth in the nation which has in a prodigious degree, facilitated the execution of all great works of improvement.[1]

Adam Smith, writing at about the same time, referred to the 'natural progress of England towards wealth and improvement', and claimed that 'the annual produce of its land and labour is, undoubtedly, much greater at present than it was either at the restoration or the revolution'.[2]

Whether this self-evident economic expansion was in its initial stages any more significant than the upturns which had occurred often before in English pre-industrial history—and been subsequently reversed—is a matter of dispute. That the trend in population, prices, output and incomes was already turning upwards by 1750 is not, however, in doubt.

[1] Arthur Young, *Political Arithmetic* (1774), p. 49.
[2] Adam Smith, *Wealth of Nations*, Cannan ed., vol. I, p. 327.

CHAPTER 2

THE DEMOGRAPHIC
REVOLUTION

Although there is still room for considerable differences of opinion concerning the exact timing of the crucial turning-points in British economic development, there is a general consensus among economic historians that sustained growth—modern economic growth some would say—can be traced back to the middle decades of the eighteenth century. Before then, economic change was generally slow (when not precipitated by non-economic catastrophes); and standards of living tended to fluctuate violently in the short run and to rise (or decline) imperceptibly in the long run. Afterwards change became continuous, evident and systematic—it was part of an indus-trialization process which was as apparent to contemporaries as it is to us in retrospect: and national output, population and incomes per head began to grow, at varying rates it is true, but with only short-term interruptions. Economic growth—sustained and perceptible—became part of the normal order of things.

Associated with the industrial revolution in time, and in a complex relationship of cause and effect, was a demographic revolution the mechanics of which are still not fully understood. One thing is clear however. One of the features that distinguishes the modern industrial (or industrializing) economy from its predecessors in the chain of economic development is that it involves sustained long-term growth in *both* population *and* output.

The rate of growth of population, of course, depends basically on the rate of natural increase, that is, on the difference between birth rates and death rates; and there are certain biological and physical limits to the extent to which these are likely to vary. In a pre-industrial economy, that is, in a primarily agricultural community, crude birth rates (i.e. live births per annum per 1,000 of the population) generally range between 35 and 50.

Within this range, the actual rate will vary according to the specific characteristics of the community concerned; for example, according to demographic factors like sex and age-composition, socio-cultural factors (such as age of marriage and attitudes to family size), economic factors (such as the demand for child labour or the costs of having children) and events such as wars, epidemics and famines. Death rates also tend to be quite high but *normally* they are lower than birth rates—the range being generally between about 30 and 40 per annum. In effect, therefore, the population of an agricultural community, undisturbed by epidemics, or wars, or cultural shocks, is generally characterized by a rate of natural increase of between 5 and 10 per 1,000, so that the population tends to grow at an annual rate of between one-half of one per cent and one per cent. Some twentieth-century developing countries have achieved much higher rates of natural increase (actually between 2 and 3 per cent) because the death rate has been sharply lowered by the introduction from industrialized economies of advanced medical techniques. But in the pre-industrial economies of the eighteenth and nineteenth centuries and before, the *normal* rate of natural increase can be assumed to have been restricted to these fairly narrow limits of 0·5 per cent and 1 per cent per annum.

In fact, however, the normal rate of natural increase was recurrently interrupted by sudden dramatic peaks in the death rate caused by particularly virulent epidemics, or wars, or a succession of harvest failures. A serious crop failure could double or treble the normal death rate of the region most closely affected, and a city struck by plague might expect to lose a third or a half of its inhabitants. Famines, wars and epidemics tended indeed to reinforce each other. For diseases that were endemic in stagnant, highly localized, agricultural communities could speedily be converted into wide-ranging epidemics in situations where harvest failures (which inevitably tend to hit some districts harder than others) produced movements of people from areas in which food supplies were virtually exhausted to areas in which they could still be obtained for the price of a man's labour. In an age when armies lived in camps rather than barracks, and were expected to live off the land, movements of troops were a common cause of the spread of infection from one region or country to another, and deaths from disease associated with military operations usually outnumbered those incurred in battle.

By the eighteenth century, however, in several countries of Western Europe—of which Britain was one—these 'dismal peaks' in the death rate became less frequent or less violent (probably both) and the natural tendency of population to grow—albeit slowly—was able to assert itself. There is also some evidence to suggest that, at any rate in certain districts, there was a rise in the birth rate. This could of course have been due to the same sort of reasons which accounted for the reduction of the peaks in the death rate. For the sort of crisis which brought an upward leap in the death rate generally involved a drop in the number of successful conceptions and a rise in the number of stillbirths. Anything which reduced the violence or the frequency of these recurrent catastrophes would tend to increase the number of live births. What does appear to be indicated by the evidence is that the population of England and Wales, which had been fluctuating above and below a level of no more than 6 million people in the first three or four decades of the eighteenth century, began to grow, possibly in the 1740's, and has been growing ever since. For population, as for output, it is by no means certain that the *crucial* change in the trend rate of growth dates from the 1740's, though it is clear that by the end of the eighteenth century the changes in birth and death rates had been such as to constitute a demographic revolution.

Let me say something about the character of the evidence on which we depend for our discussion of English population growth in the eighteenth century. Why are we so hesitant about saying exactly when and why English population began to grow?

Essentially the answer is that our population statistics are incomplete. There was no full census of population taken for England and Wales until 1801 and no official registration of births and deaths until 1839. True there had been an earlier count at the end of the seventeenth century in connection with a tax on births, deaths and marriages. But the data do not appear to have been nationally collected or aggregated. When Gregory King made his contemporary estimates of population, for example, he took the hearth-tax returns as a starting point and used some of the 1695 parish population assessments to give him an average number of persons per hearth.[1] In any case, statistics collected specifically for tax purposes are open to suspicion because there is a positive incentive to evade enumeration. Perhaps the fact that the 1695 count was used as an instrument of tax collection was part of the reason for the opposition with which all eighteenth-century proposals for a census were met. A bill for counting people and numbering marriages, births and deaths and the individuals in receipt of poor-relief was actually introduced into Parliament in 1753, for example. Though it weathered violent opposition in the Commons, where the member for York insisted that 'an annual register of our people will acquaint our enemies abroad with our weakness and a return of the poor's rate our enemies at home with our wealth',[2] it was rejected by the Lords, so that informed observers were still arguing whether the population of England and Wales was growing or declining when the first census was taken in 1801. By then the population was growing at an unprecedented rate and almost as fast as at its all-time peak.

The figures we now use for English population trends between 1700 and 1800 are, without exception, *estimates*. They are based largely on records of baptisms, burials and marriages which John Rickman, the first Director of the Census got the parish clergy to extract for him from the church registers at decade intervals through the eighteenth century. Being extracted at decade intervals they may reflect the abnormal circumstances of particular years, and without an annual series of estimates we cannot say exactly when the upward trend began. Being based on the registers of the Anglican clergy, they omit an unknown proportion of nonconformists, and moreover a proportion which cannot be assumed to have remained constant through time or as between districts. A fall in the baptisms, marriages and burials appearing in the parish records, for example, might reflect an increase in nonconformity, or a disinclination to submit to registration procedures, rather than a fall in births, marriages and deaths. Nor were the parish registers themselves always complete—there are tales of their pages being used for pot-holders or wrapping-paper or fire-

---

[1] D. V. Glass, 'Gregory King and the Population of England and Wales at the end of the Seventeenth Century', *Eugenics Review* (1946).

[2] Quoted by A. J. Taylor, 'The Taking of the Census', *British Medical Journal* (7 April 1951), p. 715.

lighters; neither were they always legible. Nevertheless, these are the data which historians have converted to estimates of total population by making reasoned assumptions concerning the relationship between recorded baptisms, marriages and burials on the one hand, and actual births, marriages and deaths on the other. Rickman, for example, derived his eighteenth-century population estimates by applying a standard coefficient (based on nineteenth-century census results) to an average of the baptisms and burials and marriages data for each year. Other investigators have chosen to depend on one series rather than the other two, and there are a variety of possible coefficients, depending on which later census one takes as a basis for estimate, and what adjustments are made to bring them into line with eighteenth-century conditions.

Consequently we are faced with a variety of possible series for English eighteenth-century population, some of which are more subtle and complex in their assumptions than the others, but none is authoritative.[1] Most of them suggest that the upward trend in English population can be dated from the 1740's, but it is generally agreed that the initial upsurge was a relatively modest affair—not greater than many earlier population upsurges which had been speedily cancelled by a single peak in the death rate. The difference was that the growth that appears to date from the 1740's was *not* reversed and indeed it accelerated to unprecedented levels in the 1780's and went on accelerating to a peak rate of growth in the decade 1811–21.

The traditional explanation of the upturn is that there was a fall in the death rate, beginning in the 1740's or thereabouts, which (it is said) was particularly marked for the infant age-groups. This would, of itself, produce a continuing rise in the rate of natural increase when the surviving infants grew up and inflated the child-bearing age groups. But it was then reinforced, so the explanation goes, by the continuing decline in the death rate due to improved medical knowledge and skill and by an upward movement in the birth rate due to rising standards of living and to the vigorous demand for labour in the early stages of the industrial revolution, from, say, 1760 or 1770 onwards. Certainly the burial figures show a spectacularly high mortality in the 1730's which is sometimes associated with the gin-drinking age—particularly in London—and they fall to

[1] See Mitchell, *Abstract of British Historical Statistics*, p. 5.

distinctly lower levels in the 1750's. Moreover there is no doubt that when the death rate is high, as it was in the eighteenth century, a relatively slight fall, if it is sustained, is capable of setting up a cumulative process of population change.

A considerable controversy has grown up around this explanation. For one thing the view that the process of population growth was set off by a decline in the death rate has been challenged by those who argue that there is at least as much evidence for an initiating rise in the birth rate. For another, the argument that the improvement in medical conditions was adequate to account for an appreciable fall in the death rate has been challenged by medical historians. For another, the view that working-class standards of living were rising during the early stages of the industrial revolution has been challenged by statisticians, who point to falling real wages as prices soared in the fourth quarter of the eighteenth century. Finally, it has been argued that an upsurge in the 1740's could be simply explained as a reaction, a compensatory adjustment, to the abnormally high mortality rates of the 1730's and that what was really revolutionary in the eighteenth-century population trend was the failure of birth and death rates to revert to 'normal' pre-industrial levels after the compensation was complete.

The first question is whether it was the death rate or the birth rate that triggered off the increase after about 1740. Professor Habakkuk's analysis of the evidence[1] has demonstrated that it is open to other explanations than those traditionally advanced by the economic historians. In particular, for example, it might be explained by postulating a fall in the age of marriage due to better economic conditions and wider economic opportunities leading to a rise in the birth rate. There seems to be plenty of evidence for an improvement in economic conditions in the crucial decades. Contemporary writings by informed observers suggest strongly (1) that standards of living among the labouring poor were improving in the decades before the industrial revolution began, and (2) that there was a shortage of labour at that stage. Malthus wrote, for example, that

During the last 40 years of the 17th century and the first 20 of the 18th, the average price of corn was such as, compared with the wages

[1] H. J. Habakkuk, 'English Population in the Eighteenth Century, *Economic History Review* (1953).

of labour, would enable the labourer to purchase with a day's earnings, two thirds of a peck of wheat. From 1720 to 1750 the price of wheat had so fallen, while wages had risen, that instead of two thirds the labourer could purchase the whole of a peck of wheat with a day's labour.[1]

Adam Smith took a similar view. Overseas trade was expanding and so was the textile industry—the major British manufacturing industry of the day. The period 1730–55 was characterized by a remarkable run of good harvests hardly paralleled before or since. At the same time, the evidence that the decline in mortality affected the infantile age-groups most strongly is far from conclusive and without this presumption it is difficult to claim that the later acceleration in the birth rate hinged on the decline in the death rate.

In effect, the argument is that the fall in the death rate which undoubtedly occurred between 1730 and 1760 was a reaction to a period of high mortality; that the greater fall suggested by the burial statistics from 1780 to 1820 was exaggerated by serious deficiencies in the system for registration of deaths;[2] and that the long-term cause of the increase in population was due to a sustained increase in the birth rate. This in its turn can be attributed to the removal of the two economic checks—first to the abnormally prolonged run of good harvests during the period 1730–55. Good harvests meant cheaper grain and a stronger demand for labour to reap the crops: they thus permitted an earlier age of marriage and larger families. Later in the century the pressure for larger families was increased by the economic opportunities for children in industrial employment and by the system of family allowances involved in the Speenhamland arrangements (see below p. 152). The increasing urbanization of the eighteenth century may also have had an impact on the age of marriage, and hence on the birth rate, for there is some evidence to suggest that women tended to marry earlier in the towns than in the country.

Until sufficient evidence is unearthed—for example in the direct investigations into parish registers which are steadily broadening our knowledge of past changes in mortality, fertility

---

[1] T. R. Malthus, *Principles of Political Economy* (1838), p. 228.

[2] This is the conclusion suggested by a careful study of the records for 1781–1850. See J. T. Krause, 'Changes in English Fertility and Mortality 1781–1850', *Economic History Review* (August 1958).

and age of marriage—the question whether it was a rise in the birth rate or a decline in the death rate that was effectively responsible for the upward surge in population that dates from the mid eighteenth century must remain open. No one denies that both factors were operative. What remains open to doubt is which of the two ratios shifted first to a new long-run position. A study of the Nottingham registers by Professor Chambers seems to support Professor Habakkuk's view that the fall in the death rate was not so much a steady decline due to improved medical, social and economic conditions, but a sharp and temporary reaction to a period of high mortality. Part of the rationale of this argument is that those who survive a period of high mortality tend to be more resistant on the whole and their mortality rates are likely to be abnormally low. Of the Nottingham death rate Professor Chambers wrote:

It is not a question...of a steady decline under the influence of the ameliorating factors of diet and environment, but rather of a sudden and temporary plunge downwards as a result of the absence of a factor which had made the preceding period one of exceptionally high mortality, followed by a return almost to the death rates of the pre-epidemic period.

In other words: 'As far as Nottingham was concerned the age of massacre by epidemic was over.'[1]

Against the view of the primacy of the birth rate in causing the eighteenth-century population upsurge it has been argued[2] that when birth and death rates are both high, as was the case for eighteenth-century England, a fall in the death rate is a more plausible explanation of a sustained rise in population than a rise in the birth rate. This is because a high death rate due to infectious disease is uneven in its incidence as between age-groups: it carries away infants and young children more rapidly than adults; and in conditions where the incidence of disease is high one would expect most of the effects of an increased birth rate to be nullified immediately by an increase in the death rate due to an expansion of the age-groups with a high death rate. Although arguments linking a rising level of economic opportunity to earlier marriages and a reduction in the average

[1] J. Chambers, 'Population Change in Nottingham, 1700 1800', in L. Pressnell, *Studies in the Industrial Revolution* (1960), pp. 116 and 110 respectively.
[2] By T. McKeown and R. G. Brown, 'Medical Evidence Related to English Population Changes in the 18th Century', *Population Studies* (1955).

number of months between successive births are persuasive, the hard evidence for either a substantial decrease in the average age of marriage, or an increase in fertility within marriage, is still limited. Wrigley's examination of the Colyton parish registers for example indicates that in this small Devonshire village the brides of the period 1770–1837 were on average younger and more fertile than women who married in the period 1720–69.[1] Hollingsworth's study of the English peerage also shows a rise in fertility for the eighteenth century, but no clear fall in the age of marriage for this group—possibly because its women already tended to marry younger than their counterparts in the rest of the population.[2] Finally, the argument that an increased demand for labour leads directly to an increase in the birth rate, rather than indirectly through a change in the marriage rate or age, implies some degree of family planning and hence of contraception: and of this there is no evidence at all for eighteenth century England. On the other hand, recent research into the demographic behaviour of today's less-developed countries, as well as an increasing volume of evidence on past practice now being assembled from parish registers in Western Europe, indicates that pre-industrial communities have been capable of postponing marriage, and restricting births within marriage, in times of economic pressure.

What does seem to stand out fairly conclusively from the evidence and the analyses carried out so far by economic and social and medical historians is that there was a sharp reduction in the death rate dating from the decade or so before 1750 (due almost certainly to a reduction in the incidence of epidemics), and an increase in the birth rate in the period *after* 1750 (due partly at least to the secondary effects of the earlier reduction in infant mortality). There is also some evidence of a pre-1750 increase in the birth rate, but, since this is based on baptism data, it could equally well have been due to a decline in non-conformity, so it must be regarded as suspect.

Why the epidemics diminished is not fully established. As far as the Plague is concerned, the reasons seem to lie partly in 'an obscure ecological revolution among rodents', and partly

---

[1] E. A. Wrigley, 'Family Limitation in Pre-industrial England', *Economic History Review* (1966).

[2] T. H. Hollingsworth, 'The Demography of the British Peerage', supplement to *Population Studies* (1964).

in a gradual improvement in standards of living and social organization. Bubonic plague was a flea-borne disease of rats— the black ship rats who travelled on the caravan routes from Northern India and were shipped with the grains they infested to Western Europe and thence to English ports. As living standards rose so that wattle and daub walls were more and more replaced by brick, thatched roofs by tiled, piles of rushes or straw by carpets, and when systematic scavenging of the streets shifted piles of rat-breeding rubbish, the disease was bound to decline. The Great Fire of London and the subsequent rebuilding of the city may have protected that major urban concentration by drastically reducing its rat colonies, and indeed the Great Plague of 1665–6 was the last serious outbreak in Britain. But, so it has been argued, it was the displacement of the small domesticated black rat with its predilection for settling in human habitations and its free-wandering flea, by the grey-brown field or sewer rat with its outdoor habits and its nest-loving flea, that eventually freed Europe from its recurrent susceptibility to Plague.[1] More important, however, than the triumph of the field rat (which is said to have reached England by sea circa 1728) was probably the development in the later seventeenth century of the sea trade between Europe and India 'which abolished the caravan routes for merchandise from the East across Asia Minor and with it the "rodent pipe line"' which brought the disease-carrying flea from India to the Levant.[2]

Plague, of course, was only one factor in the high mortality rates of pre-industrial times. It may be that we must look to similar ecological changes to explain the diminution of other kinds of endemic or epidemic disease. The decline of malaria, for example—the treatment of which was still one of the most important functions of a seventeenth-century physician—can be attributed to the reduction in the numbers of the mosquito carrier due to better domestic hygiene, swamp drainage and perhaps to climatic changes. Other investigations have linked the reduction of the 'dismal peaks' in the death rate with the run of good harvests, which reduced the movements of distressed peoples and improved the basic living conditions of the mass of the population. It is certainly difficult to over-emphasize the

[1] L. Fabian Hirst, *The Conquest of Plague* (1953).
[2] J. F. D. Shrewsbury, *History of the Bubonic Plague in the British Isles* (1970).

contribution of good harvests to standards of living and productivity in an agricultural community. Others again have argued that people were becoming more aware of the importance of sanitation and hygiene; if they were, this kind of gradual development could have brought with it a steady, if barely perceptible, improvement in the expectation of life.

One view that used to be prevalent and now seems to have been largely discredited is that the improvement in the death rate was a consequence of advances in medical knowledge.[1] It would appear that there were no *specific* improvements in medical techniques or knowledge which could have contributed substantially to a reduction in the eighteenth-century death rate. Vaccination did not become general until the nineteenth century, and in any case the evidence is that the proportion of deaths due to smallpox did not vary through the eighteenth century. 'Surgery had an almost inappreciable effect on vital statistics until the advent of anaesthesia and antiseptics in the nineteenth century.'[2] Hospitals and dispensaries were more likely to spread disease than to check it. People who went to hospital in the eighteenth century often died there, generally from some disease other than that with which they were admitted. As late as the 1870's the senior surgeon at University College Hospital was warning his surgical students that 'a woman has a better chance of recovery after delivery in the meanest poorest hovel than in the best conducted hospital furnished with every appliance that can add to her comfort and with the best skill that a metropolis can afford'.[3] There seems no doubt that doctors learned a good deal about the causes of disease in the eighteenth century, a development which was probably reflected in the gradual adoption of more hygienic methods of treatment. This is thought to have produced a substantial reduction in maternal mortality, and indeed it may have done, though it is obviously difficult to prove this hypothesis; and it is very doubtful whether the majority of the population had access to medical practitioners who were any wiser than their medieval predecessors.

[1] The medical evidence has been extensively reviewed in McKeown and Brown, 'Medical Evidence' (1955). But see P. E. Razzell, 'Population Change in Eighteenth Century England; A Reinterpretation', *Economic History Review* (1965) for evidence that inoculation against smallpox may have an appreciable effect on eighteenth century mortality rates.   [2] McKeown and Brown, 'Medical Evidence', p. 121.
[3] J. E. Erichsen, *On Hospitalism and the Causes of Death after Operations* (1874), p. 43.

In effect then, the medical historians have returned to the economic historians the responsibility for explaining the connection between the demographic revolution and the industrial revolution. The latter have traditionally attributed the fall in the death rate, or the rise in the live-birth rate, or both, to the progress of medicine. The former find no evidence of medical progress of a kind which could justify this explanation and conclude instead that improvements in the standard of living must have increased the people's resistance to infectious disease and hence reduced the incidence of epidemics.

The question whether the standard of living rose and to what extent has also been the subject of controversy. In chapter 15 I shall examine in more detail the evidence for the change in the standard of living during the early stages of the British industrial revolution. For the moment, however, I propose to take a longer view of the problem in order to make the point that in relating the standard of living to the population upsurge it matters a good deal which period or subperiod we have in mind.

I have already referred to the contemporary evidence indicating that the labourer's standard of living was relatively high in the mid eighteenth century, that is, between the 1730's and 1760's.[1] Good harvests were reflected in low meat and grain prices and these meant both cheap food and low costs for the numerous industries processing agricultural products which are characteristic of a pre-industrial type of economy. In the 1750's England was a grain-exporting country, and most of its industrial raw materials outside the metal industries were home-produced agricultural products. If these primary products were cheap it meant that the return per unit of human effort was quite high. The evidence that standards of living for the mass of the population were quite high between about 1730 and 1760—higher, that is, in relation to past periods—is rather convincing.

But later on the evidence becomes a great deal less convincing. The long run of good harvests was broken, and indeed in the last three or four decades of the eighteenth century it can be said that there was an abnormally high incidence of bad harvests. The Seven Years War, the American War of Independence and the French wars all disrupted overseas trade and

---

[1] pp. 10–11 above.

created industrial and commercial distress and unemployment. The rising population began to press on food supplies and prices began to rise. At the end of the century a marked price rise was converted by all-out war into a rapid inflation. Professor Phelps Brown's index of the price of a typical basket of consumers' goods shows no price increase between around 1730 and 1760, a rise of nearly 40 per cent between 1760 and 1792 (on the eve of the French wars) and a doubling of prices between 1793 and 1813 when the war inflation reached its peak.[1]

Certain money wages—the wages of weavers, for example, who were rendered scarce by technological progress in the spinning section of the cotton industry—rose even higher than food prices. But for the most part the rise in money wages lagged behind the increase in prices, poverty became an acute problem, food riots were common and it is very difficult to justify the view that standards of living of the mass of the population were rising over the period 1780–1815. Moreover, in so far as industrialization led to urbanization it may have tended to worsen the environment of many people and to push up the death rate, for the urban death rate was generally higher than the rural death rate. In London—'the great wen'—there was a huge excess of burials over baptisms for most of the eighteenth century.

On the other hand the poor harvests which recurred at relatively frequent intervals in the later eighteenth century were no longer associated with violent upturns in regional or national death rates. Probably the most important reason for this is the fact that standards of economic and social organization had improved substantially over the century. There had been improvements in communications (better roads, river navigations and canals), in banking (permitting an easier flow of credit facilities in times of distress) and in commerce (opening up backward regions to trade and economic opportunity). The spread of root crops, such as the potato, which were less vulnerable than grain to climatic variations (or not as susceptible to the same bad weather) provided some regions with a useful hedge against total subsistence failure. At the same time there was evidence of an increasingly humane and responsible attitude

---

[1] E. H. Phelps Brown and Sheila V. Hopkins, 'Seven Centuries of the Prices of Consumables Compared with Builders' Wage Rates', *Economica* (1956). See also E. B. Schumpeter, 'English Prices and Public Finance 1660 1822', *Review of Economic Statistics* (1938), for another price index which leads to similar conclusions.

to the vicissitudes of the poor, which was associated both with a more efficient administration of the poor law and, in some areas, with more effective techniques of famine relief. James Anderson's account of the disastrous 1782 Aberdeenshire harvest, for example, attributes to a deliberate, concerted effort by local landowners to conserve grain and to finance food imports by charitable subscription, the fact that the usual concomitants of harvest failure—famine, emigration and 'political convulsions'—were then avoided.[1] In such circumstances as these, harvest failure and trade depression would have been less lethal in their impact on the worst-affected areas and social classes than had been usual in earlier decades, when harvest failure meant starvation or near-starvation for some and increased incidence of disease for many.

What can we say then, in sum, about the relationship between the demographic revolution and the industrial revolution, about these two significant breaks in the trend of British economic development which took place in the eighteenth century—the break in the long-run trend of population and the break in the long-run trend of output? We may begin by sketching briefly the course of English population and output growth in the eighteenth and early nineteenth century.

Between about 1700 and about 1741 the population of England and Wales seems to have been virtually stagnant at between about 5·8 million and about 6 million people. From 1741 to 1751 it may have grown by about $3\frac{1}{2}$ per cent over the decade; between 1751 and 1761 the rate of increase accelerated—probably to about 7 per cent per decade, a rate which it held, more or less, for a further decade. Then it accelerated to nearly 10 per cent in the 1780's and about 11 per cent in the 1790's and reached a peak of about 16 per cent in the second decade of the nineteenth century.

We cannot describe precisely the course of death rates and birth rates because the figures of burials and baptisms are not available annually for most of the eighteenth century. It is generally agreed, however, that the death rate reached its highest levels in the first half of the eighteenth century and that the birth rate reached its peak somewhere within the period 1780–1820. When these peaks occurred is further in doubt

[1] James Anderson's account is cited in M. Flinn (ed.), *Scottish Population History* (1977), pp. 12–13.

because year-to-year changes in burials and baptisms are an uncertain reflection of the year-to-year changes in deaths and births. Estimates made by Farr, a nineteenth-century Director of the Census, and reprinted in the General Report of the Census of 1871, suggest that English birth rates per 1,000 of the population probably reached a peak of about 37·7 in the 1780's. Expressed in terms of the percentage of women aged 20–40 this represents about 25·9 per cent and it seems to have remained between 25 and 26 per cent until the 1820's and 1830's, when it slumped quite sharply to reach 21·6 per cent in 1851.[1] On the assumption that birth rates and death rates eventually tend to adjust to one another, so that the rate of natural increase does not stay explosively high, we can say that a high death rate tends to be biologically compensated for by a high birth rate and that a low death rate tends to generate a fall in the birth rate. But of course the adjustment—the 'demographic transition' as it is generally called—is rarely immediate. The birth rate reacted against the high pre-1750 death rate by rising post-1750, that is to say, and against the falling death rate 1780–1820 by falling post-1820.

Attempts to assess the pattern of output growth suggest that in the 1740's when the upsurge of population seems to have begun there was an equally marked upsurge in total output. For 20 years the rate of growth of total real output is estimated to have averaged about 1 per cent per annum (compared with under half of 1 per cent in the preceding 30 years or so), and although the pace slackened in the following two decades it seems still to have been twice the rate of the early part of the century. In the 1780's the rate again accelerated, so that by the turn of the century it was probably running at near 1·8 per cent per annum.[2] These, it should be noted, are estimates of the rate of growth of total national output. For the upsurge of the 1740's the evidence of an increase in *output per head* is largely confined to the reports of contemporaries. It does not show up in the national-income estimates. But there is certainly no evidence of

[1] See also the estimates by T. H. Marshall in 'Population and the Industrial Revolution', reprinted in E. H. Carus-Wilson, *Essays in Economic History*, vol. 1 (1954). Professor Marshall's peak as a percentage of women aged 20–40 is in 1811 rather than 1791 but the general trend of relatively high birth rates 1780–1820 and a slump thereafter is as clear in his estimates as in Farr's.

[2] Deane and Cole, *British Economic Growth* (1962), pp. 79–82. But see N. F. R. Crafts, 'English Economic Growth in the Eighteenth Century', *Economic History Review* (1970), for a critical re-examination of these growth estimates.

decline and the presumption in favour of some increase is quite strong. During the next population upsurge, which we can date from the 1780's, the national-income evidence suggests a tendency for incomes per head to increase, though contemporary reports and wage data make it obvious that substantial sections of the population were, if not worse off, certainly no better off than before. This is the period to which Rostow has ascribed his 'take-off' stage. Certainly it was a period of great change and innovation. Even if wage-earners' standards of living did not rise appreciably overall, profits almost certainly soared and there were important changes in economic organization, structure and productivity.

It is clear that there was a complex two-way relationship of cause and effect shaping these two trends—population on the one hand and output on the other—even if it is not clear exactly what form that relationship took at all times. Both trends were, it is true, determined in part by factors that could reasonably be regarded as independent: in the case of population, for example, by essentially non-economic factors which helped to reduce the long-term death rate or raise the long-term birth rate; and in the case of output, by such factors as the growth of foreign markets and the widening of the technological horizon. It is the interaction between the two trends that is of especial interest, however. It seems reasonable to suppose that without the growth of output dating from the 1740's the associated growth in population would eventually have been checked by a rise in the death rate due to declining standards of living. It seems equally probable that without the population growth which gathered momentum in the second half of the eighteenth century, the British industrial revolution would have been retarded for lack of labour. It seems likely that without the rising demand and prices which reflected, *inter alia*, the growth of population, there would have been less incentive for British producers to expand and innovate, and hence that some of the dynamism which powered the industrial revolution would have been lost. It seems equally likely that the expanding employment opportunities created by the industrial revolution encouraged people to marry and to produce families earlier than in the past, and that they increased the average expectation of life.

It is important in the last analysis not to oversimplify the story. 'For those who care for the overmastering pattern', as

Professor Habakkuk has pointed out, 'the elements are evidently there for a heroically simplified version of English history before the nineteenth century, in which the long-term movements in prices, in income distribution, in investment, in real wages and in migration are dominated by changes in the growth of population.'[1] But there were other factors to be considered in combination with the increase in the labour force. The fact was that the new technology was introduced into a country which had labour, land and capital resources in reserve. There was still waste land and common land in England that could be more intensively cultivated: there was a fund of capital that had been earned in the overseas trade of the eighteenth century. Industrialists could rely on getting ample supplies of unskilled labour. Farmers could afford to adopt large-scale labour-intensive methods of cultivation when both urban and rural populations were expanding; for this provided them with expanding markets and an ample labour force. But without some slack in other resources—in land and capital—the growth of population might have come up rapidly against an output ceiling. *With* this additional slack it provided a positive incentive to economic change and growth.

[1] H. J. Habakkuk, 'The Economic History of Modern Britain', *Journal of Economic History* (December 1958).

CHAPTER 3

THE AGRICULTURAL
REVOLUTION

Students of economic growth in today's underdeveloped countries are well aware of the fact that the route to sustained economic growth lies through an industrial revolution. What is still a matter of controversy in connection with the strategy of industrialization is the role that agriculture should play in the process. Opinion ranges from those, at one extreme, who believe that all that is required of agriculture is that it should efficiently contract and so release labour and resources for modern industry: and, at the other extreme, those who claim that a revolution in agricultural techniques and methods of organization is an essential prerequisite to modernization of the manufacturing and transport industries. Professor Rostow, for example, in elaborating his theory of the stages of economic growth has claimed that 'revolutionary changes in agricultural productivity are an essential condition for successful take-off'.[1] According to this view it is on agriculture that the pre-industrial economy must depend for the additional food, the raw materials, the markets and the capital, which permit industrialization to proceed. In this controversy the historical experience of the first country to undergo an industrial revolution assumes a special topical interest.[2]

It is well known that the British industrial revolution was associated with an agricultural revolution. What was the character of this association? To what extent did it precede, reinforce or arise out of the process of British industrialization?

There were four salient features of the British agrarian revolution. First of all it involved farming in large-scale consolidated units in place of the medieval open fields cultivated in

[1] Rostow, *Stages of Economic Growth*, p. 8.
[2] For a valuable recent assessment of the agricultural revolution published after the first edition of this book appeared, see J. D. Chambers and G. E. Mingay, *The Agricultural Revolution 1750–1880* (1966).

discontinuous strips by peasants with rights of pasture, fuel and game on the overstocked common. Secondly it involved the extension of arable farming over heaths and commons and the adoption of intensive livestock husbandry. Thirdly it involved the transformation of the village community of (largely) self-subsistent peasants into a community of agricultural labourers whose basic standards of living came to depend more on the conditions of national and international markets than on the state of the weather. Fourthly it involved a large increase in agricultural productivity, that is, in the volume of output produced per unit of the full-time labour force in agriculture.

These characteristics developed gradually over a long period of time and appeared at widely different periods in different regions. What we need to do in order to relate them to the industrial revolution is to identify the crucial period of trans-formation, to be able to say when the significant changes in agricultural practice and organization and attitudes took place. Can we specify these significant changes and can we date them narrowly enough to be able to say when the agricultural revolution effectively occurred in Britain? Can we say whether it preceded, accompanied, or followed the developments which formed the nub of the industrial revolution proper and which can be tentatively attributed to the period 1780 to 1850? These are difficult questions to answer at a national level because the regional experience was so varied. It may, however, be possible to shed some light on the question when the English agricultural revolution occurred, by reviewing three related developments on which it largely depended: (1) the adoption of new techniques of production, (2) enclosure, and (3) changes in entrepreneurial attitudes.

I. NEW TECHNIQUES OF PRODUCTION

The essential features of the new techniques of production which characterized the agrarian revolution on the light soils of England were constant tillage, new crop rotations and a closer association of crops and stock. Jethro Tull's method of drilling wheat and roots in straight lines sufficiently far apart to permit a horse-drawn hoe to cultivate the rows between them was the basis of the new techniques of constant tillage. The seed drill was built in 1700 and the method was publicized extensively in the early 1730's. It was facilitated by the Rotherham triangular plough (patented in 1730), which permitted a rapid and effective turning of the soil by means of a team of two horses and one man instead of the traditional, slow, rectangular plough drawn by four or six or eight oxen and attended by an ox-driver as well as a ploughman. Experimental threshing machines were being made in the 1780's. More important, however, than mechanization in raising agricultural productivity during the period of the industrial revolution were the improvements in the design of hand tools and the trend towards earlier cutting of grain which developed over the period 1790–1870. Dr Collins has described these changes as amounting to a revolution in hand-harvesting techniques which had been virtually unchanged since the sixteenth century.[1] They represented the first significant steps towards the reduction of manual labour in farm operations in Britain.

The abandonment of the older forms of crop rotation involving frequent fallow periods (as often as once every three years in some areas), in favour of legume rotation and field-grass husbandry, both extended the area under effective crop and provided the winter foods for livestock. Seed-grasses were recuperative crops; turnips and potatoes were clearing crops: between them they permitted the soil to be cropped continuously without fear of exhaustion and they permitted livestock to be kept in health throughout the winter. It was no longer necessary to leave land uncropped to maintain its fertility and it was worth while investing in valuable stock with the object of improving the breed. Moreover stock no longer had to be grazed exclusively on overstocked natural pastures but could contribute to and receive benefit from the new rotational techniques. Livestock, which made profitable use of hay and roots, added by its manurial residues to the fertility of the land on which it was folded. Finally, the new techniques permitted farmers to diversify their output and hence to reduce the risks inherent in the perennially unseasonable English climate. Those who went in for the new mixed farming had a chance of offsetting the losses incurred in a disastrously wet summer, and a bitterly cold winter, by a high meat and milk yield on the one hand or a good corn and straw season on the other.

It is certain that these innovations must have greatly improved

[1] E. J. T. Collins, 'Harvest Technology and Labour Supply in Britain, 1790–1870', *Economic History Review* (December 1969).

the aggregate production of the agricultural industry from a given unit of land or labour wherever they were introduced. The problem is to decide when they made an effective contribution to national agricultural output as a whole. When did the new crops, the new rotations, the new machines and the new breeds of stock become general?

On this as on many other issues economic historians used to pronounce much more confidently in the past than they do today. Fabulous fortunes were said to have been made by the innovating farmers. A formidable importance used to be, and sometimes still is attached, for example, to the turnip and to the efforts of its most famous advocate, 'Turnip Townshend'. Professor Ragnar Nurkse, for example, wrote:

Everyone knows that the spectacular industrial revolution would not have been possible without the agricultural revolution that preceded: and what was the agricultural revolution? It was based mainly on the introduction of the turnip. The lowly turnip made possible a change in crop rotation which did not require much capital, but which brought about a tremendous rise in agricultural productivity. As a result more food could be grown with much less man-power. Man-power was released for capital construction.[1]

In fact there is no evidence that the cultivation of the turnip (which is a labour-intensive crop) involved any saving in labour, nor indeed that roots or clover were in general use as field crops before the early nineteenth century. Doubt has even been thrown on the extent of the improvements achieved by the more famous of the farming innovators either in raising the output of their own estates or in immediately encouraging imitators.[2] Most of the new methods could not be effectively introduced on the open fields, which it took the enclosure movement of the late eighteenth and early nineteenth centuries to eliminate from the English farming scene, and they had to be adapted to local soil conditions. It took until the 1820's before the Rotherham plough, which has been described as 'the greatest improvement in plough design since late Iron age and Romano-British times', could work in most districts better than

[1] R. Nurkse, *Problems of Capital Formation in Underdeveloped Countries* (1953), p. 52.
[2] R. A. C. Parker, 'Coke of Norfolk and Agrarian Revolution', *Economic History Review* (December 1955). See also G. E. Fussell's introduction to Lord Ernle, *English Farming Past and Present* (1961).

the traditional types.[1] The fact is that most of the tenant farmers, who worked perhaps 80 per cent or more of the cultivated acreage of the country, had neither the incentive nor the capital to experiment, and even the richest and most efficient large landowners hesitated, for political and social reasons, to introduce labour-saving machinery into rural areas depressed by chronic under-employment. In any case, the pressure on labour came at harvest time and there was little to be gained by economizing in labour at other times. Moreover, in spite of the genuine enthusiasm for agricultural progress and the wealth of printed communications that existed in the second half of the eighteenth century, it is doubtful whether the majority of farmers became acquainted with the new technology until they saw it in action on a neighbour's farm. It has been estimated that the pace of advance of new methods was not more than a mile a year from their place of origin.[2]

Above all it should be remembered that agriculture, more than any other industry, differed in character and historical experience from region to region. We cannot assume that techniques which were shown to be effective in one region were readily adapted to the different conditions of other regions. Nor indeed is it easy to establish that the example of the enterprising improvers was generally followed even within their own regions. Observant contemporaries like Arthur Young have described one improving farmer after another: but we cannot say how far their behaviour was typical. Often there is cause to believe that it was the atypical case which contemporaries found interesting enough to record. These are some of the reasons for the doubt which still surrounds this issue. Many of the new techniques of the eighteenth century were suitable only to the light sandy soils and could not be adopted in regions of heavier soils until the use of cylindrical tiles and the application of steam to pumping machines made it possible to drain the clay soils and the fens in the middle of the nineteenth century. Much more research at the regional level of detail will be necessary before we can generalize conclusively on the impact of the new agricultural techniques on national agricultural productivity during the last

[1] F. G. Payne, 'The British Plough: Some Stages in its Development', *Agricultural History Review* (1957).
[2] C. Singer, E. J. Holmyard, A. R. Hall and Trevor Williams, *History of Technology*, vol. IV (1946), p. 40.

half of the eighteenth century and the first half of the nineteenth century.

2. ENCLOSURES

To some extent we can gauge from the parliamentary records the pace at which the enclosure movement progressed, though here again we should bear in mind two qualifications to the data. The first is that private enclosure had been going on since Tudor times and before. It was not until the mid eighteenth century that parliamentary enclosure became the usual method of consolidating land holdings. The second is that although enclosure may have been a *necessary* condition of agricultural improvement it was not a *sufficient* one. If it removed the restrictions on technological change inherent in the open-field system, it did not of itself ensure the adoption of the new techniques of production for the market and the higher productivity they entailed. Some of the smaller farmers who received an allocation under an Enclosure Act were rendered too poor, by the legal and fencing costs in which they were unwillingly involved, to invest much on improving their holdings or in buying machinery or stock. Some of the larger farmers made less intensive use of their newly acquired wastes and commons than the cottagers and squatters who had used them to support families. There is evidence that standards of food consumption deteriorated for the rural poor in the second half of the eighteenth century to a predominantly bread and cheese diet because 'the system of enclosures had taken away their pasturage and the land where they collected the fuel for cooking their hot meals'.[1] At the same time their opportunities for adding to their larder by trapping or snaring or fishing were reduced, for on the enclosed lands landowners invoked savage game-laws and protected their preserves with man-traps and spring-guns. Meat virtually disappeared from the tables of the rural poor.

Bearing these qualifications in mind, therefore, can we say when the enclosure movement developed a revolutionary momentum? It is difficult to be conclusive about this. It has been estimated that in 1700 about half the arable land of the country was still cultivated on the open-field system. By 1820 there were 'only half a dozen English counties of whose area more than 3 per cent remained to be enclosed from the open-field

[1] J. Drummond and A. Wilbraham, *The Englishman's Food* (1957), p. 206.

state by Act of Parliament: and in these a fair part of the remaining work was done before 1830'.[1] It may reasonably be supposed that private enclosure (that is, enclosures achieved by private negotiations to buy out the rights of freeholders and tenants) was going on throughout this period. It had been going on for centuries. But in villages where there were a large number of freeholders the landlord who wanted to consolidate his holdings had to make his agreements with a large number of individuals, and his prospects of doing so privately grew less promising as the eighteenth century went on, for two reasons: first because it was the most difficult cases that had survived the early centuries of private negotiation and pressure, secondly because the high prices of corn which prevailed in the second half of the eighteenth century made it worth the occupier's while to hold on to even a small strip of the open field.

The price of corn was the crucial factor which determined the eagerness of the landlord to consolidate and the readiness of the peasant to relinquish his holding. In the first half of the eighteenth century corn prices were generally low and in these circumstances the pressure to enclose was generally rather weak. The pace of parliamentary enclosure was slow and generally steady over this period, 1700–60, and it is significant that 'the only years that show distinct activity in Parliament are 1729–30 and 1742–3—both periods following deficient harvests and relatively high prices of food'.[2] It may reasonably be presumed that private enclosure also went on fairly steadily as land exhausted by the open-field system came on to the market. Often the arable open fields were enclosed because they were too exhausted to give even subsistence crops of corn, and then they were put under grass.

In the second half of the eighteenth century, however, as population rose and cities grew, the price of corn rose and the pattern changed. It is reasonable to suppose that private enclosures proceeded more slowly than in the period before 1760, because the incentives to resist dispossession were strong when the price of food was high. Would-be enclosers had to find ways of enforcing compliance. Certainly the pace of parliamentary enclosure accelerated markedly. It is worth distinguishing between the Acts concerned with the enclosure of

[1] J. H. Clapham, *An Economic History of Modern Britain*, vol. 1 (1939), p. 19.
[2] Ashton, *The Eighteenth Century*, p. 40.

arable lands and fields cultivated on the open-field system (together with their associated commons) and the Acts concerned merely with the enclosure of common pasture and waste. The former permitted (though did not ensure) the introduction of the new techniques of large-scale farming, mechanization, stockbreeding, land drainage and scientific experiment. The latter often did no more than extend the margin of cultivation to lands which had been worthless when the price of corn was low. 'Before 1760 the number of Acts dealing more specifically with the open-field system (i.e. Acts dealing primarily with arable fields and meadows) did not exceed 130. Between 1760 and 1815 the number rose to upwards of 1800.'[1] Certainly by the end of the eighteenth century English agricultural experts were convinced that the only way of expanding the output of the cultivated area, so as to keep pace with the increasing demands that were being made on it, was to break up the open-field farms and to put the commons to profitable commercial use. So in 1801 the procedure for statutory enclosure was streamlined by the first General Enclosure Act, which simplified the parliamentary machinery for enclosure of commons and thus reduced its expense. The result was a burst of expenditure relating to small acreages which had previously not been worth enclosing.

It is impossible to say exactly how far the enclosure of the open field contributed to the revolution in agricultural techniques. 'It is significant', writes Ashton, 'that nearly all the improvements in agricultural technique of which there is a record were made on lands already enclosed or in process of enclosure.'[2] There is no doubt that enclosure extended the area of productive land in England, though not all of this extension lasted into the agricultural depression that followed Waterloo. When the pressure for food was at its height, particularly in the famine periods of the Napoleonic Wars, there was a tendency to put wastes and commons under the plough, and marginal lands that would never support corn at its normal peacetime price were sown to wheat. It has been estimated that between 1727 and 1760 when corn prices were generally low, less than 75,000 acres of common pasture and waste were enclosed by Parliamentary Acts; between 1761 and 1792 the acreage was not far short of half a million—about 478,000; over the period of the French

---

[1] Lord Ernle, *English Farming Past and Present*, p. 163.
[2] Ashton, *The Eighteenth Century*, p. 34.

and Napoleonic Wars it rose to over a million; and in the period 1816–45 it fell again to under 200,000 acres.[1] This substantial contribution to the nation's land resources was an important part of the explanation for its ability to feed a rapidly growing population (even if at deteriorating standards of diet) and expanding centres of industry, and to weather an unusual proportion of deficient harvests and a major war. It must not be forgotten, however, that the new agricultural techniques, by producing high yields from the light sandy soils which had formerly been relatively unproductive, turned once-marginal lands into valuable wheat growing areas. They were worth a great deal more, in money terms, to the innovating farmer than to the peasant who had grazed his skinny stock on them.

It used to be said that the enclosures created a reservoir of cheap labour without which the industrial revolution would have been impossible. It was said that they depressed and drove out the yeomen, pauperized the cottagers and depopulated the villages. Attempts to test these hypotheses against the records available for specific regions and communities in the peak periods of parliamentary enclosure (that is, in the second half of the eighteenth and early nineteenth centuries) have thrown considerable doubt on them, however.

The evidence on population, for example, indicates that the inhabitants of the rural areas grew almost as fast in numbers as those of the industrial centres. The fencing, hedging and ditching operations required by enclosure of the common fields required more rather than less labour. There may have been cases when the land was converted from subsistence crops to permanent pasture, and hence used less labour, but as population grew and the price of corn soared this was less likely to be the case. The sowing of commons and waste to arable crops also called for more rather than less labour. So too did the new agricultural techniques which enclosure permitted—the elimination of the fallow, growing of root crops and artificial grasses, and the establishment of large herds of dairy cattle and pedigree stock. Whereas non-parliamentary enclosure must have led to absorption and consolidation of large holdings, regional research for periods after 1780 suggests that enclosure by Acts of Parliament produced an *increase* in all grades of

[1] G. Slater, *The English Peasantry and the Enclosure of the Common Fields* (1907), p. 267.

occupying owners.[1] Under the Enclosure Acts many common-right cottagers received compensation for their rights which permitted them for the first time to buy small plots of land. While the artificially inflated wartime prices prevailed they could make a reasonable living out of these marginal plots.

In effect, enclosure, stimulated by rising corn prices, tended to operate in the interests of all who could establish or buy a claim to land and made many smallholdings profitable. The radical thinning-out of the small owner-occupiers came after Waterloo when prices plunged and poor-rates soared, and only the large landowners could hope to survive. While there was undoubtedly a long-term trend towards an increase in the size of holdings which was rightly associated with enclosures it was not a direct result of the revolutionary period of the enclosures in the late eighteenth and early nineteenth centuries. Moreover, it must be remembered that England is still a country of medium-sized and small farms and that the numbers engaged in agriculture went on expanding throughout the period of the enclosures. It was not until after the middle of the nineteenth century that the numbers began to show an absolute decline. In sum, it is important not to exaggerate the impact of the burst of parliamentary enclosures which coincided with the early stages of the industrial revolution in England.

3. CHANGES IN ENTREPRENEURIAL ATTITUDES

More important, perhaps, either than the new techniques introduced in the second half of the eighteenth century or the changes in the size and organization of farms which occurred during the peak periods of parliamentary enclosure, were the associated changes in the attitudes of farmers to their agricultural activities. In this, causes and effects were inextricably entangled. Growth of population, urbanization and industrial expansion, proceeding over long periods of time, gradually widened the market for agricultural produce and created a climate favourable to innovation and to consolidation of holdings. The response of the agricultural industry to this steady enlargement of opportunity removed some of the barriers to further growth of population, of cities and of industry: and these in their turn created new opportunities for agriculture. The

[1] J. D. Chambers, 'Enclosure and the Small Landowner', *Economic History Review*, vol. x, p. 123.

crucial factor in this process of development and change, however, was the human factor. It was because the decision-takers in the agricultural industry were willing to revise their methods of cultivation and organization on a sufficient scale that they transformed the industry.

It is worth bearing in mind, when considering the relationship of the agrarian revolution to the process of industrialization in England, that both were part and parcel of the larger process of economic transformation that we are accustomed to call the Industrial Revolution. Essentially the changes that were taking place in the agricultural industry were of the same kind as those that were taking place in manufacturing and commerce. They included three significant features: (1) a widening of economic horizons in both space and time, so that agriculturalists generally became more concerned with producing for a national or international market than for home or regional consumption, and some of them began to embark on schemes of land drainage or livestock breeding which would yield their full return not at the next harvest season but at some much more distant date; (2) an increase in economic specialization reflected in the appearance of the professional farmer or the landless labourer in place of the self-subsistent peasant working for wages only in harvest and planting seasons; and (3) the application of scientific knowledge and experimental methods to activities which had formerly been rigidly regulated by tradition, communal practice and rule of thumb.

Developments of this kind are of the essence of an industrial revolution in the broad sense of the term. In agriculture they took place slowly, though cumulatively. None of them were sudden in their incidence, nor was their impact attributable to a specific narrow space of time. All of them, however, were stimulated, to an extent which is difficult either to measure or to overstress, by the high price of corn which distinguished the second half of the eighteenth century and reached its climax in the French Wars which ended with Waterloo.

The new attitude to agriculture which eventually permeated all classes of the community began to be conspicuous in the upper ranges of the social scale. 'George III rejoiced in the title of "Farmer George", considered himself more indebted to Arthur Young than to any man in his dominions, carried the last volume of the *Annals* [of Agriculture] with him in his travelling carriage, kept his model farm at Windsor, formed his flock of merino sheep and experimented in stock breeding.'[1] The aristocracy, the clergy, even the politician-landowners and industrialist landowners like John Wilkinson were passionately concerned with the craze for agricultural improvement. Technological progress in agriculture was something which concerned them all and in which the eighteenth century was evidently fruitful. A host of farming societies and associations were set up for the exchange of knowledge and ideas. The Board of Agriculture was created in 1793 to spread the new gospel. A growing number of land stewards on large estates actively propagated improved farming methods in their advice to tenants and some progressive landlords pushed their tenants along the path of innovation by writing into their leases and farm agreements the duty of taking the steward's advice.[2]

Change may have been less deliberately sought after by the smallholders, the tenant farmers and the villagers, but it was none the less apparent by the second half of the eighteenth century, though it took until the middle of the nineteenth century to become general. Gradually, however, as enclosure transformed the institutional framework, the new entrepreneurial attitudes seeped through to the smallest agricultural producer. Regional researches reveal the extent of the transformation in one area after another. Dr Hoskins, studying the process of rural change in the Midlands, has described the revolutionary effects produced by enclosure in the Midlands. 'The self-supporting peasant was transformed into a spender of money...Peasant thrift was replaced by commercial thrift. Every hour of work now had a money value: unemployment became a disaster for there was no piece of land the wage-earner could turn to.'[3] Dr Thirsk's studies of Lincolnshire are equally revealing in their description of change. In the fen villages, for example, the children and grandchildren of those who had specialized in rearing geese and catching fish and wild fowl got their living in the new agriculture as ploughmen and labourers on rich cornland. Throughout the Lincolnshire villages

[1] Lord Ernle, *British Farming, Past and Present*, p. 207.
[2] G. E. Mingay, 'The Eighteenth-Century Land Steward' in E. J. Jones and G. E. Mingay (eds.), *Land, Labour and Population in the Industrial Revolution* (1967).
[3] W. G. Hoskins, *The Midland Peasant* (1957), p. 269.

there is no doubt that enclosure and the improvements which it made possible, raised ambitions in the ordinary farmer for the first time, and that the fresh opportunities suddenly opened up brought into action stores of human energy never previously tapped. The psychological effect of change doubled and trebled the force of the original stimulus, with the result that people were willing to go beyond the economic limit in spending money and effort on their farms.[1]

In sum, then, what can we say that the agricultural revolution contributed to the process of industrialization in England? What part did agriculture play in the first industrial revolution? By definition, of course, the role which agriculture plays in a pre-industrial economy must be important. A general rise in agricultural incomes represents a rise in incomes for the majority of the population; technological change in agriculture affects the majority of producers; a fall in agricultural prices tends to lower the cost of raw materials for the sectors outside agriculture and of foodstuffs for wage-earners generally.

It is reasonable to suppose, therefore, that the run of good harvests which characterized the period from about 1715 to the 1750's reduced the costs of British industry (most of which depended on agricultural raw materials) and increased the surplus incomes which the rural and urban poor could spare from their subsistence needs to spend on manufactured goods. The gin age was one manifestation of this process. The steady development of the textile industries was another and healthier reflection. Thus the beginnings of the expansion of British population and industry which can be traced back to the 1740's may have been significantly conditioned, possible even set off by the agricultural prelude. Although landowners and large-scale farmers found that good harvests depressed their incomes in the early eighteenth century, cottagers and agricultural labourers (and these were of course the majority) certainly benefited, as did the consumers and the producers in industries outside agriculture.

In the second half of the eighteenth century the interaction between industry and agriculture took a different form. The rising price of corn, stimulated by urbanization and industrial growth, encouraged extension of the cultivated acreage, cost-reducing improvements in techniques, and professionalization

[1] J. Thirsk, *English Peasant Farming* (1957), p. 296.

of farming at all levels. Higher incomes for landowners and tenants provided both incentive and finance for agricultural progress. If the agricultural industry did not actually supply the labour which the labour-intensive techniques of the new industry demanded, it fed the increasing population from which the industrial labour force was drawn. Between 1751 and 1821 the population of England and Wales more than doubled, and still the import of corn was insignificant except in years of agricultural disaster. Had the agricultural industry not risen to the challenge, it is difficult to see how the first industrial revolution could have taken shape, as it did, in a small country with a very narrow basis of natural resources; for the foreign exchange which could be used to import raw cotton and iron and wool would have been required to buy food imports. As it was, the English industrial revolution was able to develop irreversible momentum with the aid of a leading industry—cotton—whose basic raw material had to be entirely imported from non-temperate latitudes. For many of today's under-developed countries it is precisely their inability to expand the domestic output of agricultural products at a pace sufficient to feed the rising population that constitutes the biggest obstacle to sustained industrialization.

In meeting the challenge British agriculture kept within the domestic economy purchasing power that would otherwise have leaked into foreign markets. Increased incomes in agriculture meant increased purchasing power for the products of British industry and created the solid home-market which justified large-scale production and made factories profitable. It is always difficult and risky to build up an industry on the strength of foreign demand. It was particularly difficult in the unsettled international conditions of a half-century which included the Seven Years War, the War of American Independence, the French Revolution, and the European conflagration which ended with Waterloo. Yet this was the period in which the process of British industrialization gathered unprecedented momentum. Had it been mainly dependent on foreign markets for its basic demand it is hardly likely that British industrialists, and their backers in commerce and finance, would have ventured their capital with such sturdy confidence. The exist-ence of an expanding home-market reduced the element of uncertainty to calculable proportions and provided the strongest incentive to innovation.

Finally the agricultural industry provided a substantial part of the capital required for successful industrialization. It is not possible to analyse precisely the sources of the funds which financed the first industrial revolution, but it is clear that the premier British industry—agriculture—made an important contribution. Most of the early iron-works, for example, were built originally by landowners. Farmers were prominent supporters of schemes to improve local communications by road, river or canal. Many of the new breed of industrialists came from a rural background, and found their capital by borrowing either on the strength of their own lands or from their farming friends and neighbours. It was a two-way flow, of course, because the revolution in industry and the revolution in agriculture were part of the same process. It was natural enough for successful industrialists to build up the social prestige and creditworthiness, which they needed to help them finance their industrial ventures, by putting some of their profits into landed property. It was natural too for the more enterprising of them to operate their landed estates in the same progessive innovating spirit in which they ran their factories. John Wilkinson the famous iron-master, for example, used some of his industrial and mining profits to finance agricultural improvement. He undertook large-scale land reclamation and afforestation schemes, and was a pioneer in the use of agricultural machinery: in 1798 he installed a threshing machine driven by steam-power.[1]

Moreover the agricultural industry carried much of the burden of the State. The land-tax was the traditional stand-by of government revenue throughout the eighteenth century. Even when the strains of total war forced Pitt to impose an income-tax, it was still the agricultural sector which footed most of the bill, partly because of its size and partly because it was easier to assess and to collect tax for a stable agricultural community than for an urban group. Between 1803/4 and 1814/15 gross incomes assessed for tax under schedule D (the trade and industry sector) rose by under 10 per cent despite a galloping inflation, whereas the increase for schedules A and B

[1] W. G. Chaloner, 'The Agricultural Activities of John Wilkinson, Ironmaster', *Agricultural History Review*, vol. V (1957).

(agricultural and land incomes) was nearly 60 per cent. Had the commerce and industry sectors paid their 'fair share' of the mounting cost of the French wars it is likely that the industrial revolution, then in its early stages, would have suffered a severe setback.

Briefly then, the agricultural revolution in England can be said to have contributed to the effectiveness of the first industrial revolution in three main ways: (1) by feeding the growing population and particularly the populations of the industrial centres, (2) by inflating purchasing power for the products of British industry, and (3) by providing a substantial part of the capital required to finance industrialization and to keep it going even through a period of major war, and (4) by releasing its surplus labour for employment in industry. However, the changes in technology, agrarian organization and entreprene-urial attitudes which constituted the agricultural revolution developed over a period roughly twice as long as the century 1750–1850 to which the industrial revolution is generally attributed. It is now evident that substantial improvements in farming practice were widely diffused in the period 1650–1750; and that the modernization of agriculture, through mechanical techniques, artificial fertilizers and capital-intensive drainage or irrigation projects, did not gather appreciable momentum until after 1850. Developments in agriculture were no doubt impor-tant among the environmental conditions which stimulated the initial upsurge of population and industrial output in the 1740's, and which facilitated the acceleration of British economic growth in the later eighteenth and early nineteenth centuries; and the agricultural surplus—whether of labour or investible funds—helped to power the industrialization process through the eighteenth and nineteenth centuries. It was not until the second half of the nineteenth century that the numbers employed in agriculture began to contract and that the contribution of agriculture to British economic growth began to assume diminishing importance.

CHAPTER 4

THE COMMERCIAL REVOLUTION

One of the ways—the commonest way perhaps—by which an economy can develop from a pre-industrial to an industrial state is to exploit the opportunities open to it from international trade. By selling abroad goods which are in surplus at home in return for goods which are scarce at home, it is possible both to widen the range of goods and services coming on to the home-market and to increase the value of domestic output, and so to improve the national standard of living both qualitatively and quantitatively. In widening the potential market for domestic producers, foreign trade encourages them to specialize, to develop special skills and techniques of economic organization, and to reap the economies of large-scale production. This broadening of their economic horizons constitutes an incentive to greater productive activity and helps to break up the economic inertia which so often inhibits material progress.

For any country the limits to economic growth based on international trade are set by the range of goods which it can persuade its trading partners to buy and by the intensity with which its people desire the goods that foreigners have to sell. In the eighteenth-century world of pre-industrial economies, where each country—each region in some cases—produced most if not all of its own basic needs, international trade was largely limited to luxuries and to goods which were localized in their geographical incidence—wines, tobacco, sugar and high-quality textiles, for example, or fruit, fish and minerals. For countries situated in the same geographical latitudes, the opportunities for trade are further limited by the basic similarities of the patterns of production in the trading partners, as well as by the fact, of universal significance, that the demand for any one commodity (especially a luxury) rapidly approaches saturation point in any one market. Since many pre-industrial countries depend heavily on a particular export commodity

—the crop or the skill that they happen to have in unusual abundance—the foreign demand for this commodity is not easily expanded unless new trading partners can be found and new markets can be opened up. For pre-industrial Europe the obvious way to achieve economic growth was to extend the range of its trading relationships and to open up markets in other continents, and in consequence the economic history of the fifteenth, sixteenth and seventeenth centuries is filled with attempts to expand the European trading horizon. But this was a difficult business. The underdeveloped world then, as now, was poor in purchasing power. It was often indifferent—more so than today's Third World—to the goods that Europe had to sell, especially at the high prices imposed by long and dangerous journeys over difficult seas and terrain.

In this bid to expand the economic horizon of the most rapidly developing region of the world, Western Europe, Britain was in a strategically favourable position. Britain also had a peculiarly strong incentive to succeed, for its own endowment of natural resources was comparatively narrow and in no sense unique. It was not more fertile than the rest of Western Europe: its timber and mineral resources were limited and exhaustible: its access to the northern fisheries was no easier than that of the Dutch or the French. It was thus highly sensitive, then as now, to foreign competition. It had succeeded in building up a flourishing manufacturing export by processing the wool which it had in relatively abundant supply and in good quality, and by developing the technical skills and commercial techniques which permitted it to sell quality woollens more cheaply than most of its neighbours. For most of its pre-industrial trading history England came close to being a single export economy: 'from the days of the Angevin kings to the time of the Cromwellian Protectorate, wool or woollen cloth constituted almost the whole of English exports'.[1] At the middle of the eighteenth century woollen textiles still accounted for well over half the value of English domestic exports.

But by this time the Atlantic trade had been opened and English plantations in the West Indies had greatly extended the range of commodities which English merchants could sell in Europe. Like the spices and tea of the Far East, the West Indian

[1] Ralph Davis, 'English Foreign Trade 1660–1700', *Economic History Review* (December 1954), p. 150.

products—sugar, tobacco, cotton, indigo and dyewoods—were valuable commodities unobtainable in Europe and were rapidly becoming necessities of life there. In the half-century ending in the early 1750's the volume of English re-exports had increased by 90 per cent: in the next half-century the re-export trade expanded more than twice as fast.

The immense importance of the tropical commodities lay in the fact that they increased British purchasing power on the continent of Europe. Britain needed her European imports for vital productive purposes and not merely to meet the upper-class demand for wine and brandy. She needed foreign timber, pitch and hemp for her ships and buildings, high-grade bar iron for her metal trade, raw and thrown silk for her textile trades. Her industrial expansion along traditional lines was severely restricted by the fact that the demand for woollen products was inelastic and already near saturation point in traditional markets. Had it not been for the tropical products with their income-elastic demand and growing markets in temperate regions it would have been difficult to expand British trade with Europe.

The tropical products also had to be paid for, of course, and it was not easy to buy them with woollen manufactures. The tropical demand for woollen goods was naturally limited by climatic considerations, and there were no other British goods with a special advantage in most markets. In Africa, for example, the demand for British manufactures was further restricted by low incomes, in China by the fact that local manufactures were often at least as good and always a great deal cheaper. In the end the solution to the numerous problems of matching demand and supply in the international market was found by developing a complex world-wide network of trading transactions centred on London. In this network the West Indian islands, administered by a British plantation *élite* on the basis of a slave society, constituted the most valuable and intimate link. Weapons, hardware, spirits from Britain and calicoes from India were shipped to west Africa and exchanged for slaves, ivory and gold. The slaves were sold in the West Indies for sugar, dyestuffs, mahogany, logwood, tobacco and raw cotton. The gold and ivory was shipped to the East and Near East for teas, silks, calicoes, coffee and spices. The tropical goods were sold in Europe for Baltic timber, hemp, pitch and tar (all essential naval stores), Swedish and Russian iron; and, in the fourth quarter of the century, they paid for the foreign grain which was vital when the harvest failed and which was regularly required in most years even when the harvest did not fail.

On all these transactions British merchants and shippers got their profits, generally computed by customs officials as about 15 per cent of the value of the goods imported for re-export; and as a net result British producers and consumers got vital raw materials and desirable luxuries from the ends of the earth. The domestic resources which permitted the British to expand their overseas trade in this way were fourfold: their basic human capital in seamen and navigators, their commercial advantage in the form of a merchant class with the funds and the flair for risk-taking, their organizational background in the form of a credit centre with immense financial skill and experience, and their constitutional heritage in the shape of a government which was in complete sympathy with the acquisitive aims of the mercantile classes. These advantages gave them freedom to experiment and to follow up the most promising lines of trade wherever they led. It was here in the commercial sphere that the major innovations were taking place in the early eighteenth century.

By the middle of the eighteenth century the commercial monopolies which had made it possible in the seventeenth century to support the difficult and dangerous business of overseas trade at a distance were giving way to the individual merchant, the incipient free-trader. The years about the mid-century saw a considerable relaxation in the company system by which English foreign trade had normally been conducted. The success of the system made its dissolution inevitable. There were more capitalists wealthy enough to finance voyages individually than there had been a century earlier. The risks of foreign trade, though still considerable, had been diminished by the extension of diplomatic offices, by the efficiency and strength of the Royal Navy and by the development of marine insurance. These developments reduced the need for the Chartered Company in a steadily widening area of trade. Of the great joint-stock companies, the East India and the Hudson's Bay Company survived because it seemed that the trades they served still needed the protection which only a company with permanent and collective financial resources could provide. The third, the African Company, was wound up, and in 1750 its exclusive monopoly was broken when it was formally reconstituted as a regulated company comprising all the merchants trading to Africa. In 1753 a bill was passed which threw open the Levant Company in the same way and 'brought it into line with the new fashion'.[1]

At the middle of the eighteenth century then, the bulk of British trade was with Europe, which took three-quarters of all exports from English ports. This was a natural development. Europe was relatively accessible to British traders. Its inhabitants had the same sort of tastes as the home-market and they earned incomes which, though they may have been lower on an average than British incomes, were distinctly higher than those of most non-European countries. The cities of Europe were among the richest markets in the world. But in 1772/3 Europe took only half of British *domestic* exports (that is, the goods produced within the British Isles) and this share was falling. By the end of the century it took about a third. In order to expand the markets for British domestic exports it became more and more necessary in the second half of the eighteenth century to look for markets outside Europe. On the other hand, European demand for the commodities which could not be produced in temperate climates was expanding rapidly. Britain's naval supremacy, which became virtually complete when the French were pinned down by their revolutionary wars in the last decade of the century, enabled her to meet this expanding demand from her plantations in the West Indies and her trading outposts in India and beyond. By the 1790's Europe was absorbing between 80 and 90 per cent of Britain's re-exports, and the West Indies and the Far East were supplying about half of Britain's imports. These changes in the geographical pattern of trade are illustrated in Table 2.

One of the most interesting and significant features of the change in the British trading network in the second half of the eighteenth century, however, was the growth in the importance of a new market in temperate latitudes—North America. The North American colonies were not very populous in the first half of the century. As late as 1750 there were less than a million

[1] Charles Wilson in *The New Cambridge Modern History*, vol. VII (1957), p. 48.

TABLE 2. *The geographical distribution of English trade in the eighteenth century*

	Percentages of totals for England and Wales			As per-centages of total for Great Britain, 1797/8
	1700/1	1750/1	1772/3	
Total imports from:				
Europe	66	55	45	43
North America	6	11	12	7
West Indies	14	19	25	25
East Indies and Africa	14	15	18	25
Re-exports to:				
Europe	85	79	82	88
North America	5	11	9	3
West Indies	6	4	3	4
East Indies and Africa	4	5	6	4
Domestic exports to:				
Europe	85	77	49	30
North America	6	11	25	32
West Indies	5	5	12	25
East Indies and Africa	4	7	14	13

SOURCE: Compiled from the custom-house ledgers; P.R.O. Customs 3 and 17. For a more detailed analysis see Deane and Cole, *British Economic Growth*, Table 22.

white residents. But by the time the American War of Independence had ended with the establishment of the United States of America, there were nearly 3 million inhabitants in the new country of whom more than $2\frac{1}{4}$ million were white and relatively prosperous. 'The wages of labour', observed Adam Smith in his *Wealth of Nations*, first published in 1776, 'are much higher in North America than in any part of England.'[1] He had no doubt that it was a growing and developing economy, for he went on to say: 'Though North America is not yet so rich as England it is much more thriving, and advancing with much greater rapidity to the further acquisition of riches.' The trade figures were to bear out fully Adam Smith's interpretation. In 1750/1 North America took 11 per cent of British domestic exports compared with a European share of 77 per cent: by 1797/8 its share had risen to 32 per cent of a trade which had swelled to twice the 1750 volume, and the European share had fallen to 30 per cent.

[1] Adam Smith, *Wealth of Nations*, Cannan ed., p. 71.

The fact is that the North Americans preferred British manufactures, largely no doubt because they were predominantly British emigrants themselves. Even when the colonists won their independence and were freed from the compulsion of the Navigation Laws they still bought British from choice. In 1787–90, for example, they were taking 87 per cent of their imports of manufactures from Britain.[1] Again the trade was balanced multilaterally rather than bilaterally. About a third of the exports of the United States went to Britain and were paid for largely by giving British merchants access to the credits that the United States had built up with their exports to Ireland and continental Europe.

The centre of the wide, intricate, multilateral network of world trade that grew up during the eighteenth century was London. London with its wide sheltered anchorages, its vast wharves and warehouses, its rich city banks, its specialists in marine insurance and its world-wide mercantile contacts, was uniquely qualified for this role. It drew to itself a cosmopolitan concentration of wealth and commercial expertise. According to Professor Ashton, 'Of the 810 merchants who kissed the hand of George III at least 250 must have been of alien origin. It was one of the merits of the English at this time that they opened their doors to capital and enterprise from all quarters.'[2] The London money market was the centre of the national credit system for the richest country in the world, and, largely by virtue of its immense entrepôt trade, it became a centre of credit for the whole world, finally displacing Amsterdam and Paris when these were submerged by the French wars. In the second half of the eighteenth century it was the best place in the world to find credit on reasonable terms or to invest one's capital at a lucrative return. It was this unique combination of circumstances that was to turn it into the world's financial centre for more than a century.

These developments were of importance internationally as well as nationally. Not only did they facilitate the British industrial revolution, but they helped to extend its impact to a wide range of underdeveloped areas within and beyond Europe. It was essential to national economic progress that there should have been some means of channelling the funds which

---

[1] Ashton, *The Eighteenth Century*, p. 159.   [2] *Ibid.* p. 140.

became available in the saving regions of the country into the institutions which could meet the needs of the investing regions. It was also essential that the underdeveloped areas of the new world should be given access to capital stored up in the old world if they were to become effective partners in an international trading relationship and to exploit their accessible resources in land and labour. It has been said, for example, that 'only the merchants of Great Britain with the resources being mobilized especially in 18th century London could have financed the rapid expansion of the English speaking colonies in the New world'.[1] And there is no doubt that the British colonial empire was an important means of rapidly spreading the benefits of technical progress far beyond the confines of Europe.

The expansion of the entrepôt trade, the lucrative business of collecting foreign goods and redistributing them to foreign customers, helped to turn London into the financial centre of the world, made a considerable direct addition to the incomes of British merchants, shippers and seamen, and gave merchants access to a vast network of markets in which to buy raw materials for British industry or to sell the output of British industry. Between the 1750's and the 1790's the value of English re-exports, measured at official (constant) values, expanded from about £3½ millions to about £9½ millions.[2] By 1800, as British merchants seized the opportunities created by the French wars (which crippled Britain's two chief commercial rivals, Holland and France), the value of re-exports at official values had risen to over £18½ millions.

The significance of the re-export trade in contributing to British economic growth and industrialization lay predominantly in its indirect effects on economic organization and opportunity. It was a direct source of incomes only to a limited group of merchants and seamen. Obviously the *direct* impact of international trade on British incomes and industry was more effective when exercised through the trade in *domestic* exports and *retained* imports; that is, through the goods and services which were the product of British industry or were wholly paid for out of British incomes. A substantial part of the final value of re-exports, probably between half and three-quarters, accrued to the original producers in their countries of origin. British residents benefited directly only to the extent of the value

[1] G. D. Ramsay, *English Overseas Trade During the Centuries of Emergence* (1957), p. 237.
[2] See below, p. 62, for the definition of 'official' values.

of the distribution and processing services rendered by the commercial sector. On the other hand, the export of, say, a yard of English broadcloth generated income for the farmer producing the wool, the industrial capitalist and the carrier who collected and distributed the raw material, the spinner and the weaver who worked it up, and the merchant, insurance broker, shipper and seamen who put it on the foreign market. Or to put it another way, in determining the contribution to the national income of a £'s worth of domestic exports we take the whole of its value into consideration: in doing the same for a £'s worth of re-exports we must first subtract the basic value of the commodity in its country of origin, for this made incomes for foreign producers.

In effect, expansion of the exports of woollen manufactures in the late eighteenth century meant a better market for wool, more regular employment for spinners and weavers and a higher return on capital invested in the home-country. Similarly increasing exports of other British manufactures encouraged new industrial investment and innovation and generated increased domestic purchasing power. Under the circumstances the statistics of domestic exports are particularly significant in any attempt to assess the rate of national economic growth. They are all the more important for eighteenth-century Britain because the overseas trade statistics are the only reliable *annual* records of an overall kind. We have no annual statistics of national income for this period and no other way of assessing the progress of the economy as a whole. To a considerable extent, therefore, the trade statistics have provided most of the justification for general theories of English economic growth —for example, for Professor Rostow's thesis that it was during the period 1783–1802 that the British economy experienced its 'take-off' into self-sustained growth.[1] Before going on to discuss these implications, however, let me say something about the statistics themselves, about their basic reliability and meaning.

Regular, centrally compiled, records of English overseas trade date from 1696. For Scotland (and hence for Great Britain as a whole) they date from 1755. The basic source of these data are the Inspector-General's manuscript *Ledgers of Imports and Exports* for the period 1697–1780 and the printed *Reports on the State of the Navigation Commerce and Revenues of Great Britain* for

[1] As also for his later gloss on this thesis, to the effect that there was a phase of deceleration from 1802 to 1815. See W. W. Rostow, *The World Economy* (1978), p. 383.

1772 onwards. Until quite recently students who wanted to use these figures have either had to go back to the manuscript sources or parliamentary reports, or to rely on one of the many transcriptions from these sources, made by contemporaries, which were full of copying errors and unexplained discrepancies. Now, however, the trade figures have been made a great deal more accessible. At present the best detailed source of eighteenth-century foreign-trade statistics is contained in a compilation by Mrs Schumpeter, which was posthumously edited by Professor T. S. Ashton.[1] This source has the additional advantage of being prefaced by Professor Ashton's introductory essay on the trade statistics. There are some odd omissions from the volume —it lacks the series for exports of grain or for imports of raw cotton—but all the other important overseas trade figures are there for the eighteenth century.

It is important to remember, however, that they do not appear in precisely the same form as modern trade statistics. In particular, the value figures do not reflect the amounts actually paid for imports or the amounts actually received for exports. Eighteenth-century clerks transcribed the actual quantity of the commodities as reported to them by importers and exporters and valued them in terms of an officially prescribed set of constant prices, most of which were laid down at the end of the seventeenth century. These were the famous 'official values', which were the only values applied to export statistics until the late eighteenth century and to imports until the mid nineteenth century. Actually the prices used by the Inspector-General's clerks were not completely fixed throughout the period of the official valuation of English foreign trade, though the vast majority of them were standardized by the second half of the eighteenth century; and of course new commodities had to be introduced at the prices prevailing when they were introduced. Mrs Schumpeter, however, has removed one source of confusion—changes in the official valuations—by deliberately revaluing the quantities of imports and exports at a standard set of official values throughout the century. As a result her aggregates differ somewhat from the Inspector-General's aggregates but they do constitute a genuine constant price series.

In principle, of course, there are advantages for some purposes

---

[1] *English Overseas Trade Statistics 1697–1808*, by E. B. Schumpeter. Edited with an introduction by T. S. Ashton (1960).

in valuing imports and exports at constant rather than at current prices. Such series do not permit an assessment of the true *balance* of international payments because they do not show what residents are actually getting from or paying out to foreigners. For most of the eighteenth century we have no means of judging when the balance of payments was 'favourable' or 'unfavourable'. But what a constant price series does do is to take out the effects of changes in the value of money and so give a closer approximation to what we might call the 'real' changes in the amount of trade. Nowadays when trade is originally recorded at current values, one of the first tasks of the analyst concerned with productivity or growth problems is often to remove the 'veil of money' from the statistics by constructing a volume index. This in essence is simply a matter of valuing all quantities at the constant prices of some particular year. It permits an assessment of the change in the amount of trade as if there had been no change in relative prices or the value of money over the period under consideration. Hence, in so far as we are interested in the quantity of goods entering into international trade rather than in their current values in the eyes of contemporaries, we should be grateful to the eighteenth-century clerks for giving us a rough volume-index of English overseas trade and to Mrs Schumpeter for making sure that the measure is really a standard measure by using constant prices. If the prices are not standardized the attempt to use the series as a measure of the change in the volume of trade is as unsatisfactory as the attempt to measure length with a ruler whose length and gradations are changing in the process.[1]

The fact is, however, that even Mrs Schumpeter's calculations do not provide an entirely satisfactory measure of the change in the volume of trade in the eighteenth century. When one tries to eliminate the effects of changes in the value of money over a period of time by valuing quantities at constant prices, one does so on the assumption that changes in the price *level* have been more important than changes in price *relatives* and that the *structure* of prices was much the same at the end of the period as it was at the beginning. Otherwise indeed it would be difficult to decide which set of prices to use. In effect, if there is a considerable variation in the relative values of the different

[1] Ashton, *The Eighteenth Century*, p. 153.

commodities over the period considered, one would get an appreciably different measure of the increase in the volume of trade by accepting end-year prices as the constants than one would by accepting first-year or mid-year prices. In other words the measure is indeterminate. Our ruler gives a different answer if we start measuring from right to left than it would if we started measuring from left to right. If the period is fairly short the effects of changes in tastes or techniques will be limited and confined to a minority of goods. In that case the structure of prices will have altered too little to affect the answer much. For the price structure reflects a whole host of circumstances which are fairly slow to change in the aggregate—costs of production and community standards of value or taste, for example— whereas the price level fluctuates with the amount of money in circulation or the velocity with which it circulates and is thus much more variable. But if the period covered is long enough to permit important shifts in conditions of production, and consumers' tastes, then the structure of prices can reasonably be expected to have changed significantly and different basing- points will suggest significantly different amounts of trade for a particular year.

With these problems in mind, economic historians have tended to use the eighteenth-century trade statistics cautiously, for in a whole century a great deal can happen to costs and tastes and methods of economic organization. Recent research, however, has thrown some more definite light on the margins of error involved and they do not seem to be as large as has sometimes been supposed. An attempt has been made to check the efficiency of the official value statistics as a measure of the growth in the volume of trade by doing the calculation in the reverse direction, that is, by applying the prices of the period 1796/8 to the quantity data and comparing the rates of change suggested by these results with the rates of change that emerge from the official value aggregates, based as these are mainly on late-seventeenth-century prices. Surprisingly enough, the dif- ference between the two measures is not wide *except* in the case of re-exports, where there seems to have been a considerable distortion due to the sharp fall in prices and sharp rise in consumption of certain tropical goods. Coffee and tea were the major examples, though these were not the only ones concerned. To specify: for domestic exports the official values suggest an increase in volume of 398 per cent between 1702/3 and 1797/8, whereas the 1796/8 valuations give an increase of 421 per cent. For imports (including imports destined for re-export) the official values suggest an increase of about 423 per cent and the 1796/8 values imply 328 per cent.[1]

The conclusions we can draw from this comparison are that the official values give a muted indication of the growth in the value of domestic exports and an exaggerated indication of the growth of imports, particularly certain tropical imports. Nevertheless it can confidently be presumed that the volume of domestic exports multiplied by between 2 and $2\frac{1}{2}$ times in the second half of the eighteenth century, that retained imports probably expanded to roughly the same extent and that re-exports, which quadrupled at the official values, probably trebled when measured at 1796/8 prices. Undoubtedly domestic exports grew faster than population in the second half of the eighteenth century. Measured at 1796/8 prices the value of English domestic exports rose from barely £2 per head in 1752/3 to about £2. 15s. per head of the population in 1797/8. This must have represented a substantial addition to average incomes, more especially for the sectors which were producing for the export trade.

More significant indeed than the change in the volume of domestic exports was the change in its composition—the shift from primary products to manufactured goods and from the products of the old domestic type of industry to the products of the new capitalistic factory industry. In 1750 grain accounted for a fifth of English exports: by 1800 England had become on balance a grain-importing country. In 1750 refined sugar made up less than 1 per cent of English exports: by 1800 it was $4\frac{1}{2}$ per cent. In 1750 woollens accounted for 46 per cent of exports: in 1800 their share had fallen to $28\frac{1}{2}$ per cent while cotton fabrics and yarn had jumped from negligible quantities to 24 per cent. Before the end of the first decade of the nineteenth century, cotton, which was essentially a *new* industry, had outstripped the ancient woollen industry in the value which it added to British exports.

More than any other British industry, the cotton industry depended on international trade. Mass-producing any com-

---

[1] Deane and Cole, *British Economic Growth*: table 13, p. 44, gives details of these calculations.

modity depends on access to a large popular market—much larger than the 7–10 million or so people who lived in Britain in the last quarter of the eighteenth century. Cotton, however, was the one commodity that commanded an immediate sale throughout the known world. The new factory article was cheap enough to come within the budget of the lowest income groups and fine enough to be desired by rich as well as poor: it was saleable in tropical as well as in temperate climates; and it found a market ready-made for it in the regions which Britain had been supplying for a century with Indian calicoes. There was no problem of salesmanship here, of creating a demand, of persuading people to adopt new tastes. All that had to be done was to carry this desirable commodity to the markets already opened up by British merchants and to sell it to all who had money to buy.

Cotton depended on the international trading network already built up by British merchants not only for its markets but also for its supplies of raw materials. For the first time in history a great staple industry had been established on the basis of a natural resource that could not be domestically produced. It is the classic example of the way that economic growth can be founded on international trade and the benefits of technical progress can be transmitted from nation to nation in a process of mutually beneficial exchange. British purchases of raw cotton put incomes in the pockets of the very people who were willing to buy the finished product. It provided the incentive for further technical innovation not only in the factories producing the finished product but also in the regions which were the source of the raw material. For example, Eli Whitney's cotton-ginning machine and the opening up of new cotton lands in the southern states of America induced a drop in the cost of the raw material, a further cheapening of the finished cloth and a consequent enlargement of the demand for it. For the product of the cotton industry had an important economic characteristic which made it peculiarly suitable to play a leading part in the industrial revolution. It was a commodity which enjoyed an elastic demand, that is to say: when its price fell or when purchasers' incomes rose, demand for it grew more than proportionately. The falling costs and prices generated by the opening up of new high-yielding cotton lands and the invention of the cotton-ginning machine in the U.S.A., and by the factory system and textile inventions in Britain, brought a disproportionate expansion in demand on a world-wide scale. Cotton manufacturing proved to be the first 'growth industry' in the modern sense of the term, for it stimulated a cumulative sequence of innovation and expansion which spread out over time and space and set up a wide range of income-creating repercussions. Had it not been for the lively burst of innovation in the British cotton industry at the end of the eighteenth century the new United States of America might have taken another generation to achieve complete economic independence. 'Had it not been for the productivity of the virgin upland soil of the United States the first Industrial Revolution might have been delayed quite a while.'[1] The largest profits from innovations generally go to those who adopt them first. It was the network of world trade built up by eighteenth-century British merchants that enabled Britain to take the lead in exploring the opportunities offered by innovations on both sides of the Atlantic.

If the official trade statistics do not allow us to make precise measurements of the rate of growth of British trade at different periods in the eighteenth century, they do, since they are annually available, provide a reasonably clear picture of the long-term course of this growth. Taken year by year, of course, the path looks highly erratic. In the days of sailing ships the frequent incidence of storms, or of wars in different regions of the world, often produced violent fluctuations in the value of trade as between one year and the next. Some of the more ephemeral effects of these year-to-year fluctuations can be ironed out by the statistical device of taking moving averages of the figures concerned, but the path remains fairly erratic. It is probable that if we had an annual series of national-income statistics for the eighteenth century these would look almost equally erratic, for climatic variations play a very important part in determining the flow of incomes in most agricultural economies.

The path of growth of English foreign trade is illustrated by the graph on page 68, which traces its course in terms of a three-yearly moving average of total domestic exports plus total retained imports—both series measured at offical values. This graph therefore focuses on the volume of trade which is likely

[1] K. Berrill, 'International Trade and the Rate of Economic Growth', *Economic History Review* (1960).

to have had the most direct impact in the British economy, for it excludes the value of re-exports both at point of entry into and at the point of exit from the country.[1]

An interesting feature of the pattern suggested by the graph is the existence of two marked discontinuities of trend which appear in the 1740's and the 1780's respectively. These echo the

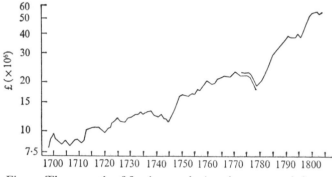

Fig. 1. The growth of foreign trade (net imports and domestic exports: three-yearly moving averages).

breaks in trend which we have already detected in the output and population figures. It is not at all surprising that the trade statistics exhibit discontinuities similar to the output indicators, for the latter are estimates which are based to a significant extent on commodities entering into international trade. But the trade graph, being based originally on annual records, illustrates the pattern more effectively than output or population statistics available only at bench-mark dates. Briefly, then, the volume of international trade traces an erratic but slowly rising course in the first four decades of the eighteenth century, moves up abruptly in the 1740's, relapses into an erratic but slow rise punctuated by wars and ending in the disastrous slump associated with the War of American Independence, and then leaps up again in the 1780's and continues to surge upwards through most of the 1790's and early 1800's. There is no question of the enormous significance of the second upsurge, dating from the 1780's, if only because it was sustained. But if we take into

[1] The graph is in two sections: one ending in the 1770's based on figures of the overseas trade of England and Wales, the other starting in the 1770's and based on figures for Great Britain.

account the fact that part of this upsurge was in effect a rebound from the artificially low level to which the economy was forced by the American war, the discontinuity of the 1780's was little more abrupt than that of the 1740's.

In sum, and in conclusion, the six main ways in which foreign trade can be said to have helped to precipitate the first industrial revolution are listed below:

(1) First of all it created a demand for the products of British industry. One of the problems which faces most pre-industrial economies is that the level of domestic purchasing power is too low to justify industrial specialization. Specialization, as Adam Smith recognized in the 1770's, depends on the extent of the market; without specialization it is not possible to obtain the economies of scale and experience which can lower costs and prices sufficiently to bring a product within the reach of the mass of the population. This is the vicious circle of a closed economy. If it is to raise output it must first raise incomes in the home-market which provides the demand for that output. It must hoist itself up by its own bootstraps. A large, well-populated country may have both the natural resources and the potential market for this kind of self-generating development. A small country with a small population has very little prospect of appreciably accelerating its rate of growth of output without access to a wider market and a wider range of resources than it can provide within its own borders. It was access to a world market that broke this vicious circle for Britain.

(2) International trade gave access to raw materials which both widened the range and cheapened the products of British industry. Without access to raw cotton Britain could not have shifted from dependence on an industry with a relatively inelastic demand (wool) to a technologically similar industry with a relatively elastic demand (cotton). Unless they had been able to import Swedish bar-iron, Sheffield cutlers could never have built up the trade in quality steel which survived into the period when British bar-iron became good enough to serve their purpose.

(3) International trade provided poor, underdeveloped countries with the purchasing power to buy British goods. Trade is a two-way process. By buying from foreigners, British importers provided them with the exchange and credit with which to buy the products of British industry. By buying American cotton,

for example, Britain provided the ex-colonists with purchasing power which raised their demand for British exports.

(4) It provided an economic surplus which helped to finance industrial expansion and agricultural improvement. The profits of trade overflowed into agriculture, mining and manufacture. Without them the innovators would have found it difficult to convert the new ideas and rotations and machines into productive enterprise. It is not enough to know about new productive methods or would-be purchasers. It is necessary also to have the capital to finance the plant, the equipment, the stocks of goods and the ships which are necessary to process and distribute the manufactured goods. A century and more of successful trading in overseas markets had enabled British merchants to build up a substantial fund of cumulated profits which was ripe for reinvestment when new profit-making opportunities arose either in trade or in the manufacture of trading goods.

(5) It helped to create an institutional structure and a business ethic which was to prove almost as effective in promoting the home-trade as it had been for the foreign trade. The elaborate network of commercial institutions in the city, with their numerous provincial contacts, helped to channel capital funds from regions where they were being accumulated to regions where they were in active demand. The systems of orderly marketing, insurance, quality-control and standardization of product which grew up out of the needs of the foreign trade were important aids to improving productivity at home. Sturdy standards of business honesty, commercial initiative and adventurous attitudes to risk-taking, which are qualities essential to sustained economic growth in any sphere, developed relatively rapidly in the sphere of international commerce, for without them foreign trade would have been impossible. A more sophisticated set of attitudes to the role of government policy in promoting economic prosperity—attitudes that were most clearly reflected in the free-trade movement—was another major factor facilitating British economic progress.

(6) Finally, it is worth noting that the expansion of international trade in the eighteenth century was a prime cause of the growth of large towns and industrial centres. It is the essence of an industrial revolution that the balance of the economy shifts from a primarily agricultural basis to an industrial/commercial basis. The beginnings of the process lie generally in the growth

of large towns and the scope that these offer for specialization in economic activities. It was the growth of really big towns like London, Liverpool, Manchester, Birmingham and Glasgow that directly stimulated the large-scale investments in transport which were such an important feature of the early stages of the British industrial revolution. All these towns owed a large part of their growth to the overseas trade, and the spectacular expansion of Liverpool and Glasgow was almost entirely a function of the foreign trade.

The effect of the commercial revolution, generally attributed to the period of the late seventeenth century and the first half of the eighteenth century, was thus to bring a special kind of maturity to the English pre-industrial economy.[1] The merchants trading overseas had learned to operate confidently in an impersonal, international economy, where the scale of operations was large and far-flung, and where both risks and rewards were potentially high. To reduce the uncertainties of these operations, they had created in the City of London an information system, an institutional structure and a business ethic which together provided a strategic base for expansion of national and international markets during the period of accelerating industrialization. By the second half of the eighteenth century, Britain was a commercially and financially mature economy in a sense that few mid twentieth-century developing economies were when they began to promote industrial growth. She already had an effective home-grown network of institutions which could channel surplus capital from regions and activities where it was piling up, to regions and activities where it was needed, and a body of entrepreneurs capable of calculating, and insuring against, the risks inherent in operating on a large-scale, and also capable of locating new markets and guaranteeing the quality of final goods. The fact that Britain was already the centre of a world wide network of international trade and of commercial knowhow was a crucial element in the process whereby a small pre-industrial economy with a narrow resource base was able to become the workshop of the world.

[1] Charles Kindleberger, 'Commercial Expansion and the Industrial Revolution', *Journal of European Economic History* (Winter, 1975).

CHAPTER 5

THE TRANSPORT REVOLUTION

One of the most significant differences between a pre-industrial economy and an industrialized economy is that the latter has a larger stock of capital; in other words, each member of the industrial labour force has a great deal more physical capital to assist him in the process of production. This is one of the reasons for the higher level of productivity that characterizes an economy which has gone through an industrial revolution. To the extent that the additional capital is purchased by private entrepreneurs as they innovate and expand, then the accumulation of the larger national stock is achieved by raising the proportion of profits which the average entrepreneur ploughs back into his business.

There are some kinds of capital, however, which cannot be accumulated in this automatic way because they require capital outlays out of all proportion to current or immediately expected levels of profit. This is recognized to be a major stumbling-block to the economic growth of some of today's underdeveloped countries. A great deal has been written in recent years about the 'social overhead capital' which must be provided before an underdeveloped economy can expand its output of goods and services at a rate which will produce an appreciable growth in incomes per head. If we begin to define this 'social overhead capital' in concrete terms, most of it seems to consist of capital embodied in basic transport facilities—harbours, roads, bridges, canals and, nowadays, railways. Without this sort of capital an economy's richest natural resources may remain inaccessible and underdeveloped.

Now it is characteristic of such investments (1) that they require much greater outlays of capital than the individual entrepreneur can normally be expected to get access to, (2) that they take a long time to construct and an even longer time to yield a substantial profit, and (3) that the gross return on the investment comes indirectly to the community as a whole rather than directly to the initiating entrepreneurs. The consequence is that social overhead capital generally has to be provided collectively, by governments or international financial institutions rather than individuals, and that the mobilization of the large chunks of capital required is most easily achieved through taxation or through foreign borrowing. The interesting thing about the British experience, however, is that it was almost entirely native private enterprise that found both the initiative and the capital to lay down the system of communications which was essential to the British industrial revolution.

Roads, it is true, had always been collectively provided, largely because they were closely associated with questions of military security. The Roman roads were built almost entirely by soldiers, and so at public expense. In manorial times all landowners were theoretically responsible for the highways adjacent to their own land, but only where the maintenance of law and order was at stake was the medieval State likely to intervene by enforcing the responsibility and levying rates on those who failed to repair the roads. Except for a few roads of strategic importance, road building and repair was a matter of purely local concern, and landlords enforced road-making obligations on their tenants in the interests of particular estates. In the towns, and at some bridges, tolls were levied on road-users to cover the cost of repair. In the sixteenth century, however, the regulations always implicit in the common law were tightened up, parish surveyors were appointed and each parishioner was made formally liable for spending a given number of days each year on the repair of the highways. This was the system of statute labour which remained the normal method of keeping the English roads in repair until it was abolished in 1835. It was not very efficient, but while domestic industry prevailed, and traffic in heavy produce was limited and highly localized, it worked well enough for the pack-horse trade. By the eighteenth century, however, English roads were reputed to be amongst the worst in Europe. The accounts of contemporary travellers on the one hand, and on the other, a mounting flood of legal enactments dealing with the weight of wagons, the number of horses and the width of their wheels bore ample testimony to the fact that the traffic was outrunning the capacity of the roads to carry it. The growing number of

Turnpike Acts, which gave private enterprise the task of repairing the roads, in return for rights to collect tolls from users, showed the inadequacy of the statute labour system in maintaining an economic road system. By 1750 many of the main London routes and some busy interprovincial routes had been turnpiked and it has been estimated that the costs of land carriage were lower in the 1750's than they had been at the beginning of the eighteenth century.[1] Over the period 1751–72, a turnpike mania developed, giving rise to 389 Turnpike Trusts, more than in either the preceding four decades or the following $6\frac{1}{2}$ decades.[2] Another sharp, but less well-sustained, upsurge in Turnpike Acts took place in the 1790's, and by the mid 1830's— on the threshold of the railway age—there were over 20,000 miles of main road controlled by Turnpike Trusts, collecting an annual total of over £0·5 millions in tolls.[3]

Not all turnpike roads were good roads. Contemporary travellers had some hair-raising stories to tell about their perils. But the evidence suggests that the Trusts were generally more effective in providing roads suitable for the continuous carriage of heavy traffic than the system of statute labour. In most villages the days devoted to statute labour on the roads were social occasions rather than working days. Many a small parish on a busy national route, such as the Great North Road, could not afford to keep its stretch in adequate repair. Many of the turnpike operators were also inefficient, irresponsible and corrupt, but the fact that their profits depended directly on their roads being passable was a stronger incentive than that motivating the parish authorities; they were more likely to employ specialized and successful road engineers and new techniques than was the parish. Moreover the existence of the toll-gates on the turnpikes made it easier to enforce legislation against the heavy wagons and narrow wheels which tended to tear the road surface to ribbons.

What the new techniques of road-making did, in effect, was to produce the kind of roads which would stand up to heavy traffic over long periods of time and were passable throughout a normal British winter. Actually the techniques were not as new as they may have seemed. John Metcalf's system was essentially the same as that used by the Romans: he began with

[1] William Albert, *The Turnpike Road System in England 1663–1840* (1972), p. 186.
[2] *Ibid.*, p. 49.   [3] *Ibid.*, p. 189.

a solid foundation of stone blocks and covered them with several layers of stone chippings, ramming them down hard into the cracks and producing a slight camber to assist drainage. Other methods were merely a variation on this. Telford, for example, started with two layers of three-inch stones before laying seven inches of broken stones and finishing with one inch of gravel. Macadam made a less expensive, if less durable, surface by using several layers of broken stones instead of the larger blocks and then finished with several layers of small chips which eventually settled to form a smooth hard surface. The new roads were passable in wet weather and durable and they served their purpose well. Except for the introduction of the steam-roller in the 1860's to hard-pack the stones, there was little development in the technique of road-making until the advent of the motor-car at the end of the nineteenth century.

It was not until well into the nineteenth century, however, that the scientific road-making methods developed by the new genus of road engineer, typified by Metcalf, Macadam and Telford, were applied generally. As late as 1815 it is doubtful whether more than 1,000 miles of highway had been laid down according to their principles and hence laid down to last. Nevertheless, though good roads remained rare, there is evidence to suggest that, taken over-all, standards of road maintenance rose markedly over the period 1750–1830 and that improvements made to certain crucial main roads had had notable effects on the speed, regularity and comfort of travel. This was the era of the stage-coaches. Whereas it had taken four days to go from London to York in 1754, by 1785 one could go from London to Newcastle in only three days. The journey from London to Birmingham, which took two days in the 1740's, was accomplished in 19 hours in the 1780's. In 1754 the coach from London to Bristol took two days for the journey: by 1784 some coaches did it 16 hours. As the journeys became speedier and more comfortable the traffic thickened. In 1756 only one coach a day went between London and Brighton—by 1811 there were twenty-eight coaches a day. By 1820 it was calculated in a contemporary periodical that 'a person has 1,500 opportunities of leaving London in the course of twenty-four hours by stage coaches'.[1]

[1] Quoted from the *Scots Magazine* of 1820 in L. Gardiner, *Stage-Coach to John o' Groats* (1961), p. 6.

Goods, of course, moved much more slowly than passengers. The 'fast' vans which plied on certain main roads could reach five miles an hour on the well-kept London–Birmingham route, but most goods that went by road travelled at a more leisurely pace in stage-wagons, and if the district was hilly the pace was a crawl. It took 24 hours for stage-wagons to do the 45 miles between Manchester and Leeds and 40 hours to accomplish a similar distance between Sheffield and Manchester: even as late as 1829 the normal speed of the wagons between Newcastle and Carlisle was 19 to 20 miles a day.

Some improvement in the roads dates from the 1750's, *before* the industrial revolution had gathered momentum sufficiently to add greatly to the internal traffic of goods. It was largely a consequence of the growth of towns with their mounting demands for basic food and fuel supplies which had to be drawn from a wider and wider agricultural hinterland. The main driving force for road improvement throughout the country was London. Most of the new roads and the best-kept roads led to London, although the influence of other towns—Liverpool, Birmingham and Manchester for example—began to show itself in the quality of their feeder-roads as the century wore on. The growing towns called for rapid and regular transport of foodstuffs and fuel over distances of 30 to 50 miles or so, and for comfortable, safe and speedy transport of passengers and mail between the main towns; and it was this kind of localized or light traffic that benefited most directly and impressively. The extent of the improvement may perhaps be gauged from the evidence of a clergyman before the 1808 Highways Committee, to the effect that three horses could then do what five had been required for 30 years before, and from Jackman's avowedly conservative estimate that 'on the great highways of trade the time consumed on a journey between the termini of the longer routes was in 1830 only from one third to one fifth of what it had been in 1750'.[1]

If Britain had had to depend on her roads to carry her heavy goods traffic the effective impact of the industrial revolution might well have been delayed until the railway age. She started off, however, with transport advantages which none of her contemporary rivals could equal. The cheapest way of trans-

---

[1] W. T. Jackman, *The Development of Transportation in Modern England*, vol. 1 (1916), p. 339.

porting bulky, weighty, goods was by water and Britain scored heavily in this respect by being narrow and insular—no part of the British Isles is more than 70 miles from the sea—and by having a considerable length of river which, if not naturally navigable, could readily be made so. The sea-coast route was the main highway of the British Isles in the eighteenth century and that required relatively little in the way of maintenance except to harbour installations. Adam Smith, exaggerating a little perhaps, declared that 'Six or eight men by the help of water carriage can carry and bring back in the same time the same quantity of goods between London and Edinburgh as 50 broad-wheeled wagons attended by a hundred men and drawn by 400 horses'.[1] London indeed was built up on the strength of its sea routes, and the growth of this vast city—it had more than half a million inhabitants at the end of the seventeenth century and more than a million at the end of the eighteenth —was an important factor in England's transition from a regionally based subsistence economy to an integrated exchange economy. A fleet of vessels averaging a little over 200 tons in weight plied along the eastern coast between the Scottish ports and Newcastle, Hull, Yarmouth and London bringing coal, stone, slate, clay and grain, commodities whose transport through the miry roads of eighteenth-century England would have cost a fortune. According to Clapham the major portion of the coasting trade existed that Londoners might be housed, warmed and fed.[2]

The sea had its hazards and delays, of course. Shipping might be held up in the Tyne and the Thames for weeks in succession in stormy seasons. When war broke out ships and seamen were liable to be summarily pressed into the navy and foreign privateers menaced the English sea lanes. Heavy duties were put on coastal shipping and enormous losses are reported to have resulted from the pilfering of the London dockers. Nevertheless, for all its vicissitudes coastal shipping was the main means of handling bulky, heavy commodities in the eighteenth century and without it there could have been no large-scale heavy industry and no large towns.

No revolutionary developments took place in coastal shipping during the late eighteenth and early nineteenth centuries and

[1] Adam Smith, *Wealth of Nations*, Cannan ed., vol. I, p. 20.
[2] Clapham, *Economic History*, vol. I, p. 4.

it is to the transformation of the inland system of water navigation that we must look for the most spectacular and typical innovations of this period. The industrial revolution called for a reliable, high-capacity, low-cost transport system and this is what the canals provided. Moreover they were of the essence of the industrial revolution in that they were man-made, that they represented an application of scientific knowledge to practical engineering problems, that they catered for a mass market (albeit a producers' market) and that they involved heavy capital outlays involving a long time-horizon.

The canal age took place mainly in two hectic bursts of construction; the first in the 1760's and early 1770's was inspired by the success of the Duke of Bridgewater's canal between Worsley coal mine and Manchester and then stifled by the trade recession resulting from the American War; the second started up in the 1780's, after the war was well over, and became a national mania in the 1790's. It had been preceded by a century and a half of steady river improvement also financed capitalistically by groups of local landowners and businessmen.

It has been established that by the end of the eighteenth century some 2,000 miles of navigable water existed in England, of which approximately one third was in the form of canals built between 1760 and 1800: one third was in the form of 'open' rivers which were naturally navigable: and the remaining third had been created as a result of the work of engineers, chiefly between about 1600 and 1760.[1]

It may seem surprising that a few hundred miles of canal could make a significant addition to the basic industrial communications of an economy of the size and complexity of England. But the canals were not cut into an empty map. Often a short canal represented the last strategic link in a network of navigable rivers and its construction might bring to fruition investments on river improvement made over a century before.

The main motive-power behind the early development of the canals was the same as that which was gradually pushing up the standards of the roads at this period. It was the growth of the towns. Later the prospects and needs of large-scale industry helped to rocket the canal age into its grand mania; but, to begin with, the operative force was the towns with their

---

[1] Skempton, in Singer, Holmyard, Hall and Williams, *History of Technology*, vol. III, p. 456.

insatiable demand for coal to supply fuel for domestic needs and for the whole host of little industries that are required even in a pre-industrial community—bakeries, smithies, tanneries, sugar-refineries, breweries. It must be remembered that apart from coal there was no fuel available in eighteenth-century England other than wood and this was already an exhausted resource in most centres of population and industry. 'The fuel famine of the eighteenth century would have stopped the growth not solely of industry but of population in many districts had not means been found for overcoming it.'[1] The canals were the means. More than half the Navigation Acts passed between 1758 and 1802 to set up a canal or river-improvement company were for concerns whose primary aim was to carry coal. This was one of the crucial bottlenecks that had to be broken before the industrial revolution could take shape in England. It was crucial, first because it removed the main barrier to the urbanization which is generally associated with industrialization as both cause and effect; and secondly because the first industrial revolution grew up on a basis of coal and iron and it was necessary to be able to move these bulky raw materials and their finished products quickly and cheaply across the face of the country.

The first wholly man-made inland navigation in this country was the Sankey Brook, inspired by the coal needs of Liverpool, then Britain's premier port outside of London. But it was the Duke of Bridgewater's Canal from Worsley to Manchester that is generally regarded as the first great achievement of the canal age. Built by James Brindley, it was designed to carry coal from the Duke's colliery at Worsley to the up and coming industrial town of Manchester. It was an immediate social and commercial success. Its tunnel at Worsley and its aqueduct at Barton were engineering achievements which stirred the imagination of a public that believed passionately in man-made improvement. The fact that it halved the price of coal in Manchester further impressed itself on hard-headed businessmen and wealthy landowners and encouraged them to risk their savings, mortgage their lands and borrow from their relatives to finance similar expensive schemes of capital accumulation. Eight years later Birmingham businessmen had a similar success with the opening

---

[1] Clapham, *Economic History*, vol. 1, p. 78.

of the first section of the Birmingham canal, and by the end of
the century the Hereford–Gloucester canal had reduced the
price of coal at Ledbury from 24s. to 13s. 6d.[1]

Success on this grand scale was bound to encourage imitation.
It is amazing nevertheless that so much private capital was
raised in England to finance the construction of costly capital
assets which generally took several years before they began
earning at all and which could not, in the nature of things, be
expected to yield a quick return. The Duke of Bridgewater's
canal cost nearly a quarter of a million pounds to complete
—which was a great deal of money at a time when the average
Lancashire labourer earned less than £20 per annum; it took
five years to complete it as far as Runcorn and another nine
years to link up with the Mersey so that vessels could go on to
Liverpool. The Leeds and Liverpool Canal took 46 years to
complete and there were many which took 10 years or more.
Yet by 1790 between £2 and £3 millions had been spent on
canal construction, and in the nine years (1788–96) of the canal
mania Parliament had authorized the expenditure of nearly
£10 millions on canals and inland navigations. The work thus
enthusiastically begun continued steadily in the first quarter of
the nineteenth century, and by the beginning of the railway age
in the 1830's about £20 millions had been invested in the
construction and improvement of British inland navigation. At
their peak in 1858 the inland waterways of Great Britain
reached a length of about 4,250 miles.

Where did all this capital come from? For the most part it
was raised locally in the region the canal was to serve. 'It was
only among men to whom solid advantages were promised that
money could be got for a canal that might take many years to
build.'[2] Sometimes a local landowner or industrialist took the
initiative and used his lands or his stock as collateral for
borrowing the money; colliery owners like the Duke of Bridgewater or industrialists using heavy raw materials like Josiah
Wedgwood, the pottery manufacturer, had most to gain.
Occasionally a local merchant was able to raise the bulk of the
funds necessary to cut a short canal. In most cases the new
navigations were the product of corporate enterprise initiated
by local businessmen and landowners and supported by local

[1] Clapham, *op. cit.* vol. I, p. 78.
[2] Charles Hadfield, *British Canals* (1959), p. 34.

shareholders and bankers and city corporations and even sometimes by universities. During the mania the geographical basis of the capital raised for the canal companies began to spread beyond the regional level and many individuals with quite small capital resources and no direct interest in the enlargement of transport opportunities were tempted by the offer of glittering prizes to have their flutter among the canal shares.

There is no doubt that some of these ventures paid off extremely well. 'Fantastic dividends were sometimes paid—the Oxford Canal for instance paid 30% for more than 30 years——although the average dividend was under 8%.'[1] The shares of the old Birmingham Canal, originally £140 each, were selling at £900 in 1792, at the height of the canal mania, and by 1825 an eighth share of this canal, originally worth £17. 10s., was selling for £355. A writer who picked out the ten most successful canals in 1825 calculated that they were then paying an average of 27·6 per cent.[2] Not all the canal companies fulfilled the hopes of their investors, however. Some of the projects foundered on unexpected engineering difficulties, some on post-war depression and some on the inefficiency of their managers. Jackman has estimated, for example, that 'fully one half of the number of canals and probably considerably more than one half of the capital expenditure realized returns that were inadequate in order to maintain the canals as effective agents for the work they were intended to accomplish'.[3]

In the last analysis, however, it is inappropriate to judge the contribution of the canals to British economic growth in terms of the returns they yielded to their shareholders. What mattered was that the coal got to the consumers at reasonable prices, that the iron-foundries and potteries could reduce costs, that the factory worker could warm his family in winter and still have some money left over to buy the products of British industry and that the bread-and-cheese-eating labourers of Southern England could have cooked meals occasionally. In these terms the Canal Age made a massive contribution to the first industrial revolution and was a worthy forerunner of the railway age.

---

[1] Asa Briggs, *The Age of Improvement* (1959), p. 30.
[2] *Quarterly Review*, XXXII, quoted Clapham, *Economic History*, vol. I, p. 82.
[3] Jackman, *Development of Transportation*, vol. I, p. 426.

Throughout the country, stone for building, paving and roadmaking; bricks, tiles and timber; limestone for the builder, farmer or blast furnace owner; beasts and cattle; corn, hay and straw; manure from the London mews and the mountainous London dustheaps; the heavy castings which were coming into use for bridge-building and other structural purposes—all these and whatever other bulky wares there may be, moved along the new waterways over what, half a century earlier, had been impossible routes or impossible distances.[1]

In effect, what the canals did was to make possible enormous ultimate savings in man-power and horse-power at the cost of heavy preliminary outlays of capital. A single horse plodding along a canal towpath typically dragged a load of 50 tons of merchandise; on the banks of a navigable river its average load was 30 tons: on iron rails it pulled 8 tons and on macadam roads 2 tons. The typical goods carrier of the early eighteenth century, the pack-horse, carried an average load of only about one-eighth of a ton. The effect was to produce what a development theorist would describe as a 'radical transformation of production functions'; for it revolutionized the respective contributions of the main factors of production—labour, capital and natural resources—to the business of transport; and it permitted significant savings in raw materials and in the kind of capital that gets tied up in stocks of goods when delivery dates are uncertain.

In addition it is worth noticing that the canals produced a new class of investor, the canal shareholder, a non-participant investor who was readily transformed into a railway shareholder when the infinitely greater demands for railway capital were made in the 1830's and 1840's. This was an important new development. Most economies in the early stages of industrialization have some economic surplus, the problem is to channel it into the kind of large-scale investments which do not guarantee immediate return and which may be of more value to the community as a whole than to the chief investors. Even where incomes are unequally distributed it is rare to find many individuals with the enterprise, the far-sightedness *and* the access to capital necessary to launch one of these ventures. The Duke of Bridgewater was a rarity in eighteenth-century England. Hence the development of the joint-stock company system,

[1] Clapham, *Economic History*, vol. I, p. 79.

whereby a large group of impersonally associated individuals could pool their capitals in a corporate venture, was a major step in permitting private enterprise to undertake costly capital projects on a wide scale. The joint-stock company established by Act of Parliament was not, of course, a new institution in the second half of the eighteenth century but it was the canal age that familiarized the small saver with this type of investment.

One consequence of building up the social overhead capital involved in the canal network by the agency of private enterprise was that it was not very efficiently done. The miscellany of widths, depths and transport charges made the network less integrated than it could have been. The opportunities open to some carriers to charge monopolistic rates limited the social gain and restricted the potential traffic; the nil returns which characterized a large proportion of the capital invested and the fantastically high share prices of the mania resulted in some capital wastage: and many of these wastages could have been avoided had there been effective centralized planning of the canal network. Nevertheless the job was done, and before the railway age revolutionized the transport situation a second time, England had been endowed with a solid and worth-while capital asset in the shape of more than 2,000 miles of heavy-traffic lanes, many of which are still in economic use today.

The canals were not the only examples of heavy, privately-initiated expenditure on social overhead capital in the late eighteenth and early nineteenth centuries though they were certainly the most spectacular. Even while the canal age was in progress a considerable extension of British dock and harbour capacity had been achieved. It began effectively with the foreign-trade boom in the last quarter of the eighteenth century. During the whole of the first three-quarters of the eighteenth century less than 150 acres of dock and basin accommodation were constructed in England: but during the last quarter of the century this accommodation was doubled and in the first three decades of the nineteenth century the total area of dockland expanded by over 4,700 acres; that is, by more than ten times its area in 1799.

In London, whose trade had doubled in the course of the eighteenth century, nothing was done to extend the docks until the French war made their improvement desperately urgent and precipitated the first London dock boom. Between 1799 and

1815 capital authorized by Parliament for the London docks exceeded £5½ millions; and before the 1820's Liverpool and Bristol in the west and Hull and Grimsby in the east had spent nearly £2 millions in dock construction. This was only the beginning. 'There was hardly a port of any size or a threatened part of the coast where improvements had not recently been undertaken or were not in hand during the middle twenties.'[1] Moreover, this was a sphere of capital formation in which private enterprise was not the only operator. Government (central and local) also played a direct, if unspectacular, part. Public expenditure on docks and harbours was averaging over a million pounds per decade in the second and third decades of the nineteenth century.

On the face of it, the new forms of capital formation (the canals, for example, the macadamized roads and the bigger and better docks and harbours) were expensive in terms of a factor of production in which a pre-industrial economy is generally poor, namely capital. Certainly they required massive initial outlays on projects which often did not yield a commercial return for a period of five to ten years from the raising of the capital. To begin with it would appear that the transport innovations of the period 1750–1830 were capital-intensive, in that they required a relatively high input of capital per unit of output produced.

This is true up to a point, but only up to a point. First it must be remembered that when it is said that a pre-industrial economy is short of capital what is meant generally is that it is short of *productive* capital. By the standards of most of the rest of the contemporary world and of many present-day under-developed countries in Asia and Africa, England was a relatively affluent country in the eighteenth century and was not absolutely short of capital in the broader sense. There was a good deal of capital invested in the Funds, in land, and in game preserves and country-houses in the second half of the eighteenth century, that was yielding a very low return indeed, in either money or in goods and services, compared with what it could be made to yield in- canals and turnpike trusts. To the extent that the canals drew finance away from the Funds or from the building of country houses, say, they were making more productive use

---

[1] Clapham, *Economic History*, vol. 1, p. 6.

of existing capital resources and to that extent might be regarded as capital-saving in their effect.

Secondly, and more importantly, the successful canals and the well-managed turnpikes made it possible to economize directly in capital resources in a number of significant ways. A large part of the capital of a pre-industrial economy has to be tied up in stocks of goods. By shifting goods rapidly and regularly across the face of the country, the canals made it possible to reduce the volume of goods in transit at any one point of time and to save incalculable loss through deterioration or highway robbery or petty pilfering: for the longer a consignment was *en route* the less likely was it to reach its destination intact and in good condition. The new roads and canals also achieved spectacular reductions in the costs of heavy raw materials. All these factors permitted the commercial and industrial community to economize in their stockholdings. Traders who could rely on placing an order for vital supplies and of obtaining delivery within a matter of days, not weeks, could keep smaller stocks in their warehouses. Factory owners who had been dependent on delivery of coal by sea had been forced to hold substantial stocks on the site to ensure continuous working during the winter storms that kept the coasting ships in port; when they had a regular supply floating down the canals they could dispense with a large part of these emergency stocks. The fact that coal was cheaper in the industrial areas served by canals further reduced the amount of capital required for stockholding. For some goods—foodstuffs in particular—costs of efficient storage were high, and small stocks combined with safe and sure regular deliveries meant a considerable saving in wastage costs.

Capital economies were also achieved through the rapid and regular movement of people on the stage-coach and posting routes. London bankers could send their agents regularly to the country towns. Commercial information—on gluts or scarcities of particular commodities for example, or on the state of the uncut harvest—could be quickly sent from one region to another. Credit and insurance facilities were more easily arranged on the basis of personal contact. Currency could be swiftly and relatively safely shifted to areas where it was in short supply. The fact is that an efficient market, whether it be in goods or capital or men or ideas, depends largely on a rapid and free flow of information as well as of things. It is this freedom

of communication that keeps prices down, renders entrepreneurial decisions more likely to be the right decisions and
helps to facilitate the rapid spread of cost-reducing innovations.
It is always difficult to assess the value of easy personal contact
in facilitating trading relationships but there seems little doubt
that it was an important factor in creating a more integrated
and confident business community in this country.

On balance, then, it is doubtful whether the developments
in transport which occurred during the period 1760–1830 were
capital-intensive in their final effects on the national economy.
They may have raised the level of national saving by attracting
to capital formation resources that would otherwise have been
spent on current consumption purposes by governments or
individuals. If they did, the evidence does not point to a
substantial increase in the rate of saving due to this cause. What
they certainly did was to permit a more economical and
productive use of existing capital resources and there is no
evidence that, except very temporarily at the height of the canal
mania, they competed with other industries for the supply of
capital. On the contrary, there were a number of ways in which
they evidently freed capital for other uses—by economizing in
traders' and industrialists' stocks, for example, by freeing horses
for agricultural purposes, by saving entrepreneurial time and
by facilitating credit negotiations.

The transport revolution did not of course end in 1830, for
of all the industries whose transformation made the industrial
revolution, transport seemed to have the most inexhaustible
capacity to innovate. Railways, steamships, tram-cars, motor-
cars, aeroplanes—the list seems endless and the economic
consequences of each have been complex and far-reaching. For
the moment, however, it seems particularly worth emphasizing
that the transport revolution had effectively begun and was
affecting the productivity of the economy as a whole before the
changes in other industries were at all sizeable in their impact,
and that it was an absolutely crucial factor in facilitating the
cost-reducing innovations which characterized the other
transforming sectors of the first industrial revolution.

CHAPTER 6

THE COTTON INDUSTRY

It is convenient to regard the first industrial revolution as consisting of not one but a galaxy of revolutions in the traditional system of economic activity, each springing in part from an independent set of causes and each interacting with the others to produce cumulative effects, the causes of which it is very difficult to disentangle. The four associated revolutions which have been considered in the four preceding chapters can each lay some claim to having helped to precipitate and condition the industrial revolution proper. So long as we do not fall into the trap of supposing that they effectively preceded it in time, instead of being an integral part of it, we might say that the demographic revolution, the agricultural revolution, the commercial revolution and the transport revolution were the most important preconditions of successful industrialization and the sustained economic growth which goes along with it.

Now it is time to come to grips with the process that is generally assumed to be at the heart of the first industrial revolution, that is the growth of modern manufacturing industry and all that this implies—large-scale units of operation, labour-saving machinery, and regimentation of labour, for example. There were two industries which more than any others first experienced the early revolutionary changes in technology and economic organization that made Britain the 'workshop of the world'. They were cotton and iron. It seems to be generally agreed that the prime mover was the cotton industry. This is the industry which Professor Rostow, for example, has described as the 'original leading sector in the first take-off'[1] and to which Schumpeter referred when he asserted that 'English industrial history can (1787–1842)...be almost resolved into the history of a single industry'.[2] There seems to be no doubt of the

[1] Rostow, *Stages of Economic Growth*, p. 53.
[2] J. A. Schumpeter, *Business Cycles*, vol. 1 (1939), p. 271.

tremendous importance of the cotton industry in the British industrial revolution. The interesting question is why cotton rather than any other industry should have led the way and how a single industry came to play such an important part in reshaping the economy of a nation.

Textile manufactures had constituted an important part of the English national product for centuries. But it was in the woollen manufacture that England especially excelled on the eve of the industrial revolution. There were reasons for this. Sheep flourished on the English pastures and yielded a high-quality wool. The finished product was particularly acceptable in cool latitudes and English manufacturers had developed skills which had enabled them to produce exceptionally fine woollen cloth.

By contrast the cotton industry was backward, small, and unable to compete with Indian calicoes or muslins in either quality or price unless protected. Its finished product was a compound of linen warp and cotton weft; its expansion was restricted, on the demand side by the limited market for these coarse cottons, and on the supply side by the relatively low productivity of spinners dependent on the ancient hand-wheel. Like wool it was a domestic industry in which all members of the household played their part. Children did much of the labour of the preliminary operations such as cleaning and carding the raw cotton, and they assisted the weaver. Women span the yarn; men wove the cloth. Many households treated it as a subsidiary occupation to agriculture and it provided casual employment in seasons when the demand for labour was at a low ebb. Except in Manchester itself, most weavers were also farmers. The raw cotton came largely from the Levant, the southern States of America and the West Indies and was dearer per pound than best English wool. The final product was rough, difficult to sew and difficult to wash. The aggregate gross value of cotton textiles produced was quite small: a contemporary estimate put the value of its annual sales at a mere £600,000 in the early 1760's. At that time its exports averaged an annual value of a little over £200,000 at official prices: for woollen goods the corresponding export value was about £5½ millions.

The first of the series of major textile inventions applied to wool as much as to cotton but they were slow in developing in either branch. They were (1) Kay's flying shuttle, which was first introduced in the 1730's and began to be adopted widely by the cotton weavers in the 1750's and 1760's, and (2) Paul's carding machine, patented in 1748, which began to find its way into Lancashire about 1760. These two inventions intensified the bottleneck which was already in evidence in the spinning branch of the cotton industry. It took three or four spinners to supply one weaver with material by the traditional methods, and where the fly-shuttle speeded up the weavers' operations the shortage of yarn became acute. It was practically impossible to get any yarn for weft in the harvest season when women could earn an equivalent wage less laboriously in the fields.

Meanwhile there was pressure on the demand side too. There was a marked improvement in the foreign market for cotton manufactures in the 1750's (largely due to the East India company's difficulties in maintaining the Indian supply) and this continued into the 'sixties, as continental markets were developed. At the same time British population and domestic incomes were increasing and it may be supposed that home demand was rising in step. It is not therefore surprising to find that prizes were being offered in the early 1760's to encourage inventions which would increase the productivity of the spinner and the quality of the yarn.

Hargreaves' spinning-jenny, invented probably around 1764 and patented in 1770, was not the first spinning machine—the inventor Paul had been machine-spinning cotton at his mill in the 1740's and there were other early attempts too—but it was the first wholly successful improvement on the age-old device of the spinning wheel. In its earliest form it contained eight spindles: the patent specification in 1770 mentioned sixteen spindles: by 1784 the number had increased to eighty and by the end of the century the large jennies were capable of holding 100 to 120 spindles. At once therefore the effect of the invention was to multiply many times the amount of yarn that could be spun by a single operator. It saved labour just where labour had been so scarce. The success of the jenny was immediate. It was not perfect, but it produced a satisfactory yarn for weft; in the smaller sizes it was relatively cheap to buy and to house and its mechanism was so simple that it could be operated by children, again in the smaller sizes. The very large factory-jennies were generally operated by a man with several child helpers. It was adopted rapidly and it was rapidly improved. The family spinning-wheels were hastily consigned to the lumber room and their place taken by the new jennies. In the words of a manufacturer who lived through this era: 'From the year 1770 to 1788 a complete change had gradually been effected in the spinning of yarns. That of wool had disappeared altogether and that of linen was also nearly gone: cotton, cotton, cotton has become the almost universal material for employment.'[1]

But the invention which more than any other laid the basis for the revolution in cotton was the water-frame, patented by Arkwright in 1769. For this, for the first time, produced cotton yarn strong enough to serve as warp as well as weft and thus created a new product—a British cotton cloth that was *not* a linen-mixture. Unlike the jenny the water-frame was a factory machine from the beginning: it was designed to be horse-operated but was powered first by water and later by steam. This was the real beginning of the departure from domestic industry. A few years later Crompton's mule (patented in 1779) combined the principles of the jenny and the water-frame and produced a smoother and finer yarn. This enabled the British producer for the first time to outclass the Indian producer in the quality of his cloth, and with later improvements the finished product grew finer and stronger. In 1785 Arkwright's patent was cancelled and the water-frame became available to all; and in the same year a Boulton and Watt steam-engine was used for the first time to operate a spinning-mill. Thus within a few years the most crippling limitations on the output of the industry were removed; a new system of production, large-scale factory industry, became feasible; and the way was opened to the development of what was for British industry an entirely new range of products suitable for a mass market.

The effects of the water-frame and the jenny show up in the statistics of raw cotton imports as early as the 1770's, but it was after the end of the American War, in the 1780's and 1790's, that they begun to multiply. Between 1780 and 1800 there was an increase of about eightfold in raw-cotton imports; and since the yarn spun grew finer on the average, as well as stronger, the raw material imports understate the increase in yardage and real value. The machinery was elaborated and improved. By 1812 'one spinner could produce as much in a given time as 200 could have produced before the invention of Hargreaves'

[1] W. Radcliffe, *The Origin of Power Loom Weaving* (1828), p. 62.

jenny'. These developments changed the whole character of the industry. Spinning began to be concentrated in factories. Weavers could rely on uninterrupted supplies of yarn and could afford to give up their agricultural activities, which had once provided most of their income, in order to engage full time in manufacture. Their numbers increased rapidly. They began to crowd into the towns. Improvements in other technical processes helped to accelerate the rate of growth of the cotton industry and to remove it further and further from the domestic system. There were improvements in bleaching and dyeing; carding, scutching and roving machines were introduced; steam-power made it possible to locate factories where no water-power was available; the introduction of Whitney's ginning machine in the United States in the last decade of the century provided another major impetus by greatly reducing the price of the raw material.

Curiously enough the weaving branch of the industry lagged behind in the modernization of the cotton manufacture. There was distress among the weavers of coarse cottons even before the end of the eighteenth century—their markets had never been unlimited and were easily saturated. The power-loom was adopted only very slowly. Cartwright invented an imperfect machine in 1787 and set up a factory at Doncaster which closed two years later when the inventor went bankrupt. A Manchester firm which introduced it experimentally in 1791 found itself in opposition to its workers and had its factory burned down in consequence. A number of improved machines were tried out in the following decades but the power-loom remained experimental until after the Napoleonic wars. When eventually the power-loom began to be introduced on a considerable scale in the 1820's, 1830's and 1840's the displacement of the hand-loom weavers, still clinging to their independence in spite of the relentless downward pressure on their wages, was achieved at the cost of much social distress.

Within a little more than a quarter of a century the cotton manufacture graduated from being one of the least significant industries (Adam Smith's *Wealth of Nations*, published in 1776, has one glancing reference to it) to one of the most important. By 1802 it probably accounted for between 4 and 5 per cent of the national income of Great Britain, and by 1812 when its share was estimated to be between 7 and 8 per cent it had outstripped the woollen industry in national importance. At this stage there were about 100,000 workers in cotton-spinning factories and probably another quarter of a million weavers and their auxiliaries working on cotton goods. By 1815 exports of cotton textiles account for 40 per cent of the value of British domestic exports and woollen goods for 18 per cent, and by 1830 more than half the value of British home-produced exports consisted of cotton textiles. In real terms (i.e. in yards of cloth produced) the growth of the cotton industry was even more impressive, for prices fell at a speed which has no precedent in the history of manufacturing industry, while quality rose. Since the innovations were mainly concentrated in the spinning branch of the industry it was at the yarn stage that the price fall was most impressive, particularly when falling costs in spinning were reinforced by falling raw-material costs, due to the introduction of the cotton gin, in the southern States of America. Prices of cotton yarn fell from 38s. per lb. in 1786 and 1787 to under 10s. in 1800 and 6s. 9d. in 1807. Demand proved to be elastic, and as prices fell the amounts sold expanded more than proportionately. Even so, the market would have been readily saturated by the immense capacity of the factory system, had it not been possible to exploit the international contacts which British merchants had been building up for the previous century and to supply a steady succession of new foreign markets. By the 1780's the volume of exports (i.e. exports valued at constant official prices) was flowing at a rate which was between three and four times its volume in the 1760's, before Hargreaves' jenny had come on the scene; by the first decade of the nineteenth century the flow was ten times that of the 1780's; and by the end of the Napoleonic wars it had trebled again. All this was something quite new in industrial experience. It caught the imagination of contemporaries and provided a dramatic object-lesson in the profitability of mechanization.

Various explanations have been advanced for this spectacular breakthrough in the cotton industry. It has commonly been argued that the relative insignificance of the industry at the beginning of the transformation militated in its favour. Economic change in the woollen industry, for example, was inhibited by the opposition, or inertia, set up by powerful vested interests. The silk industry, to take another example, had proved itself to be a convenient source of public revenue and was crippled by import duties: and like the linen industry it was hindered by the fact that its raw material was in any case in inelastic supply.

But if the cotton industry was new it was not so different from the other textile industries that it was technologically strange. Most English families had eked out their earnings by engaging in some kind of textile-manufacturing process. The skills, the techniques, the institutions and the processing industries which had long served the other textile trades could serve the new industry just as well. The new factory system did not immediately displace the old domestic industry: for a while it supplemented and strengthened it. The tens of thousands of little men who operated jennies and looms in extensions to their cottages provided the industry with buildings and machinery which would have required hundreds of wealthy capitalists to set up on a factory basis. It was this more than anything else that permitted the *immediate* expansion of capacity in response to technological opportunities and market demand. The costs and risks of the new industry were more widely spread than they would otherwise have been and were more readily undertaken because of this. 'One cannot avoid the conclusion', writes an authority on the eighteenth-century cotton industry, 'that the new machinery spread quickly in England because the whole community was interested in it.'[1]

Another way of looking at it is to say that the cotton industry's success depended largely on the fact that it made demands on factors of production which it was well within the power of the British economy to meet. It was labour-intensive, for example, rather than capital-intensive. In so far as it needed skills—the weaver's skill for example—these were in relatively abundant supply: there was a veritable army of under-employed weavers in eighteenth-century England. It also used the labour of women and children; and in a pre-industrial country with a rapidly rising population an industry which makes use of female workers and pauper children is an industry with an abundant labour supply. In so far as it required capital this was not large in relation to the return that was expected of it—in terms of modern growth-theory it was an industry with a relatively low capital–output ratio—and the task of providing and maintaining capital equipment could, as it happened, be spread over

[1] Julia de L. Mann in A. P. Wadsworth and J. de L. Mann, *The Cotton Trade and Industrial Lancashire 1600–1780* (1931), p. 506.

a fairly large number of individuals. Some of it was already in existence. Looms which had never clacked for more than a day a week found material for more or less continuous operation when the jennies got to work.

Moreover the final product was not so new that it had to create its own demand through changing tastes. Indian calicoes and muslins had long been in active demand in the markets served by British merchants, including Britain itself, where unsuccessful attempts had been made to exclude the Indian article. When a commodity as good—in time it was better—was produced by British manufacturers it found a market ready-made. As its price fell so as to bring it within the reach of the poorest people, and its quality improved so as to enable it to compete with other textiles like linen and silk the market widened to mass proportions. This gave it a momentum which few other industries could have attained. The basis of Professor Rostow's argument that cotton was a leading sector in the British industrial revolution, for example, lies in its relatively massive impact on the national economy, and in the secondary repercussions which such a massive impact could produce on related sectors. 'Industrial enterprise on this scale had secondary reactions on the development of urban areas, the demand for coal, iron and machinery, the demand for working capital and ultimately the demand for cheap transport, which powerfully stimulated industrial development in other directions.'[1]

Another characteristic of the eighteenth-century cotton industry which may have helped it to respond as rapidly as it did to the opportunities offered by the new inventions was the fact that it was highly localized. It is not entirely clear why it should have been so concentrated in Lancashire, though a number of reasons can be advanced which might have contributed significantly to this result. The tendency towards concentration can be traced back to the first half of the century, and the traditional explanation is that geographical conditions were peculiarly favourable to a Lancashire home for the cotton industry—its damp climate, for example, and its lime-free water are said to have assisted the spinning and cleaning processes. It may have been important that labour was relatively abundant, and therefore cheap; the evidence on baptism, births and marriages points to an upward movement in the curve of

[1] Rostow, *Stages of Economic Growth*, p. 54.

population growth in the north-west *before* this appeared in Britain as a whole. No doubt the expansion of the port of Liverpool, a point in the triangular trade in cottons to West Africa, slaves to the West Indies and the southern States of America and raw cotton back to Britain, helped to encourage the cotton manufacture in Lancashire. The fact that this was also a flax-producing and -spinning region in the early eighteenth century was another reason for siting the cotton industry in its vicinity at a time when linen yarn was required to provide the cotton warp.

It is unlikely that any one of these reasons was strong enough to determine the increasing concentration of the eighteenth-century cotton industry. But taken together they may explain it. Later in the century, when the water-frame produced a demand for power, the fast-running streams of Lancashire, and later still the coalfields, reinforced these tendencies. But, whatever the reasons, the concentration of the industry helped to increase the economies of scale and to accelerate the progress of innovation. In a country as little integrated as eighteenth-century England it often took many decades for an innovation to spread from one end of the country to another. Within one county the force of successful example was more easily manifested and the jennies appeared rapidly in one cottage after another.

Finally, of course, in looking for an explanation for the sustained character of expansion in the cotton industry and the strength of its impact on the national economy, it must be remembered that Britain was first in the field with the new machines and with the cheaper, finer cottons and that she was therefore able to reap the innovator's profits. By the time her rivals had followed her lead and were turning out comparable products, prices had fallen to more competitive levels and the boom profits had been won. The initial lead was particularly important for an industry producing for a mass market and operating under conditions of increasing returns. For it meant that the country which was first in building up the capacity and the ancillary industries and the commercial contacts could go on getting higher-than-average profits for a considerable time, simply because it was enjoying larger economies of scale and could go on supplying its products at keener prices.

In retrospect, the progress of the cotton industry looks

spectacularly rapid: and so it did to contemporaries. By the end of the eighteenth century an industry which contributed less than half a million pounds to national income in the early 1760's and exported goods worth probably no more than a quarter of a million pounds overall was adding over £5 millions to national income and a similar amount to the declared value of exports. The speed with which the imports of raw material multiplied is staggering—from under 10 million pounds per annum in the early 1780's to ten times as much in the period of Waterloo and fifty times as much in the early 1840's.

Yet in some ways the transformation of the industry was quite gradual, and it was partly this that permitted the expansion in output to be strongly sustained through wars and depressions. To begin with, expansion was achieved by taking up the slack in existing under-employed resources rather than by diverting resources from other uses. The jenny multiplied the productivity of labour in the spinning branch and enabled weavers to work regularly at their looms. The water-frame and the mule were more than mere labour-saving devices; they were substitutes for human skill, for they permitted the production of stronger, finer yarn by relatively unskilled labour. They were the beginning of a new era in economic organization, for they required a docile labour force working in the disciplined atmosphere of the factory.

The factories, however, provided only part of the immense increase in output that put cotton at the head of the British manufacturing industry. Most of it was produced by a multitude of outworkers—the domestic spinners to whom the capitalist mill-owner served out raw cotton, and the hand-loom weaver whom he supplied with the appropriate yarn. When trade was bad it could be largely concentrated in the factories and it was the domestic spinners and weavers who took the full brunt of depression. When trade was good it was generally possible to attract new spinners and hand-loom weavers without having to raise the level of wages, for there remained a dearth of alternative avenues of employment; so that the capitalist employer reaped the main benefit of the boom, and escaped the worst effects of the slump. Having a minimum of overheads to carry on his own costs he still had a virtually inexhaustible reservoir of surplus labour and machine capacity to draw upon at will.

The persistence of the domestic cotton industry is thus not altogether surprising. On the one hand there was the natural and dogged resistance of the independent head of household to being dragooned into factory employment. The hand-loom weavers paid heavily for their independence, but they held out in force until the 1830's. On the other hand, there was the capitalist employer's reluctance to sink his capital into buildings and plant that might reduce his profits in depression when he could meet the boom demand by turning to outworkers. These two factors delayed the general adoption of the power-loom for three to four decades after it was effectively available. 'So eminent a factory owner as John Kennedy was still doubtful in 1815 whether the saving of labour by the power loom counterbalanced the expense of power and machinery and the disadvantage of being obliged to keep an establishment of power looms constantly at work.'[1] It was not until the early 1840's that the number of power-loom weavers exceeded the number of hand-loom weavers and not until the 1850's that the latter were effectively extinguished.

Throughout the period of mechanization of the cotton industry, which could be said to have been virtually complete by 1850, the capitalist manufacturer was in a very strong position. He could shift the main burden of adjustment to technical change to the domestic producers who owned the hand-looms which were being rendered obsolete. He could readily contract or expand the working time of a large unorganized labour force composed mainly of women and children or young persons, for it was not until the 1850's that maximum-hours legislation became effective. In 1835 not many more than a quarter of the operators in cotton factories were men over the age of eighteen; 48 per cent were women and girls and 13 per cent were children under fourteen. There was not much competition for this unskilled semi-dependent labour force until the industrial revolution gathered momentum in other industries and provided additional openings for women and children in light industry. At the same time the cotton manufacturer was producing a commodity with a mass market at a price which sheltered it from competition until technical change had had time to spread to other textile industries and other countries.

There is no doubt that the sustained progress of the cotton

[1] Wadsworth and Mann, *The Cotton Trade*, p. 405.

industry in the period 1780–1850 and its leading role in the industrial revolution owed much to the favoured position in which its capitalist manufacturers found themselves. For the British industrial revolution was a spontaneous industrial revolution, not a forced industrialization as some of its successors have been. Its development depended on the unfettered response of private enterprise to economic opportunity.

A great deal of stress has been put on the role of the textile inventions in stimulating the industrial revolution and hence, understandably, on the leading role of the cotton industry. It is important, however, not to overstate their importance. For it is arguable that the fact that the cotton industry led the way at this period was due more to the drive of its entrepreneurs than to the skill of its inventors.

In examining the process of economic growth through technological change it is convenient to distinguish, as Schumpeter has done, between invention and innovation, for it is the latter which is revolutionary in its economic effects, not the former. Invention is the basic original discovery, the crucial breakthrough in the realm of either theoretical or practical knowledge which makes a change in productive methods possible. Innovation is the application of this new knowledge or the use of the new machine in practical economic activity. Thus invention can be and often is a purely external factor to the economic situation: of itself it has no economically relevant effects and it does not necessarily induce innovation. A new machine or a new technique may be known to its original inventor and accessible to producers for years or decades before it is put into practice.

Innovation, on the other hand, is the heart and core of technological progress. It is this that enlarges the possibilities of production, requires new combinations of factors of production, and creates new cost structures. Not all innovations are the product of what we should classify as invention, traceable to some identifiable conquest in the realm of theoretical or practical knowledge made in the immediate or remote past. On the other hand an invention—the steam-engine, for example —may give rise to a variety of innovations. Indeed the essence of Schumpeter's theory of innovation is that innovations tend to occur not in a steady stream, but in a series of bunches emanating from some specially fruitful invention, and hence that growth tends to take place not steadily but in waves. In any case, whether we subscribe to the theory of 'bunched innovations' or not, it is evident that what we want to focus on in tracing the course of economic change is not the initial inventions or new knowledge which made it possible, but on the response of businessmen which made it real, that is, on what is sometimes called the 'technological dynamism' of the economy's entrepreneurs.

The reward for innovation in a private enterprise economy is profit. The first entrepreneur to carry an innovation into effect sells a commodity at the old price but at a lower cost and takes the whole of the difference as profit. He becomes that much richer than his rivals. His example, or rather the size of his profit, encourages imitation and, as the number of his imitators increases, two factors tend to narrow the gap between price and cost: (1) competition between producers to invade existing markets, which tends to diminish price, and (2) competition for existing factors of production which are in inelastic supply. If the gap narrows too quickly the rate of innovation falls off smartly both because entrepreneurs have less incentive to change their methods and because they have smaller profits with which to finance new kinds of capital equipment.

The interesting thing about the cotton industry at this period is that although prices fell steeply—between 1815 and 1845 for example, the prices of cotton cloth exports fell by about three-quarters—profits were well maintained. In part of course this was because producers continued to innovate, though perhaps not as fast as they could have done. I have already referred to the slowness with which the weaving section turned over to steam-power and 'there were still plenty of wooden spinning jennies, turned by hand in the Lancashire mills in 1824'.[1] However, a series of innovations in related industries helped to reduce costs in the first quarter of the nineteenth century: improvements in cotton-ginning machinery reduced the price of raw cotton; specialization on the part of textile-machinery firms produced better and cheaper machines; mechanization in the bleaching, dyeing and printing trades reduced processing costs; the introduction of gas-lighting made it possible to reduce the weight of overhead costs by operating plant and machinery day and night through a multiple shift system; and

[1] Clapham, *Economic History*, vol. I, p. 86.

improvements in road and canal communications reduced distribution costs.

But possibly the most important reason for the cotton industry's ability to maintain its profits and hence its rate of investment was the fact that it enjoyed an almost inexhaustible low-priced labour supply. While women and girls and pauper children could be put to work for 12 to 16 hours a day in cotton-mills at bare subsistence wages and while there remained a 'reserve army' of domestic handloom weavers prepared to work longer and longer hours for a smaller and smaller return, the cotton industry could nearly always command as much labour as the demand for its products warranted and wages stayed low. Between about 1820 and 1845 the industry's total output roughly quadrupled but the wages of its operatives barely rose at all.

In this surely lies one of the most important reasons for the powerfully sustained growth of the cotton industry over the period 1780–1850. An increasing proportion of the incomes that it generated went to the entrepreneurs, and they in their turn were ready to plough back a substantial proportion of earnings into more plant and machinery. This high rate of plough-back meant two things: (1) that the industry went on expanding its capacity to produce and increasing its economies of scale (i.e. the kind of internal economies that accrue to concerns that can produce on a scale large enough to minimize the cost of their overheads in each individual unit of product, and the kind of external economies that arise from the development of specialized ancillary industries in merchanting, bleaching, dyeing, etc); (2) that the industry went on improving its equipment even though radical changes in technique were not as rapid as they could have been, given the accessible range of inventions; the fact is that even where technical change is unspectacular it tends to be continuous wherever there is a high rate of investment, for new machines tend to be better than their predecessors, even if they are not substantially different from them, so that a high rate of investment, which involves a high rate of introduction of new machines, generates a continuous flow of these minor improvements.

When the supply of labour became somewhat less elastic in the late 1840's and after, the industry's rate of growth slackened. The reasons for the tightening up of the labour supply were several. First of all there was the fact that certain pockets of technological unemployment—the hand-loom weavers constitute the classic case—were liquidated by depression and sheer starvation. Secondly, the social conscience was beginning to revolt against the callous exploitation of child and female labour and the shorter-hours legislation was gradually beginning to take effect. Thirdly, other industries were beginning to compete for labour, particularly when the railroad boom developed and stimulated trade and industry in general, and when the other textile trades began seriously to mechanize. These factors slowed the rate of expansion of the industry but accelerated the growth of incomes from employment in the industry. Between 1845 and 1870, for example, the cotton industry's output roughly doubled, that is to say it grew at about half the pace of the preceding 25 years, but the workers' share in the incomes which it generated grew a little faster than the total. By this time cotton had no claim to be the leading sector in the industrial revolution or to be setting the pace for national economic growth.

To sum up, then, it is not difficult to see why and how the cotton industry grew from insignificance to principal manufacture within little more than a generation and became the first British industry to adopt labour-saving power-driven machinery on a large scale and to produce for an international market. There is no doubt that its spectacular success inspired the imagination of contemporaries and set an example which may well have been an important factor in encouraging technical change in other industries. The demonstration effect was clearly influential in other textile industries. The new spinning techniques, for example, were relatively readily adaptable for worsted and linen mills. The power loom was applicable in principle to woollen and linen weaving. Technological change in the primary processes—carding, spinning and weaving—stimulated output and innovation in the finishing trades. The multi-storeyed cotton spinning mills were the first factories to introduce the new building technique of iron-framed construction,[1] and the first to adopt gas-lighting with the round-the-clock working schedule that this permitted. It was not chance that put the first modern railway service, regularly

---

[1] T. Bannister, 'The First Iron-framed Buildings', *Architectural Review* (1950).

moving both goods and passengers, between Liverpool and Manchester.

It is possible, nevertheless, to exaggerate the strategic role of the cotton industry in stimulating and pushing forward the broader process of industrial change and growth. The principal raw material was entirely imported so that the crucial links in this direction were with non-British rather than with British industries. It was a long time before cotton manufacture became a major consumer of coal. The industry was highly localized so that it did not create a spreading demand for new transport and building facilities. It was not until the second quarter of the nineteenth century that a textile-machinery industry developed on any scale. In short, the industry's links with other major producing sectors were quite limited and its repercussions on the rest of the economy were largely indirect. How significant these indirect effects were in precipitating and sustaining the overall process of industrialization must remain a matter of judgment rather than measurement. What is clear is that the transform-ation of the cotton industry was an important part of the industrial revolution. In order to complete the picture, however, we need to examine the changes taking place in other industries which were independently transformed over the period 1780–1850.

CHAPTER 7

THE IRON INDUSTRY

The other British industry whose technology was revolutionized in the last quarter of the eighteenth century was the iron industry. As with cotton, the effect of the technological transformation was to satisfy a long-established need with the production of a commodity which was so different, both in quality and in price, from what had hitherto been produced in Britain that it was virtually a new commodity.

In certain other respects the changes in the iron industry's system of production which were involved in the industrial revolution were less radical than the changes in the cotton industry. The textile industries were transformed in organization as well as in technology. There the domestic-handicraft type of manufacture gradually changed into a capitalistic factory industry. But the iron industry was already capitalistically organized. Its development in the sixteenth century was one of the outstanding examples of technological and organizational change which Professor Nef adduced to support his argument that the origins of the industrial revolution lie in the period 1540–1640.[1] Professor Ashton makes the point forcibly in his study of the iron industry in the Industrial Revolution:

From the earliest period of which we have exact information, iron-making in this country has been conducted on capitalistic lines—capitalistic not only in that the workers are dependent upon an employer for their raw material and market, but also in that they are brought together in a 'works', are paid wages and perform their duties under conditions not dissimilar to those of any large industry of modern times. The scale of operations has increased enormously: the sapling has become an oak, deep-rooted and widespread; technique has been revolutionized. But in structure and organization there is no fundamental change.[2]

[1] J. G. Nef, in Carus-Wilson, *Essays in Economic History*, vol. I. See especially p. 95.
[2] T. S. Ashton, *Iron and Steel in the Industrial Revolution*, (1924) p. 1.

Another feature of the industrial revolution in iron and steel which distinguishes it from that of the cotton industry is that the former expanded on the strength of domestic raw materials. The eighteenth-century innovations enabled British industries to turn from charcoal (a dwindling resource) to coal (which was abundantly available) and from imported to native iron. Whereas the cotton industry achieved its spectacular economies largely by saving labour, the iron industry did so by economizing in raw materials, that is by using materials that were abundant and cheap in place of materials that were scarce and dear. It has been estimated that a big eighteenth-century blast furnace could work for ever with about 7,000 acres of woodland at its disposal,[1] but growth in population and urbanization, the pressure for more farmland and the rising demand for woodfuel by both domestic and industrial consumers were pressing hard on the limited British woodlands by the middle decades of the century. Abraham Darby had successfully smelted iron with coke as early as 1709. In a sense this was the beginning of the end of the charcoal iron industry. But recent research on the furnace accounts of some of the ironmasters indicates that it was not until the 1750's that the rising price of charcoal and the falling price of coal (associated with steadily increasing efficiency in its use) combined to turn the balance of advantage decisively in favour of coke-smelting.[2] Later innovations in the refineries completed the move from wood to coal as the staple fuel of the iron industry.

Once the switch from wood to coal was complete the effective constraint on an ironmaster's expansion of his output depended not so much on his access to fuel resources as on his power supply. Coke was a slow-burning fuel compared with charcoal and needed power to secure an adequate blast. Water power could be used, of course, but was subject to seasonal variation and was also limited in supply at any particular location. It was when Boulton and Watt's steam engine was introduced around 1775 that the iron-masters were freed from the restrictions on location and size of plant characteristic of the wood and water level of technology, and were able to move into areas rich in coal and high-class iron resources and began to reap the

[1] G. Hammersley, 'The Charcoal Iron Industry and its Fuel', *Economic History Review* (1973), p. 606
[2] Charles K. Hyde, *Technological Change in the British Iron Industry, 1700–1870* (1977).

economies of scale of modern industry. A third distinguishing characteristic of the industrial revolution in iron then is that its final breakthrough seems to have depended at least as much on an invention that was external to the industry as on the innovations in ironmaking.

Finally there was a fourth reason why we might expect the iron industry to have played a very different role from that played by cotton in the British industrial revolution. This is the fact that iron was primarily a producer's good, subject to a derived rather than a direct demand and, partly in consequence, was subject to an inelastic demand. The expansion of a producers' good industry depends on economic conditions in general or on the growth of industries which consume its products. In some ways the iron industry was able to widen its market when its price dropped, to create new demands by replacing other products—iron began to be used widely in construction work (bridges, and building for example), in the last quarter of the eighteenth century, and in 1784 the plant of a London flour-mill was built largely of cast-iron. But until towards the middle of the nineteenth century when the demand for iron to construct railroads, locomotives, ships, machinery, gas and sanitation systems greatly expanded the range of its outlets, the industry's expansion was severely limited by factors on the side of demand. So that although the changes in its production function were radical enough and its price fell steeply, demand was too inelastic to permit a *corresponding* rise in the amount sold. There had to be some progress in industrialization before the iron industry could develop and sustain an accelerating momentum comparable to that of the cotton industry.

These characteristics of the iron industry in the last quarter of the eighteenth century—its traditions of capitalistic large-scale organization, its new demand for domestically produced raw materials, its dependence on the steam-engine, and its inelastic demand—rendered the role it played in the British industrial revolution very different from that of cotton. Whether it was less or more important in this respect is a matter of legitimate doubt. Professor Rostow, who gave cotton the role of leading sector in his model of the British take-off, apparently considered iron less important, but this view seems to be largely a consequence of the rather rigid frame of thought imposed by his 'stages of growth' analysis. If it is necessary to think of the

Industrial Revolution, as Rostow did, in terms of a specific period of two to three decades within which the crucial changes in methods of production had *decisive* consequences, then the fact that he ascribed the British industrial revolution to the period following 1783 and the fact that the cotton industry did (and the iron industry did not) reach a relatively massive proportion within the British economy in that period, lead inevitably to the conclusion that cotton must have been the leading sector. If, on the other hand, we regard the Industrial Revolution as having effectively evolved over a longer and less rigidly defined span of years—roughly within the period 1770–1850—and judge an industry's importance in the process by the weight and range of its repercussions on the rest of the economy, then the iron industry's claim to have played the key role is quite impressive.[1] Here surely in its forward and backward linkages with the rest of the economy—in the demand for coal and iron and extensive transport and capital facilities on the one hand, and in the reduction of costs for a wide range of manufactured goods as well as in the building and transport industries on the other—we can see the iron industry playing a more powerful and pervasive role in the process of British industrialization than did cotton.

But it is not really necessary, or even useful, to persist in the attempt to identify a single industry to which can be ascribed the leading part in precipitating the British industrial revolution. A more satisfying and convincing, if less dramatic, case can be made for the view that the first industrialization was the result of a cluster of innovations in Schumpeter's sense of the term. Some of the relevant *inventions* belong to an earlier period: but it is the *innovations*, the general adoption of the inventions, that counts. This cluster of innovations was decisive for three main reasons: (1) because they occurred at roughly the same period of time, (2) because they came when Britain's naval supremacy and commercial contacts enabled her to take advantage of rising European and North American incomes, and (3) because they reinforced each other in certain important respects. The concentration of the cluster was all-important. It made the process of industrialization a great deal more profitable than it would otherwise have been, and gave the British economy a lead over its rivals which ensured that the process would go on being profitable so long as the lead was maintained.

[1] See W. W. Rostow, *The World Economy*, p. 383, for a less rigid periodization of British stages of growth than that suggested in his earlier writings.

With this kind of interpretation of the industrial revolution in mind, let us try to assess the part played by the iron industry in the first industrial revolution. Let us ask ourselves first what was the character of the technological changes which transformed the industry—and when did they occur? And secondly what kind of impact did they have on the national economy as a whole? To begin, then, consider the process of technological change in the eighteenth-century iron industry. What kind of industry was it at the pre-industrial stage?

The evidence suggests that the English iron industry in the first half of the eighteenth century was scattered, migratory, and tightly constrained by its resource limitations. It has been estimated that the peak output of the English charcoal industry was achieved between 1625 and 1635 when the output of pig-iron probably reached 26,000 tons per annum. By the 1720's it is estimated that the pig-iron output was between 20,000 and 25,000 tons per annum and most of this went to produce cast-iron objects. Most of the wrought-iron and steel produced in this country was made from imported bar-iron, largely Swedish.

The reason for the industry's stagnation was that it faced acute raw-material problems. On the one hand its native iron-ore resources were very low grade—full of impurities which made it difficult to evolve a tough, hard, final product. On the other its main fuel, charcoal, was a dwindling resource which was so fragile that it was virtually non-transportable. This of course is what made the industry scattered and migratory. The first requirement of a successful iron-works in the early eighteenth century was that it should be situated in a large area of woodland. Nowadays the iron and steel industry is characteristically the hub of a dense complex of industry and population. The charcoal-fired blast-furnace was generally found in a remote area, isolated from other industries and from other furnaces, and there were furnaces scattered all over the country from the Scottish Highlands to the Weald of Kent, wherever there was a sufficiently large woodland to supply their voracious needs for charcoal.

The industry was vital to the economy, even in pre-industrial times, and much thought and effort was put into trying to overcome the obstacles to its expansion. There was a close association between land-holding and iron-making, and the iron-masters were relatively wealthy men who had the financial resources and the incentive to experiment with new methods.

The first patent for the use of coal in iron-making was granted in 1589 and a series of similar patents were taken out in the late sixteenth and seventeenth centuries. None of them seems to have resulted in a commercially viable product until 1709 when there is evidence that Abraham Darby's works at Coalbrookdale actually did smelt iron with coke, but until the 1750's the only blast furnaces dependent on coke were operated by the Darby family. Various reasons have been advanced for this long technological lag, of which the most convincing is the fact that there was a quality difference between charcoal pig and coke pig which significantly raised the costs of converting the latter into acceptable bar iron.[1] The Darbys found it profitable to use coke because the bulk of their output went to cast iron rather than wrought iron products, and also because they had developed a technique of making thin-walled castings for which coke pig was actually a superior material. This was the technique which Darby patented in 1707 and which 'remained a well-guarded industrial technique long after the expiration of his patent'.[2] Meanwhile Benjamin Huntsman achieved a similar kind of success in steel-making, by perfecting in the 1740's a process which used coke to generate an intense heat and so to produce a cast-steel that was relatively free from impurities.

Neither of these innovations, however, solved the basic problems of the forging branch of the iron industry, the branch which produced bars intended for wrought-iron or steel. Benjamin Huntsman had to use Swedish iron for his steel-making because English pig was too brittle. Wrought-iron still required a charcoal fire. The coke furnace somewhat eased the problem by making cast-iron an acceptable substitute for wrought-iron in many products. The new cast-iron products of the coking furnaces could be used for a variety of household utensils: for gates, gun-carriages, cannons, cheap nails, joists, pipes and bridges. Because cast-iron is less costly to produce than wrought-iron, these products were cheaper and displaced the wrought-iron versions. But for plough-shares, hoes, tools of all kinds, locks and bolts and stirrup bits the coke furnaces would not produce an acceptable product: and for the better articles of this kind and for cutlery and all steel goods the British ores were unsatisfactory, even when processed by charcoal furnaces.

[1] See Charles K. Hyde, *op. cit.*, pp. 26–8 for a discussion of the nature of the quality difference.　　　　[2] *Ibid.*, p. 41.

Through most of the eighteenth century the search for charcoal supplies went on and reached out into the wooded areas of Scotland. A furnace was built at Inveraray as late as 1775. Clearly an industry with a product as heavy as iron could achieve little in the way of economies of operation if it had to set up its workshops so far from the consuming centres. Except where there was navigable water, transport costs were prohibitive in the eighteenth century. 'It has been estimated that the cost of inland transportation for 20 miles was about equal to the cost of freight from the Baltic.'[1] British charcoal iron-making was thus a high-cost industry in the eighteenth century. Swedish iron was not only better but cheaper in many areas, even though it had to run the gauntlet of both a £3 export duty and a £2 import duty on its way to the British market.

It has been said that the turning point in the history of the iron industry came in 1775, when Watt's steam-engine made it possible to apply increased power for blowing the blast furnace and mechanical power for forging. There is no doubt of the immense and immediate importance of the steam-engine to the iron industry. The first steam-engine to be applied for purposes other than pumping water was installed at the factory of John Wilkinson the iron-master, but the switch from charcoal to coke in the blast furnaces was already well underway by the 1760's. In 1760 the Carron iron-works coke blast-furnace was opened and was powered by a steam blowing-engine; the standard method of blowing till then had been by waterwheel-driven bellows. In 1760 there were only 14 coke furnaces in blast in Britain, but the number doubled in the 1760's and early 1770's. Meanwhile investment in the charcoal iron-industry had come to a standstill: there is no evidence of a charcoal furnace being built after 1775, and by 1790 the number in use had fallen to 25, whereas the number of coke furnaces had risen to 86. With the development of steam-driven blast in the late eighteenth century the iron industry lost its migratory character and began to concentrate in large-scale units of production grouped in regions where coal and iron were in ample supply and where water-borne transport was available. By 1806 87 per cent of the pig-iron production of the country was located on the coalfields. With up to 10 tons of coal required to produce

[1] H. Roepke, 'Movements of the British Iron and Steel Industry 1720–1851', in *Illinois Studies in the Social Sciences*, volume 36, p. 38.

1 ton of pig iron in the 1760's and 1770's it is understandable that the coalfields should have been the main attraction.

The main disadvantage of using coal in the forge, that is in the refining process whereby pig-iron was converted into bar-iron, was that coal introduced impurities which made the bar-iron brittle and the final product unreliable. Using coke pig-iron added further impurity. These technical problems inhibited the output of British forges through most of the eighteenth century and the evidence suggests that the first commercially viable technique designed to eliminate both sorts of impurity was the potting process patented by the Wood brothers in 1761 and adopted widely—after a period of experiment and modification—from the late 1770's.[1] This early break-through has, however, been overshadowed in the literature by the technique which was to supplant it from the mid 1790's—Cort's puddling and rolling process patented in 1783 and 1784.

There were three features of Cort's method that made it an important advance: (1) it used coal fuel throughout and so escaped the dependence on charcoal which made British bar-iron such a costly product, (2) it converted native pig-iron to bars which were at least as good as the Swedish product, and (3) it made a single process of a series of operations—puddling (i.e. melting and stirring), hammering and rolling—which had hitherto been disconnected. Successful application of a complex discovery of this kind was not automatic. It required capitalists with the capital to spare and the inclination to risk it on innovation, experienced managers and foremen to design the production process and introduce the minor modifications and improvements that were needed to put the finishing touches on its efficiency, and skilled workmen to build the equipment and put the plans into execution. Such factors of production were scarce in eighteenth-century Britain as they must be in all pre-industrial economies. In the beginning progress came where these factors were available. Most of the immediate expansion in iron-making that followed in the decade after Cort took out his patent occurred in South Wales, where Richard Crawshay had been quick to introduce the process. As late as 1791 the Carron Company, a large and progressive concern, had tried

[1] Hyde, *op. cit.*, p. 194.

Cort's method and—to quote from a letter in the Company's records—found that it 'made iron far from being bad, but the extraordinary waste rendered it a very losing process'.[1] Moreover it took some time for consumers at home and abroad to realize that British iron, so long an unreliable product, could be as satisfactory as foreign iron.

Nevertheless, like Arkwright's water-frame, Cort's discovery was actually adopted more rapidly than most successful eighteenth-century inventions, partly because the inventor was unlucky enough to lose his patent rights prematurely. Cort was ruined by the bankruptcy and suicide of one of his main creditors and was unable to protect his patent, which lapsed in 1789. From then on the iron-masters could experiment with his process as they chose, introducing whatever improvements occurred to them, without costs in the way of royalties. In the 1790's and the first decade of the nineteenth century the industry expanded on all fronts. The possibility of using British pig-iron for wrought as well as cast iron products greatly expanded the demand for pig. Between 1788 and 1805 output of British pig-iron almost quadrupled: it had already doubled in the previous wave of expansion which resulted from the wider use of coke in blast-furnaces dating from the 1760's. By 1812, although Swedish bar-iron was still being imported for the steel-makers, Britain was exporting more bar-iron than she was importing.

By the first decade of the nineteenth century, then, the output of British pig-iron was running at over a quarter of a million tons per annum compared with perhaps 30,000 tons in 1760. Over 60,000 tons per annum were being exported. Taken broadly—from the iron mines to the final product, that is to say—the iron industry may have generated something like 6 per cent of the British national income in the first decade of the nineteenth century, compared with perhaps 1 or 2 per cent in the 1760's. Its expansion in the fourth quarter of the eighteenth century owed much to the steam-engine, not only through the use of steam-power in its own furnaces, hammers and mills but also through the cheaper, better coal and ore which steam pumping-machines in the mines made accessible.

The main consequence of the innovations in the iron industry

[1] R. H. Campbell, *Carron Company* (1961), p. 60.

in the second half of the eighteenth century was to effect spectacular economies in its raw-material costs. But the basic innovations stimulated others which resulted in important savings in time and labour. A steam-hammer introduced by John Wilkinson in 1782 could strike 150 blows a minute. Cort's rolling mill when powered by steam could process 15 tons of iron in the time originally required to turn out 1 ton of bar-iron by the standard hammering process. By the first decade of the nineteenth century it was estimated that English puddled bar-iron was selling at prices varying from £20 to £28 per ton, whereas the rival Swedish product varied from £35 to £40 a ton. Cheaper supplies of pig and bar iron stimulated innovation in further processes. In the 1780's and 1790's new machines were introduced for a variety of intermediate stages: machines for drawing, cutting and working the metal, for example, drills for boring cannon, metal turning lathes, and machines for forging nails or turning screws.

The result of this cluster of innovations was to change completely the structure and character of the industry. Between 1788 and 1805 the average make per blast-furnace grew from 750 tons to 1491 tons, an increase of 99 per cent in less than two decades;[1] by 1839 it was 3,566 tons. The iron-founders had always been relatively wealthy men—they had to be in an industry which required such heavy capital outlays as were involved, for example in the construction of a blast furnace, but the iron-masters of the last quarter of the eighteenth century operated on a scale which was beyond all previous experience. John Wilkinson's industrial empire included collieries, tin mines, iron foundries, forges, warehouses, and landing-stages; it extended over Wales, Cornwall, the Midlands, London and France; he even coined his own money. Moreover when Cort's process enabled the forging sector of the industry to go over to coal, it finally removed the barriers to integration of the iron industry. It was this that facilitated its concentration and permitted it to grow into the industrial giant that it character-istically is today. 'In Staffordshire, Yorkshire and—above all—South Wales, all processes from the mining of coal and ore to the slitting of rods and the production of finished wares were henceforth carried on in the same locality, by the same firm,

[1] Hyde, *op. cit.*, p. 113.

and most of them in single establishments.'¹ This resulted in
enormous operational economies and by producing good cheap
iron of uniform texture and reliability provided the British
economy with the raw material of a new industry—mechanical
engineering.

In effect, the innovations which began to spread through the
iron industry in the last three to four decades of the eighteenth
century determined the character of technical change in the
industry until the 1860's, when Bessemer demonstrated his new
steel-making process and Cowper's regenerative stove was
perfected. The only major discovery affecting the industry in
the first half of the nineteenth century was Nielsen's discovery
in 1828 that heating the air used in the blast resulted in much
lower coke consumption and greatly increased output. Within
less than a decade the use of hot blast had been adopted
generally. This innovation brought with it a number of advantages: it permitted considerable economies in the use of fuel, it
facilitated the use of larger furnaces, it gave economic value to
the Scottish black-band ironstone which had been almost
unusable for iron smelting until the hot blast was used, and it
enabled those regions of Scotland and South Wales which were
without good coking coal to use raw coal. After the introduction
of the hot blast, Scotland produced pig-iron at the lowest cost
in Britain and probably in the world.

But if there was no new major development apart from hot
blast in the first half of the nineteenth century, technical
progress in the iron industry did not come to a standstill. There
were three related trends. (1) There was a steady increase in
the size of the unit of production. (2) There were continuing
economies in the amount of coal consumed: by 1840 the weight
of coke used in making pig-iron was no greater than the weight
of iron ore required; in 1788 the ratio had been 7 tons of coal
to one of pig, in 1810 5 tons and in 1840 $3\frac{1}{2}$ tons. (3) There were
continuing improvements in the design of plant and machinery:
there were changes in the design of the blast-furnace in the
1830's, for example, which raised the height of the furnaces and
saved fuel and accelerated the output of metal; there were
improvements in the puddling process which reduced the
pig-iron required to make a long bar from 30 or 35 hundred-

¹ Ashton, *The Eighteenth Century*, p. 117.

weight at the beginning of the century to 26 or 27 hundredweight in the 1840's; there were improvements in the steam-hammer and in the rolling mill which saved time and labour.

Actually, after the breakthrough of the 1780's which quad-rupled output in less than a couple of decades, the iron industry grew very much more slowly. The expansion of the 1790's and the 1800's was associated with the abnormal wartime demand for iron products inflated by naval and military needs and it was assisted by the improvement in transport facilities created by the canal mania. When the war ended there was a pro-nounced depression, and growth was not resumed until the military demand was replaced by demand for a variety of other purposes. Iron began to be used in increasing quantities in constructing buildings, bridges, machinery, canal boats, gas and water pipes, lamp-posts, railways, and pillars; 'London even made experiments with iron paving—near Blackfriars Bridge and Leicester Square'.[1] It was not until the railway age, however, beginning in the 1830's, that the industry resumed the rate of growth which had characterized it over the period between the 1780's and the 1800's. Yet, if output grew more slowly in the period after the Napoleonic wars than before, it grew faster than in any other country. Britain's share of the world output of pig-iron grew from 19 per cent in 1800 to 40 per cent in 1820 and to 52 per cent in 1840. What can we say then about the impact of the iron industry's progress on the British economy as a whole? Consider, for example, the linkages on the demand side—the 'backward linkages' with the rest of the economy in Professor Rostow's terminology.

First of all the iron industry created a demand for British iron-ore resources: and the significant point here was that it gave a value to mineral resources which had hitherto been so low grade that they were practically worthless. It was one of Britain's special advantages as a location for the first industrial revolution that her iron and coal resources co-existed in the same regions, often within the same mines. The ore that was used at this time was almost entirely from beds within the coal measures: indeed in 1850 it was estimated that 95 per cent of the iron ore used was coal measures' ore.[2] For more than a century following the rapid development of coke smelting in the

[1] Clapham, *Economic History*, vol. i, p. 149.
[2] Roepke, 'Movements of the British Iron and Steel Industry', p. 27.

industry (dating from about 1760) it relied almost exclusively on domestic sources of iron ore, although these were of relatively low quality. It was not until the 1870's and the 1880's that imports of iron ore became significant.

In addition to iron ore the industry used large quantities of British limestone and British coal. The iron industry was the most important single factor in the rising demand for coal in the first half of the nineteenth century, and through its demand for both coal and ore it created an associated demand for transport facilities. The canals, as we have seen, were built primarily to ship coal, and a sizeable proportion of this— probably about a fifth in the early nineteenth century and about a quarter by 1840—was required to meet the needs of furnace and forge.

Finally, it may be said that if a modern industry is a large-scale, heavily capitalized and mechanized factory industry, the iron industry was its prototype and it demanded the factors of production appropriate to a modern industry. It needed steam-power (though water-power was often made to serve in the earlier years) for a whole variety of purposes: for pumping water out of coal and iron mines, for crushing ores, for the blast-furnace, the foundry hammer and the rolling mill, and for fashioning the final products. There are no factory returns for the iron industry in the first half of the nineteenth century, but by 1871 blast-furnaces, iron mills and foundries absorbed about 25 per cent of the steam-power generated in the factories and workshops of Great Britain and about 40 per cent of their labour force. It cannot have required a much smaller proportion in the first half of the century. It also required a semi-skilled adult male factory labour force and large doses of capital and specialized machinery, and thus helped to build up the national reserve of these essential elements of a modernized economy.

On the other side of the account—the forward linkages—the iron industry supplied a cheap and tough industrial material that was an absolute necessity for an industrialized economy; and the existence of this commodity in such cheapness and abundance was an important part of the reason for Britain's success in achieving an industrial revolution in advance of its rivals. Good cheap iron was required for implements and tools of all kinds from plough-shares to lathes, for military and naval purposes of all kinds, from anchors to guns and gun-carriages, for hardware, for telegraphic wire, for building purposes and above all for industrial machinery. The new method of casting and forging developed at the end of the eighteenth century laid the basis for the engineering industry that was to serve all British industry and supply the world with machinery during the nineteenth century. It stimulated inventions which not only saved labour and made large-scale production possible on a scale hitherto out of the question, but also laid the basis for the standardized products and precision instruments which are the basis of modern industry. By developing its own machinery the metal industry helped to introduce technical improvement into a wide range of the other industries. Machines and the machines that make machines have proved to be capable of an infinite sequence of improvement, and it is this process of continuing, self-generating technical change that is the ultimate cause of the sustained economic growth that we now take for granted.

For the characteristic of the iron industry that makes it a crucial factor in modern economic growth is that it was to a large extent, though not exclusively, a producers' industry. A reduction in the price of iron meant a reduction in costs of production for a wide range of other industries, and it also permitted the substitution of iron for other less durable products that had hitherto been employed because the price of iron was prohibitive. The substitution of cheap cast-iron products for expensive wrought-iron or imported products was one example. But more important by far was the substitution of iron for wood, which made it possible to produce textile machinery, for example, with semi-skilled labour instead of with scarce wheel-wrights, and to create a product which was not only more precisely made than the old hand-made product but would stand up to the rigorous day-and-night shift work and was more easily repaired. Iron pipes were more efficient and more durable for gas and water piping than wood or pottery pipes, and iron joists added greatly to the strength of public buildings. In time, of course, iron began to be found the most efficient material for many other industrial purposes—shipbuilding, for example, carriage making, brewers' and distillers' vats and so on. The country which could supply this vital industrial material in virtually unlimited quantities and at a relatively low price was a country with a high growth potential.

But the sector which eventually made the biggest demands

on the iron industry, the development of which really tested the iron industry's capacity to grow, was the railways. In the first quarter of the nineteenth century iron-railway construction was not negligible, but it was limited to small-scale localized railroads, most of them attached to a mine or iron works and dependent on the draught power of horses or stationary engines. Those that went beyond the bounds of a private estate and were more than adjuncts to a mine or an iron works required an Act of Parliament, so we have surviving records of their length. During the first 20 years of the nineteenth century nearly 200 miles of this kind of public railroad were opened to the public. Within the decade of the 1820's nearly 100 more miles were opened and the steam railway age began. The peak of railway building activity was reached in 1847 when nearly 6,500 miles of railway were under construction. By the 1850's the railway construction boom was over and the main skeleton of the British railroad network had been laid down. The speed at which it had been constructed was quite phenomenal. Clearly it could not have been achieved in such a fantastically short span of years had it not been for the existence of an iron industry with a tremendous capacity for expansion. Equally clearly, the speed at which the network was completed was one of the reasons for its high rate of profitability. By the late 1850's operating profits on the railways began to be of the same order as the increase in capital invested in the railways. In spite of manias and crises, mismanagement and bad planning, the story of the railway boom is an impressive success story.

Nor was this the end of the story, of course. When the British railway network had been virtually completed, the expanded iron industry was able to supply the railroad iron for foreign railways. Already in the 1850's exports rose to be 39 per cent of the gross product of the industry—during the first half of the century they had averaged only 25 per cent. Till then three-quarters or more of the output of the industry had gone to supply the domestic demand and incidentally to support British industry.

In short, the iron industry played a role in British industrialization that was both pervasive and stimulating. It provided cheaply and abundantly the commodity on which, more than on any other single material except coal, modern industry was to depend for its essential equipment. Nineteenth-century industrialization may indeed have been started by the textile innovations of the end of the eighteenth century. But continuous industrialization depended on the availability of coal and iron, and would have been inconceivable without the steam-engine and the technical progress in the iron industry which also took effect in the last three decades or so of the eighteenth century. Even today underdeveloped countries seeking a means of escape from economic stagnation are inclined to see the establishment of a steel industry as a first step. They may not always be right in this assessment of their current problem but it is not difficult to see why they drew this lesson from nineteenth-century British experience.

CHAPTER 8

THE SOURCES OF INNOVATION

The process of industrialization which gathered momentum in Britain during the second half of the eighteenth century and initiated the sustained upward movement of real incomes that the western world now takes for granted, involved revolutionary changes in the structure and organization of the economy. The origins of some of these changes can be traced to earlier centuries. Some of them are still working themselves out. It is generally agreed, however, that the crucial transformation occurred fairly rapidly—certainly within the century between 1750 and 1850, probably in a considerably shorter time. The temptation to time it narrowly, to identify a relatively short period of time within which the crucial change can be said to have taken place, is very strong. The discontinuities of history are more dramatic than its continuities, and it is natural to want to give them a precise time reference.

So the chronology of the industrial revolution has become a fruitful source of controversy. There are those who would like to trace its beginnings back to the beginnings of organized manufacturing industry itself and others who insist that it is not over yet, even for a fully industrialized country like Britain. There are those who find overwhelming evidence for significant discontinuity in the last quarter of the eighteenth century: and others like Clapham and Schumpeter who are equally convinced that 'if one wishes to refer the industrial revolution to a definite historical epoch it can be located more justifiably in the second quarter of the nineteenth than in the end of the eighteenth century'.[1]

What answer one gives to this kind of problem of interpretation depends of course on what precise question one is asking of the data; in particular, in this context, what one means by

---

[1] Schumpeter, *Business Cycles*, vol. 1, p. 254, ascribes this view to Clapham, Tugan-Baronowsky and Spiethof.

the 'crucial' changes. Crucial in what sense? Was it the very beginnings of organized industry that constituted the significant change? If so, one must go back as Nef did to Tudor times and earlier and give up all hope of ascribing the industrial revolution to a definite epoch. Was it when technical change assumed a distinctively modern character, involving the substitution of machinery for man-power, of mineral for biological sources of energy, of factory organization for domestic industry? If so, presumably it is the cluster of innovations which took effect in the last three decades of the eighteenth century which must engage our attention. Was it when manufacturing industry grew massive enough to shape the structure of the national economy, to set the pace of economic growth, to determine standards of life and ways of living for people in general? If so, we should probably focus on the beginnings of the railway age in the second quarter of the nineteenth century.

Professor Rostow has given a special interest to the problem of identifying and of timing the British industrial revolution by making it the basis of his theory of the stages of economic growth; that is, viewing it as the prototype of the take-off, 'that decisive interval in the history of a society when growth becomes its normal condition'.[1] This of course is going much further than his predecessors have done in the ancient controversy over the chronology of the industrial revolution. Their main purpose was to sketch a chronology of British industrialization which could be useful in the attempt to analyse the causes, character and consequences of the central process. What Professor Rostow has tried to do is to interpret British economic history in a way that has strategic policy implications for those concerned with the problems of today's pre-industrial economies, and this leads him to view the industrial revolution as something nearer to an *event* than to a *process*. So that although he claims that his is a return to an 'old fashioned way of looking at economic development' it is indeed a highly novel way of looking at economic history. If he is right and it *is* possible to identify, in the history of those countries which have successfully industrialized, a period of two to three decades within which the transformation was sufficiently decisive to ensure a continuance not only of the process of industrialization, but also of the growth in average productivity

[1] Rostow, *Stages of Economic Growth*, 2nd ed., p. 36.

and standards of living, then it is certainly important for today's policy makers to understand the mechanics of the change. For presumably in principle the changes which took place spontaneously in past 'take-offs' can be induced by appropriate government action in today's underdeveloped countries.

Examination of the historical record for particular countries in the light of the 'take-off' as formalized by Professor Rostow has proved immensely fruitful in focusing the attention of economists and economic historians on the significant discontinuities implied in the fact of an industrial revolution.[1] However, it is clear that the concept of the 'take-off' is a dramatic simplification which does not stand up to a systematic attempt to relate it to the known facts in any detail or to give it a definite chronology. In the British case, for example, the choice of the period 1783–1802 as the one in which the process of industrialization became in some sense irreversible is, while understandable, not justified by detailed analysis.[2] The period contained some significant developments in the cotton and iron industries, it included the canal mania, it saw an acceleration in the pace of enclosures and of population growth and above all it was characterized by a sharp upsurge in the amount of overseas trade entering and leaving British ports. Each of these developments, however, formed part of a historical continuum in which the period 1783–1802 was not unique. Population, for example, and enclosures had begun their acceleration earlier and reached their peak later. The canal mania was preceded by an earlier burst of activity in canal construction which, if it was less powerful was certainly unprecedented; and it was followed a generation later by the more spectacular and important railway mania. The cotton and iron industries had begun to transform their techniques in earlier decades and by 1802 were still too small a part of total economic activity to carry the national economy along by their own weight. The most significant change of trend distinguishing this period is that for overseas trade; any estimate of national output which is heavily dependent on the foreign-trade series suggests an acceleration in the national rate of growth during this period. On the other

[1] W. W. Rostow (ed.), *The Economies of Take-off into Sustained Growth* (1963), reports a conference of the International Economic Association on this theme.
[2] See Phyllis Deane and H. J. Habakkuk, 'The Take-off in Britain', in W. W. Rostow (ed.), *op. cit.*

hand, overseas trade was highly vulnerable to the fortunes of war, and the upsurge of the 1780's and 1790's can easily be explained by war conditions; the growth of trade in the 1780's, for example, can be seen as a rebound from the abnormally low levels to which it had been pushed by the American War, and the prolonged growth of the 1790's must have owed a good deal to the fact that Britain's main continental competitors were so largely kept off the seas by the French wars. If we allow for these special circumstances, the upsurge in foreign trade which characterized the period 1783–1802 is not as spectacular as it might appear at first.

What all this amounts to, in effect, is that we cannot justify the choice of such a tightly specified and narrow period as 1783–1802 to represent the span of years within which the industrial revolution took the kind of shape that made continuing future industrialization inevitable. Yet the questions raised by Professor Rostow's attempt to give a time reference to the crucial changes in the industrial revolution remain interesting and important. We know, for example, that some of today's underdeveloped countries have begun to industrialize and have failed either to maintain their original impetus or to generate sustained economic growth. If we knew more about the mechanics of past industrial revolutions, in particular if we could say whether there was an identifiable stage in the process beyond which growth seemed to be inevitable, it might help us to understand the conditions of successful industrialization. In this connection the first industrial revolution, because it was spontaneous, has a special interest.

One thing that is clear about modern economic growth is that it depends on, more than anything else, a continuing process of technical change. What the industrial revolution did was to increase substantially the flow of innovations embodied in the nation's economic activity and to turn it into a continuous, if fluctuating, flow. In a pre-industrial economy technical progress tends to be exceptional and intermittent. In an industrialized economy it is accepted as part of the normal order of things. Each generation expects to be able to improve on the productive techniques of its fathers. Each new machine is designed to be in some way more efficient than the machine it replaces in the production process.

From this we may deduce that an industrial revolution

implies certain conditional changes. One condition of an industrial revolution, for example, is a change in the attitude of mind of the representative producer. For in a traditional type of economy techniques are normally handed on from father to son without change or thought of change. Another condition is a change in the market environment. Where there is no economic surplus or where the prospects of expanding sales are limited or uncertain, producers have neither the freedom nor the incentive to experiment with new methods. A third condition is an increase in the flow of inventions or of ideas for change suitable for incorporation into the productive process. How near were these three conditions to fulfilment by the end of the eighteenth, or the beginning of the nineteenth century?

I. CHANGES IN ENTREPRENEURIAL ATTITUDES TO INNOVATION

There is no doubt that innovation was high fashion by the middle of the eighteenth century. 'The age is running mad after innovation', said Dr Johnson with characteristic sarcasm. 'All the business of the world is to be done in a new way: men are to be hanged in a new way; Tyburn itself is not safe from the fury of innovation.'[1] What we have to ask ourselves, however, is how far this was a fashionable craze and to what extent did it affect the behaviour of the representative producer, of the multitude of relatively inarticulate, uneducated and far from affluent individuals who took the day-to-day decisions about the conduct of the nation's business. This is a difficult question to answer because while it is nearly always possible to time the first appearances of new methods—novelties get themselves into the news—it is rarely possible to trace their gradual spread and adaptation over a wider field.

Agriculture was still the principal industry and there seems no doubt that the actively improving farmer was still uncommon in the late eighteenth and early nineteenth centuries. Nevertheless there must have been many small farmers who were forced by enclosures to find new ways of organizing their time and their acreage. Traditional methods would no longer suffice to earn a living for many of those affected by enclosures. They had either to experiment with new crops or to spend more time

[1] Quoted by Charles Wilson and William Reader in *Men and Machines* (1958), p. 2.

at domestic handicrafts like spinning or weaving or to go out of business on their own account and join the agricultural and industrial proletariat. But enclosure had been going on for centuries. We cannot identify the period at which the enclosure movement began to affect the methods of the majority of farmers but it may be reasonable to associate it with the period when forcible enclosure—parliamentary enclosure that is to say— reached its peak. Enclosures of common land and waste by Act of Parliament, which had involved about 75,000 acres in the period 1727–60, affected 478,000 acres in the period 1761–92 and over a million acres in the period of the French and Napoleonic wars, 1793–1815. By the 1820's the open-field type of agriculture was becoming a rarity, though the antiquated rotations and attitudes had by no means disappeared by the middle of the nineteenth century. When James Caird toured the country in 1850/1 the old 'two crops and fallow' rotation of the open-field system was still common in many parts of England and there were still farmers who regarded manure as useless muck.[1]

Trade was the other major industry of pre-industrial Britain, and here there is evidence of changes in methods of organization and procedure that probably widened the opportunities and reduced the uncertainties for all merchants engaged in trade on a large scale. Within the restrictions imposed by the Bubble Act, businessmen were actively experimenting with new forms of organization. By the end of the century the joint-stock association, without incorporation or limited liability but with freely transferable shares, was a common form of unit. There was, too, a steady development through the eighteenth century in the business of insuring traders' stocks against fire, which must have greatly reduced the element of uncertainty in the merchants' business. Marine insurance, which had been barely distinguishable from frivolous speculation in the early part of the century had become a skilled professional service of some consequence by 1771, when the Society of Underwriters at Lloyd's Coffee House subscribed to build a new Lloyd's Coffee House and to separate itself from the miscellaneous gamblers and brokers of all kinds who frequented the old Coffee House.[2]

Developments in transport also revealed new entrepreneurial

[1] J. Caird, *English Agriculture 1850 and 1851* (1852).
[2] See H. E. Raynes, *A History of British Insurance* (2nd ed. 1961).

attitudes in the eighteenth century, and by changing the pattern of economic opportunity for the trading community in general they must have had significant secondary repercussions. In the business of providing communications, private enterprise was beginning to encroach on sectors hitherto regarded as the province of local government and the new decision-takers were often less conservative than the old. The managers of turnpike trusts, for example, realized more readily than the parish councillors the advantage of employing a skilled engineer—even a self-made expert like John Metcalf—in building cheap durable highways, and a new career was thus opened up for the new genus of road engineer. Similarly, canal builders gave employment to engineers like James Brindley who brought new dimensions into the thinking of the inland navigators and opened up a new range of economic opportunity to those whose livelihood depended on transporting heavy raw materials across country.

In manufacturing industry the technical transformation was most evident and most complete in the textile industries, particularly cotton, and in the metal-using industries, particularly iron. In textiles it was only the cotton industry that had been revolutionized by the early years of the nineteenth century, but it was clearly just a matter of time before the other textile industries responded to competition and example by adapting the new machines to their special needs. Wool-carding engines were being power-driven in Yorkshire in the early 1770's, and attempts were being made in the 1790's to comb worsted and to prepare flax and silk so that the spinning machines which had been so spectacularly successful in cotton could be applied to other textiles. The Jacquard loom, a French invention originating in the hard-pressed silk industry and patented in 1805, spread rapidly in England in the 1820's when an English improvement permitted a more compact version suitable for cottage industry as well as factory industry. In the iron trade events moved as rapidly at the end of the eighteenth century as they did in cotton. The transition from charcoal-fired furnaces was virtually complete by the first decade of the nineteenth century and the traditional technology was thus completely displaced. Even the village blacksmith was adopting new techniques where coal was accessible and cheap, though in these more localized branches of the industry the full effect of the change had to await the spread of canals and later of railways, which eventually made coal cheap throughout the country. Similarly techniques in the other metal industries, and coal, were altered at the mining stage by the use of the steam-engine for power-pumping and hoisting machinery, and at later stages by the use of coal instead of charcoal. It was not until later in the nineteenth century, however, that radical changes were introduced into the non-ferrous metal manufacturing processes.

In the building industry, too, there were important changes in technique which dated from the early stages of the industrial revolution. The shortage of timber was already a significant factor in the early part of the eighteenth century, and it led first to a greater use of stone in building (at any rate in the areas where it was easily quarried), and then to a more extensive use of brick. The clay deposits from which bricks were made were widespread and the spread of the canals first, and even more so of railways later, made it easier to feed the brick kilns with cheap coal. The growing output of bricks prompted the imposition of an excise tax in 1785, and from that date consequently we have a record of the country's brick output. Within a couple of decades after 1785/9 the output of bricks expanded by 80 per cent, a development which reflected more than anything else the effectiveness of the canals in providing the brickmakers with a cheap means of transport for both fuel and final product. It took another 30 years to bring a further expansion of 80 per cent in the annual output of the brick industry and by then, in the late 1830's, the railway age was well under way and was creating not only another channel of transport but also a new source of demand for bricks. There were important developments, too, in other building materials before the end of the eighteenth century—in plaster for wall-facing, for example, in mortar for joining bricks or stone and in concrete for foundations; but it was not until the 1820's that the many experiments in cement-making led to Portland cement, the material of which the London main drainage system was constructed a generation later.

In most other manufacturing industries the only major technological change which dates effectively from the late eighteenth century was the use of steam-power instead of water- or horse-power. This, however, had a very limited impact for it was important only in units of production which were already operating on a large scale. The first two steam-engines set up in London, for example, were both at breweries, but it was only in big established centres of population like London or Bristol or Dublin that the individual brewer's market was on a scale sufficient to warrant the purchase of a steam-engine. Where the market was less securely large the attempt to operate a steam-engine was more likely to land the entrepreneur in financial difficulties. The ill-fated Albion flour-mill, for example, the first mill to be powered by steam, was set up in London at a cost of £60,000, began operations in 1786 and after several unsuccessful years was completely destroyed by fire in 1792. This was an object-lesson to other manufacturers who had the capital and the enterprise to start such a project but not the long purse required to carry it through the period of problems and miscalculations which must attach to every radical change in existing practices. Even in the textile mills of Lancashire, Cheshire and Yorkshire, the bulk of the power was still provided by water in 1800.[1] The fact is that major innovations require a period of development before they become commercially viable and few eighteenth-century manufacturers were rich enough to face a potentially long period of loss or nil return. Most 'manufacturers' were still 'handicrafts' at the start of the nineteenth century; most machinery was wooden, clumsy, easily broken or worn and dependent for its efficiency more on the acquired skill of its operator than on its basic design. There was little shortage of unskilled labour and few producers would have found it profitable to substitute machines for human effort. Scotswomen were still carrying coal on their backs up ladders reaching 100 feet and more, though the steam-engine could have hoisted it to the surface more quickly and effectively. As late as 1831, the census list of activities headed 'retail trade and handicraft' included shipbuilding, wood and furniture, watches, toys and musical instruments, food and drink, fur and leather, printing and paper industries as well as blacksmiths and some of the iron-founders, weavers and dyers.

On the other hand, a catalogue of the various kinds of innovation which were introduced into Britain in the second half of the eighteenth century produces an impression of

[1] D. S. L. Cardwell, 'Power Technologies and the Advance of Science, 1700–1825', *Technology and Culture* (1965), p. 192.

accelerating technical progress and it is evident that significant changes were already taking place in the character of the entrepreneurial decision-making process as a result of organizational and institutional developments. In agriculture, for example, the effect of the long enclosure movement on the structure of English landownership and tenure was to shift more of the power, and the funds, for technological change towards the class of agrarian capitalists who had the incentive and know-how to experiment with new ideas, to adopt radical cost-reducing techniques, and to influence more conservative farmers. By 1780, according to the land tax returns, more than four-fifths of English land was cultivated by tenant farmers or large landowners. The latter were well placed to develop new techniques to the point of commercial viability and to propagate best-practice farming. A growing number of professional land stewards helped to raise technological standards both by their own actions and by advising tenants. Progressive tenants were much sought after by landowners who saw that their rent incomes hinged on the technological dynamism of their tenants and these in their turn were prepared to offer high rents on estates where the owners were known to spend generously on capital improvements such as farm buildings.[1] Since most tenants were on fixed-term leases, increasingly on short leases, there was considerable scope for renegotiating rents in response to fluctuations in prices and costs. As a result, English farmers tended to be more responsive to opportunities for technological change than their peasant contemporaries in Europe.

Changes were also taking place in the organization of industry in manufacturing which had implications for the character of entrepreneurial decision making. On the eve of the industrial revolution, the decisions which determined the manufacturers' response to market forces and the ways in which productive resources were deployed to meet changes in conditions of demand or supply were generally taken by the merchant-capitalist. Except at the purely local level of the village shop where the producer met each customer's specifications individually, the typical eighteenth-century manufacturer worked to the orders of a merchant who supplied him with his raw materials and took up his finished product. The

---

[1] H. J. Habakkuk, 'English Landownership 1680–1740', *Economic History Review* (1939/40).

exact way this was done varied from industry to industry and (with the development of regional specialization) from region to region. Broadly speaking, however, the system was similar over a wide range of trades. In the textile industries, for example, merchants operating from Norwich, Leeds, Manchester, Nottingham and London, gave out raw and spun wool, cotton, flax or silk to an army of spinners and weavers to work up in their own homes, and received back the yarn or cloth which they might then reissue for further processing (finishing, dyeing, printing) in other homes or small workshops. Sometimes a merchant had his own finishing sheds. Occasionally, as in the West of England woollen trade which specialized in fine quality cloth, the merchant was also a manufacturer and had weaving sheds which he could keep under closer supervision for quality-control than was possible under the putting-out system. Generally the worker in domestic industry had to do his own fetching and carrying, either on his own back or in his farmcart, and to buy his own capital equipment or tools. In the hosiery industry where the basic equipment—the stocking frame—was relatively expensive, the merchant who supplied the yarn and took up the completed hose also rented out frames, and sometimes floor space, as part of his bargain with the independent knitters.

Even in the metal trades, the domestic putting-out system prevailed in all but the heavy smelting branches of the industry. Only at the blast furnaces, where the need to keep the furnace at a constant level of heat required a continuously employed labour force, was the iron manufacturer making all the technological and marketing decisions in relation to his product. Potters, or builders, generally worked directly to the local customer's specific requirement and there the productive unit consisted of the individual potter (or jobbing builder or small master) and the craftsmen and labourers were employed on a day-to-day or task-by-task basis. In the pottery townships, where potters tended to congregate because of the availability of suitable clay, small workshops with some division of labour were common; but the men were all skilled craftsmen and both their coming together and their specializing were ad hoc arrangements of mutual convenience rather than a form of industrial capitalism. Whether working independently or in groups, they normally produced on a bespoke basis directly to the requirements of an individual customer or merchant.

In most other manufacturing units, especially those processing agricultural products, the majority of producers operated in small domestic units for strictly local markets, though in the larger towns (especially London) sizeable workshops and even factories could be found by the early eighteenth century. Sugar-refining, dependent on imported raw material, was already a factory trade concentrated in the main receiving ports—Bristol, Liverpool, Glasgow and London. Beer was produced for sale in units of all sizes from large-scale brewers to innkeepers and victuallers supplying their own premises. Indeed, in most industries there were units of production representing the whole spectrum of industrial organization from household production through small workshops to large factory, from bespoke trade to mass-produced goods. Typically, however, manufacturing industry in the mid eighteenth century was carried on by skilled craftsmen working on their own, *either* for direct sale to the customer on materials bought from local farmers or tradesmen *or*—as market horizons widened to national and international proportions—as outworkers for merchants who took the marketing decisions (i.e. how much of each kind of commodity to produce and at what price) and who earned the profits arising from successful speculation in the markets for raw materials and finished goods.

Under this domestic system of industry, technology was thus under the control of men whose craft tradition and long apprenticeship was better designed to maintain standards of quality than to develop new processes of production or new products. The fact that, for many of those producing on a small scale, incomes earned in manufacturing were secondary to those earned in agriculture made them even less ready to contemplate changing their traditional techniques. The dynamic profit-seeking entrepreneur was more likely to be a merchant than a manufacturer in the early eighteenth century and his innovations tended to take the form of opening up new markets (for raw materials or finished goods) or developing new techniques of commercial organization (e.g. in management, insurance or finance). The shift to a factory system of organization that was associated with mechanization and the use of steampower in the industry transformed by the industrial revolution involved a crucial change in the nature of the decision to innovate. Once the productive process came fully under the control of the professional capitalist entrepreneur, accustomed to assess the profits implications of changing the structure of his inputs, the probability that opportunities for profitable innovation would be rapidly identified and taken up became distinctly higher. The change in the character of the decision to innovate is an important part of the explanation for the acceleration in the pace of technical progress associated with the industrial revolution and for the fact that the acceleration was sustained through the nineteenth and twentieth centuries.

The conclusion suggested by this survey of the evidence on innovation in the eighteenth and early nineteenth centuries is that it was only when the potential market was large enough, and demand elastic enough, to justify a substantial increase in output, that the rank and file of entrepreneurs broke away from their traditional techniques and took advantage of the technical opportunities then open to them. This occurred in a few industries where the economic stimulus and the technical opportunity were present in strength. Elsewhere innovation was the prerogative of an enterprising few and had often in fact been developing since the early decades of the eighteenth century. There is no evidence to suggest that, except in a few industries and regions, the majority of producers were any more ready to innovate in 1815 than they had been in 1750.

2. CHANGES IN THE MARKET ENVIRONMENT

Innovation required an economic stimulus and a technical opportunity. If innovation was to be widespread the stimulus had to be massive and the opportunity accessible. Probably the most effective stimulus to innovation is a change in the market environment. What evidence do we have for changes in the market environment towards the end of the eighteenth century?

There are two sides of the market to be considered—the domestic market and the overseas market. What can we say, first of all, about the domestic market? Here there seems to have been a significant set of changes in the distribution of incomes in the first half of the century, which stemmed from the abnormal proportion of abundant harvests occurring in the three or four decades preceding 1755. A good harvest meant low prices for foodstuffs and higher labour costs, hence it also meant low profits for farmers who bought their labour and falling rents for landlords. A succession of good harvests meant that farmers and landlords had no chance of recouping their losses. This in effect was a period of acute agricultural depression.

On the other hand, the reverse was true for the rest of the community. Cottagers and paupers and agricultural labourers found that a good harvest meant more work and more wages and abundant food from the cottage plot or as gleanings from the big estate. A succession of good harvests meant that the granaries were always full and prices stayed low so that at the end of the harvest year, when they had to make up their own shortfall by purchasing food, they could do so cheaply. Labourers in non-agricultural occupations, who expected to buy nearly all their food, benefited still more from a good harvest. They found that their wages went further and they had more money left over to spend on luxuries like drink (this was also the gin age), sugar and clothing. Industrialists who got their raw material from agriculture (and a large proportion of them did so in this pre-industrial economy) found that their costs fell in a year of good harvest and that most of their customers were more affluent, so that their profit and sales tended to rise. A succession of good harvests encouraged them to hire more labour, to invest more capital, to expand their output, and to reap the economies of scale which were obtainable from a higher level of output. Merchants who sold British agricultural products in foreign countries found that they could lower prices without reducing their profits per unit of output and that as their markets expanded in response to lower prices their profits soared. Encouraged by the corn bounty (which gave subsidies of 5s. for every quarter of wheat exported and smaller, though still substantial amounts, for the cheaper grains) they managed to raise English exports of corn to over a million quarters by the early 1750's. This made the balance of trade more favourable than it would otherwise have been, increased the national supply of money and further stimulated trade.

In sum, the effect of a succession of good harvests was to make farmers and landlords poorer and to make all other members of the community richer. In terms of Gregory King's analysis of the families of England and Wales we may say that freeholders, farmers and all gentlemen and members of the nobility who got their incomes from land (probably less than 20 per cent of the nation's families) found their incomes lowered by a succession of good harvests: and the other members of the community, the majority, found themselves richer. Or to put it another way, the profits from agricultural enterprise fell, the profits from non-agricultural enterprise rose and the lower income groups in general got more regular wages and more goods for their money. All this represented a marked stimulus to British industry and trade which was sustained for rather more than a generation. It is hardly surprising that the evidence is strong for an acceleration in the pace of economic growth dating from just before the middle of the eighteenth century.

In the later 1750's the run of good harvests was broken and in the second half of the eighteenth century the pattern accordingly changed. But the evidence does not suggest that the level of domestic demand was falling back in the 1760's and 1770's.[1] On the contrary, the upsurge of investment in turnpikes and in canals, the increasing shipments of coal from Newcastle to London (29% higher in the 1770's than in the 1750's), and the strong rise in net raw cotton imports which were more than 70% greater in the 1770's than in the 1750's all point to a buoyant domestic market in spite of the relative stagnation in the volume of domestic exports. There were two ways in which changes in the domestic market may have been important in stimulating British industry and trade at this period. The first was through the effect of a growing population, which raised the volume of national expenditure even if it did not raise expenditures per head proportionately. The second was through the enlargement of the money economy which resulted from enclosures. The dispossession of the cottager from common and waste, and the buying out of the smaller smallholders who were too poor to afford the necessary investment in fencing and ditching, meant that fewer and fewer families were producing the food and clothing that they themselves consumed. Of course this enlargement of the money economy had been going on as long as (indeed longer than) the process of enclosures, whether voluntary or statutory. But it is reasonable to presume that in the period of rising prices which characterized the period from the 1750's to 1815 the cottager and small smallholder found it more difficult to resist the consolidating landowner and the

---

[1] See D. Eversley, 'The Home Market and Economic Growth in England, 1750–80' in *Land, Labour and Population in the Industrial Revolution*, ed. Jones and Mingay, *op. cit.*, for a systematic presentation of the evidence for the view that the situation continued to be favourable to home demand from 1750 to 1780.

expanding farmer than in the years of agricultural depression. By the beginning of the nineteenth century the 'cottagers', who had comprised about a quarter of the families of England and Wales when Gregory King drew up his table, and whose real incomes depended to a considerable extent on goods and services which never reached the market, were no longer important enough for Colquhoun to distinguish separately in his corresponding table of families. The subsistence producer had by then been eliminated from all but a few relatively inaccessible regions.

The other aspect of the market environment was the overseas market. To the extent that prices and costs declined in British agriculture and industry this must have made it easier to sell British goods abroad and one would expect British domestic exports to rise in consequence. The rising trend in domestic exports in the 1730's, 1740's and 1750's can thus be regarded as a secondary repercussion of the contemporary changes in the home-market. The fact that the big upsurge of domestic exports in the 1740's (an increase of about 50 per cent in volume) coincided with a decline in re-exports seems to confirm the view that the cause of the increase lay not so much in a spontaneous growth of foreign demand as in the more favourable terms on which British goods were being supplied.

Nevertheless there were significant signs of change in the overseas market situation which became increasingly evident in the second half of the century though they were obscured at first by the dislocation caused first by the Seven Years War and then by the American War of Independence. The fact is that populations and incomes were growing in Western Europe and North America and the potential markets for British goods were widening rapidly. The rebound from the American War was spectacularly sharp and a high rate of growth persisted through the 1790's when the French wars crippled Britain's major European competitors. The domestic-export and the re-export trades expanded strongly together in face of this widening horizon of economic opportunity. Hence although British merchants and industrialists had to grapple with rapid inflation and high taxation, they were so favourably placed in command of the world's trade routes that they could hardly fail to expand their sales. In the products of the cotton and iron industries they had the additional advantage of being able to supply better qualities of goods at lower prices.

We may conclude then that factors on the side of demand appear to have been positively encouraging to innovation through most of the eighteenth century. When population and national income were relatively stagnant in the early decades the low prices for food and industrial raw materials associated with an abnormal run of good harvests were redistributing incomes in favour of the agricultural poor, the urban working classes and manufacturers generally. As a result, the period of 'agricultural depression' was stimulating to industrial expansion even if it reduced the investible agricultural surplus. When the upsurge in international trade which had characterized the second quarter of the century slackened in the third quarter, domestic demand seems to have maintained a healthy momentum. Finally, in the last two decades or so of the century Britain found herself in a peculiarly advantageous position to exploit the rapidly expanding markets in Western Europe and North America.

3. CHANGES IN THE PACE OF INVENTION

It is not enough to have the economic opportunity to innovate: it is also necessary to have the technical opportunity. Can we time the flow of new inventions and ideas which became available to British producers in the course of the eighteenth century? Can we assess their significance in the light of current bottlenecks and limiting factors to economic growth?

Some idea of the pace of invention can be obtained from the annual record of patents taken out by inventors, though not all inventors tried to protect their copyright, and not all inventions were productive. The break in this series comes quite clearly in the 1760's when for the first time the number of patents sealed exceeded 200 in a single decade. Only once before—in the booming 1690's—had they exceeded 100. From then on the numbers expanded steadily, increasing by about 50 per cent per decade until the 1810's and 1820's, when they rose more modestly, and accelerating again in the 1830's and 1840's, so that in this latter decade they were twenty times as numerous as they had been in the 1760's.

The number of inventions patented is unfortunately a very weak index of the number of new processes becoming available to British entrepreneurs, still less of the productive significance of these new inventions. The quality and character of inventions was a great deal more important in determining their impact than the number of patents. Clearly the immediate significance to potential innovators of a new invention depends on the extent to which it breaks a current bottleneck, or reduces some of the limiting factors to expansion of supply, or meets an unsatisfied demand. Kay's flying shuttle, for example, patented in 1733,

TABLE 3. *Numbers of English patents sealed in each decade*

1630/39	75	1740/49	82
1640/49		1750/59	92
1650/59	4	1760/69	205
1660/69	31	1770/79	294
1670/79	50	1780/89	477
1680/89	53	1790/99	647
1690/99	102	1800/09	924
1700/09	22	1810/19	1124
1710/19	38	1820/29	1453
1720/29	89	1830/39	2453
1730/39	56	1840/49	4581

SOURCE: B. R. Mitchell, *Abstract of British Historical Statistics* (1963), p. 268.

permitted an energetic weaver to do the work of two. Yet it spread slowly and brought its inventor little profit since the current shortage was not of weavers but of spinners and Kay's invention merely made that shortage more acute. Similarly a quarter of a century after Cartwright had introduced his power-loom there were still only 2,400 in the whole of the country, for there was no shortage either of hand-looms or of people to operate them, and coal was still an expensive commodity. On the other hand, Hargreave's spinning-jenny provided a machine which multiplied the output of the individual spinner some sixteen-fold and spread like wildfire through cottages that had hitherto depended on the old hand-wheel: and Arkwright's water-frame produced yarn of sufficient strength to serve as warp as well as weft and so satisfied from British sources what had hitherto been a largely frustrated demand for Indian calicoes.

The most crucial and general of the bottlenecks limiting the expansion of the British economy on the eve of the British industrial revolution (that is in the middle of the eighteenth century) were two: they were the shortage of wood and the shortage of power. These were closely related problems. Wood was the universal material of which capital assets were made.

It was needed for ships, for machinery, for vehicles, for drain-pipes, and for buildings; it was also needed for fuel in areas where coal was inaccessible or where technical problems prevented the use of coal (as in the iron industry). It was unsatisfactory as a construction material because it was clumsy, rapidly worn out by weather or friction and easily burnt, so that it had a short life on the average and was not very adaptable when used for the moving parts of machinery. Its shortage restricted the output of industries which depended on it for fuel, of which the most important was the iron industry.

The only forms of power available to the pre-industrial economy were muscle-power, water-power, and wind-power. None of these was capable of development to a form which would support a modern industrial economy. The watermill and the windmill had been available for centuries and a good deal of ingenuity had been put into their design. But they were subject to two inescapable limitations—they were erratic and unpredictable in that they depended on weather conditions (and there is nothing less predictable than the British weather), and it was necessary for the power they generated to be used on the spot.

The most important achievement of the industrial revolution was that it converted the British economy from a wood-and-water basis to a coal-and-iron basis. Wood was a dwindling resource with a strictly limited future as a construction material in an industrial context. Water-power and wind-power were only partially under the control of their operators and had a very limited potential. The power of the average windmill or water-wheel was in the region of 5–10 h.p. and in their most elaborate and expensive forms they seemed unable to generate more than 30 h.p.

If we were to try to single out the crucial eighteenth-century inventions which set the stage for the industrial revolution by precipitating a continuous process of industrialization and technical change, and hence sustained economic growth, the strongest candidates would seem to be the steam-engine on the one hand, and on the other Cort's puddling process which made a cheap and acceptable British malleable iron. Watt's steam-engine, first constructed in 1775, had a wide range of immediately feasible applications. Applied to water-pumping and to hoisting-machinery it made it possible to get cheap coal from deeper and deeper seams. Applied to the blast-furnace, it provided a blast strong enough to burn coke instead of charcoal and ensured continuous operation of expensive blast-furnace equipment wherever coal and iron ore were available, instead of being dependent on a seasonal localized water supply. Applied to industrial machinery it powered spinning and weaving factories, breweries, flour-mills and paper-mills and effectively removed an important limiting factor to the large-scale operation of a wide variety of industries. These possibilities were already apparent by the first decade of the nineteenth century. They might have developed faster and further had not Watt restricted the spread of his engine by means of a patent. Water-power was still by far the main source of power in most fields of manufacture at the beginning of the nineteenth century.[1] Later in the nineteenth century, steam applied to locomotives made it possible to transport coal and iron and bricks and other heavy raw materials or producers' goods to any part of the country; and later still, applied to iron ships it permitted the import of cheap food from the New World and so carried the process of industrialization to the ultimate conclusion of international specialization.

The other crucial invention, Cort's puddling and rolling process, which was diffused from the late 1780's, put the finishing touch to the series of inventions which were involved in the change-over from charcoal to coal in iron manufacture. It permitted the industry to escape rapidly from dependence on diminishing supplies of native timber and expensive foreign bar-iron, and to exploit the relatively abundant British resources of iron ore and coal. Again, a tightly restrictive bottleneck was broken quickly and effectively. But it was the longer-term results which were most significant. The use of iron as the material of which producers' durable goods were most commonly constructed had revolutionary consequences. Iron machinery was long-lasting, could be run continuously with little wear, would stand up to stress, could be fashioned into standard shapes which ensured more accurate results than the eye of the skilled craftsman, and above all it was cheap. The introduction of cheap iron was the beginning of the machine age and of the engineering industry. Applied to steam-engine

[1] G. N. von Tunzelmann, *Steampower and British Industrialization to 1860*, p. 125.

boilers, for example, British wrought-iron was cheaper than copper and safer under high pressure than cast-iron. Applied to machine-tools it made precision work possible for the first time, and thus was susceptible of infinite development. Henry Maudslay, for example, the first great British machine-tool manufacturer in the modern tradition, set a new standard of accuracy by using metal alone as his material of construction. In 1802 he set up in Portsmouth dockyard a set of woodworking machines designed to mechanize the manufacture of pulley blocks. 'Driven by a 30 h.p. steam-engine the machines made 130,000 blocks a year, cut the labour force from 110 skilled men to 10 unskilled men and saved the Admiralty almost a third of the capital outlay in a year...Some of the machines that Maudslay built for Portsmouth remained in use, for more than a century after his death in 1831.'[1] Finally, applied to railways and ships, iron was a construction material of extraordinarily high strength and with the aid of the steam-engine revolutionized the transport industry.

The distinctive feature of both these inventions is that they introduced radical technological changes into the industries producing capital goods and it was this that gave them their tremendous continuing impact in the process of industrialization. By their effects on the price of capital goods they eventually raised national investment from pre-industrial to industrial levels, and they economized in capital by making existing funds go farther in terms of the income-creating assets that they would buy. By affecting the rate at which new techniques could be introduced into different sectors of the economy they stepped up the rate of innovation. The adoption of a metal-using technology employing decentralized sources of power, which the inventions permitted, lies at the heart of the first industrial revolution.

What conclusions can we draw, in the light of the above discussion, about the timing of the technical changes which made the first industrial revolution? At this point we may reasonably focus on a consideration of manufacturing industry, on the grounds that the associated innovations in agriculture, commerce and pre-railway transport were merely permissive factors which could equally well have been associated with the continuance of a pre-industrial economy.

[1] T. K. Derry and Trevor I. Williams, *A Short History of Technology* (1960), p. 352.

(1) The first point that seems to stand out fairly clearly is that the eighteenth-century environment was generally favourable to technical change. Over a large part of the century, beginning somewhere before the middle and accelerating in the second half, there seems to have been a tendency for the demand for British manufactures to exceed their supply. The resultant stimulus to technical change was reflected in the wide interest in innovation. Innovation was fashionable, if not yet common, and it was sometimes, though by no means always, highly profitable.

(2) The fashion for innovation was made more effective by changes in the mode and scale of production associated with the new technological opportunities that emerged decisively in the late eighteenth century. The industrial-capitalist who owned the plant and equipment of factory industry had more incentive and scope for rethinking the basic technology of manufacture than either the merchant-capitalist or the artisan craftsman. What is particularly striking moreover, about the industrial scene of the second half of the eighteenth and early nineteenth centuries is the active and fruitful collaboration between industrialists and scientists interested in technical progress.[1] This collaboration was to prove important not only in shortening the process of trial and error which lay between a major invention and a commercially profitable innovation, but also in the less revolutionary, but in the long run equally important, cost-reducing improvements in the efficiency of machines or processes already widely adopted.

(3) There were some sectors in which the generalized stimulus to expand output was intensified by an increasing technical difficulty in so doing. Innovations that broke through these technical limitations were particularly successful and particularly rapidly diffused.

(4) The number of these sectors of highly successful, rapidly diffused technical change was for a long time rather few. Before the 1820's they were virtually limited to the cotton industry and to the iron industry. In addition there was the steam-engine, which was successfully applied over a wide range of industries, but which before the railway age was important only in cotton and iron and mining.

[1] A. E. Musson (ed.), *Science, Technology and Economic Growth in the Eighteenth Century*, p. 62.

(5) Nevertheless, if the industries whose techniques had been effectively revolutionized by the second decade of the nineteenth century were few and accounted directly for a relatively small proportion of total national output, they contained the seeds of continuing industrialization. To some extent this was because there were other industries with similar technologies. It was only a matter of time, for example, before the innovations which began in the cotton industry were adapted to other textile industries. To some extent it was because they directly stimulated other industries—as iron stimulated coal-mining and coastal shipping, and textiles stimulated processing and clothing trades. But largely it was because the development of the steam-engine and of the iron industry had such far-reaching implications for producers' goods industries in general and through them for investment and innovation in all manufacturing industry.

CHAPTER 9

THE ROLE OF LABOUR

An inescapable condition of successful economic development is the existence of an expanding, mobile and adaptable labour supply. To achieve the shifts in the structure and rate of growth of national output of which an industrial revolution is composed, there must be profound changes in both the quantity and the quality of the labour force. In this chapter we shall consider the character of these changes as they appeared in the first industrial revolution and try to explore some of their causes and consequences.

To begin with, it is important to see the factor of production labour in some sort of perspective. If we ask ourselves what are the basic determinants of economic growth, for example, we can classify them under four main heads: natural resources, technical progress, accumulation of capital and increase in the quantity and quality of the labour supply. Basically, that is to say, the rate at which any economy can expand its output of goods and services depends on four fundamental factors:

(1) The rate at which it can enlarge its stock of natural resources. Thus for example, a country which can bring new land into cultivation or open up new mineral resources or make passable roads or rivers that were formerly impassable or passable only at certain seasons can effectively extend its resource base and so increase its product per unit of labour or capital. Generally there are limits to the extent to which a country can increase its natural resources, though a country such as nineteenth-century America can go on doing so for a considerable period of time through the medium of an advancing frontier; and in late eighteenth- and early nineteenth-century England the same kind of process was in operation, though of course to a lesser extent, through the enclosure of waste lands and the elimination of crucial transport bottlenecks whose removal opened up hitherto inaccessible mineral resources.

(2) Technical progress also permits the production of a larger output of goods and services with a given input of labour and capital. An innovation in productive technique (a new rotation of crops for example or the use of coke instead of charcoal fuel) or a new machine will reduce costs and so enable entrepreneurs to increase output per unit of input.

(3) The third determinant of the rate of economic growth is the rate of new investment; that is, through an increase in the input of capital into the productive process. More ships or more canals carry more trade; more pumping machinery and hoisting equipment means more coal raised; and so on.

(4) The fourth determinant of the rate of economic growth is the rate of expansion of the labour supply. If people work harder or longer or more regularly or more skillfully, or if the numbers of the actively occupied population grow, this leads to a larger output of goods and services.

These determinants are closely interrelated. It is not usually possible, for example, either to enlarge the national stock of natural resources or to introduce technical change without increasing the rate of investment. In the end, the capital required *per unit of output* may be smaller, but at the outset the absolute amount of capital required for the productive process is almost invariably larger. Conversely, of course, a rise in the rate of investment will often make the existing natural resource supply more valuable or will raise the rate of technical progress or will bring into use unemployed labour. A new machine is generally more up-to-date and more efficient than the one it replaces, and even if the differences are individually trivial a continuous stream of such minor improvements in techniques or machines, associated with a continuous increase in capital formation, will mean a steady rise in the efficiency of capital, a steady technological advance. Moreover, any substantial enlargement of the nation's stock of natural resources, or any appreciable increase in capital investment, or any significant technical advance can be expected to require *either* some increase in the numbers engaged in productive activity, *or* some movement of workers between occupations *or* both. It is difficult to conceive of a way of enlarging the natural resource endowment or of adding to the national capital which does not involve an increase in the labour supply to the sector affected. Even where technical change in the industrial revolution was labour-saving in its effects, the immense impetus that it gave to the expansion of investment promoted an eventual increase in the demand for labour.

In principle, of course, it is always possible for an expanding sector of the economy to attract labour to itself by offering workers a higher wage than they can get elsewhere. Where the existing labour force is fully employed this represents the only way of expanding output. If the immediate cost-reducing effects of a given innovation are large enough and the risks are slight it may be worthwhile offering quite considerable increases in wages. On the other hand, if there is a certain amount of unemployment or under-employment of labour, so that labour does not have to be lured away from other occupations, it may not be necessary to offer wages that are above the prevailing rates. Clearly, however, the lower the increase that is necessary to attract an adequate labour supply, the more lucrative will be the prospects of a given innovation or a given new investment. Hence an elastic labour supply—access to an abundant supply of labour at a relatively low price—is immensely encouraging to potential investors.

The fact that British entrepreneurs in the late eighteenth and early nineteenth century were able to increase industrial output and capacity without facing correspondingly increased costs due to a rise in the real wage-rate meant that the reward for successful innovation was largely shared between the investor and the consumer. This greatly increased the incentive to industrialize. Profits rose and prices fell. To the extent that profits rose, investors were encouraged to plough back a high proportion of their earnings into further investment and so to increase output and opportunities for employment still more. As prices fell demand rose, and, since the demand for manufactures tended to be elastic, total expenditure grew in spite of the price fall, and by widening the market stimulated further investment and further demand for labour. The process was cumulative. Increased investment raised the rate of technical progress, by increasing the extent to which producers were adopting the newer machinery and the newer techniques, and this in its turn meant more output for less input of either capital or labour. Thus abundant cheap labour promoted new investment and so maintained technical progress which, by economizing in both capital and labour, generated a cumulative self-reinforcing expansion in economic activity.

Although not all producers found it easy to get all the labour they needed in the second half of the eighteenth century, there is no doubt that the labour force was far from fully employed and that it was growing at a faster rate than ever before. After stagnating in the early decades of the century the population of England and Wales began growing at a rate of $3\frac{1}{2}$ per cent per decade in the 1740's and had reached it peak rate of increase of nearly 17 per cent per decade in 1811–21. It was still about 16 per cent in the following decade; and for the rest of the nineteenth century the decade rate of increase continued to be above 11 per cent, though it never again rose above 14 per cent.[1] At the height of the industrial revolution the population was growing at a rate of about 1 per cent per annum. This was slow compared with the explosive rates of population growth characteristic of some of today's developing countries, but it was nevertheless appreciably above any previous experience in Britain.

Because in its early stages the increasing population was largely due to the combined effects of a falling infantile death rate and a rising birth rate, the increment was largely composed of infants. Consequently until 1821 or thereabouts the active labour force was growing a little more slowly than the total population. On the other hand, it did not take long for eighteenth-century babies to grow up to the stage at which they could be made to earn at least part of their own keep. Domestic industry found work for children almost as soon as they could crawl and the early textile factories were taking batches of pauper children from the age of five upwards. Moreover the continued high rate of infantile mortality meant that the average size of family did not increase to a very marked extent. Thus the burden of dependants so often created by a growing population tended to fall less heavily on the British economy of the late eighteenth century than it does on today's developing countries with their more humane standards set by international example and with their large surviving families of young children. Although the community's conscience became more tender as the nineteenth century wore on, and although Factory Acts and factory inspectors and national schools began to get the children out of the factories, child labour continued in some

---

[1] See Deane and Cole, *British Economic Growth*, p. 288, for rates of population increase in England and Wales, Great Britain and United Kingdom where available.

form or another for more than a century after the industrial revolution began. Even as late as 1871 the Medical Officer of Health for the Local Government Board reported finding a child of three making lucifer matches in Bethnal Green.

Another factor which helped to increase the input of labour into the productive process was the increase in the average number of hours worked per worker and per day. It was of course particularly conspicuous in the factories as compared with domestic industry. The factories used full-time labour which stayed at the machines as long as the machines were turning, which was as long as there was a demand for their products. While they depended on water-power there were seasonal interruptions in their operations, but when steam-power was introduced, and still more when gas was employed to light the factories day and night, only trade depression stopped them. Men, women and children worked 12–16 hours per day or per night in continuous shifts. Whether the input of labour wrung from children working a daily 15 or 16 hours in temperatures of 80° and above was more productive than, say, 11 or 12 hours worked in more humane conditions in one of the better-run factories is questionable. There must have been a point beyond which the extra time worked gave negative rather than positive returns even in the unskilled operations of child labour. Nevertheless there is no doubt that as more people abandoned the kind of domestic industry which was an off-season activity of agriculturalists and went into full-time manu-facturing in factory and workshop, the effective input of labour per member of the labour force rose. Nor was it only in manufacturing industry that labour input increased. As yields per acre rose, as farmers turned land from fallow to labour-intensive root crops, and as animal husbandry became more sophisticated, the average agricultural labourer of the late eighteenth century found himself spending more hours of each day and more days of each year in active gainful employment than his predecessors had done.

It used to be argued that the process of enclosures, by drawing smallholders and cottagers off the land and depopulating the rural areas, created the large proletarian labour force which made the industrial revolution possible. This is the view which was romanticized in Oliver Goldsmith's poem *The Deserted Village* and, much later, was given political point by Karl Marx.

But it seems to have been a grossly oversimplified view of what happened.[1] That the enclosure movement helped to destroy some of the traditional rigidities in the agricultural labour force and also, by taking away rights of common, to drive out the few remaining self-subsistence cottagers seems plausible enough. What is not confirmed by the evidence, however, is that there was an immediate connection between enclosure and the movement of the labour force from agriculture to industry. The true exodus from the land did not develop until the second half of the nineteenth century, and although there was some growth in the numbers of the rural proletariat in the course of the industrial revolution it was not so sudden and radical a transformation as was traditionally supposed. Clapham, comparing the results of the 1831 census with Gregory King's table of families, concluded that by the later date there were still only about 2 rural proletarian families to each rural occupying family, compared with a ratio of about $1\frac{3}{4}$ to 1 a hundred and forty years before.[2]

The fact is that the complex process of economic change and growth that we call the industrial revolution—whether it concerned agriculture or transport or trade or manufacturing—was a process which called for a massive increase in the input of labour and itself provided part of the occasion for that increase. The factories gave full-time gainful employment not only to men but also to women and children, groups which had rarely enjoyed more than seasonal or part-time work for pay in the domestic industry era. It would be wrong to exaggerate the new opportunities. Only a small percentage of the community had access to factory employment, and there were many would-be part-time workers whose incomes from manufacturing had been taken from them by the factory operators. But there seems very little doubt that on balance both the range and the number of economic opportunities were enlarged whenever output grew appreciably faster than the costs of producing that output—in other words whenever technical progress gathered appreciable momentum.

That the labour became available to satisfy the new demands can be judged from the relative stability of wages. Special

[1] See J. D. Chambers, 'Enclosure and Labour Supply in the Industrial Revolution', *Economic History Review*, vol. v, no. 3 (1953).

[2] Clapham, *Economic History*, vol. i, p. 114.

categories of workers—like weavers in the early years when the spinning-mills turned out more cheap yarn than there were hands to process it, or like engineers when the demand for machinery soared—earned boom wages at times. But for the mass of the employed population there was little evidence of a marked or sustained improvement in daily wage-rates over the period 1780–1830, once allowance had been made for rising food prices during the war years. This in itself is a remarkable fact, and it has sometimes been claimed that the elastic labour supply which it reflects constituted one of the main reasons for the enormous and unprecedented expansion of the British economy over this period. In a famous footnote, for example, Professor Hicks suggests that 'the whole Industrial Revolution of the last 200 years has been nothing else but a vast secular boom, largely induced by the unparalleled rise in population'.[1]

To say that abundant cheap labour was a crucial factor in maintaining the impetus of the British industrial revolution does not, however, amount to advocating a low-wage economy of the kind favoured by the mercantilists of the seventeenth and eighteenth centuries. This was an argument which went out of favour as industrialization progressed. Mandeville, for example, asserted in 1705 in his *Fable of the Bees* that 'in a free nation where slaves are not allowed of, the surest wealth consists in a multitude of laborious poor'.[2] Arthur Young put the point more trenchantly in 1771: 'Everyone but an idiot knows that the lowest classes must be kept poor or they will never be industrious.'[3] A more sophisticated view of economic development, with a curiously modern ring about it, was put forward by Sir James Stewart in his *Principles of Political Economy* published in 1769. Stewart recognized that high wages meant high consumer purchasing power, which stimulated demand and hence output, but he saw rising wages as a limiting factor to the expansion of the export sector. In the absence of continuing technical progress, he argued, rising wages would eventually check national economic growth by raising domestic prices above those of foreign competitors and thus by reducing the market for exports.[4]

[1] J. R. Hicks, *Value and Capital* (1946), p. 302.
[2] Quoted by E. Hecksher, *Mercantilism*, vol. II (1955), p. 164.
[3] A. Young, *Farmer's Tour through the East of England*, vol IV (1771), p. 361.
[4] Quoted by A. W. Coats, 'Changing Attitudes of Labour in the mid-Eighteenth Century', *Economic History Review* (August 1958), p. 50.

Adam Smith took a more optimistic view. In his *Wealth of Nations*, originally published in 1776, he pointed out that on the one hand poverty resulted in a high child death rate and hence reduced the supply of labour: and that on the other hand high wages provided the labourer with incentives to work harder. 'The liberal reward of labour', he wrote, 'as it encourages the propagation, so it increases the industry of the common people...Where wages are high accordingly, we shall always find the workmen more active, diligent, and expeditious than where they are low; in England, for example, than in Scotland; in the neighbourhood of great towns, than in remote country places'.[1]

Significantly, too, Adam Smith dealt quite specifically with the theory of the 'backward sloping supply curve' for labour, which is often used today as an explanation for the behaviour of the labour force of some of the modern pre-industrial regions of the world. Briefly, this theory says that the labour force behaves quite differently in certain economically backward areas than we should expect. Instead of being ready to offer more labour for higher wages—in which case the supply curve would slope 'normally' (i.e. it would rise from left to right)—it does the opposite. The reason is that workers in these areas have a limited demand for money income; and since a higher wage enables the workman to reach his target-income in less time than before, he works fewer days in the week. While Adam Smith admitted the existence of this attitude he denied that it applies to the majority of workers. 'Some workmen indeed, when they can earn in four days what will maintain them through the week will be idle the other three. This, however, is by no means the case with the greater part.'[2]

The interesting thing about Adam Smith's interpretation is that it marks a transitional stage in English economic experience. A target-income is the goal of an economically static community, and the English economy was already growing markedly both in average incomes and in numbers of inhabitants by the 1770's. The transformation which we have come to call the industrial revolution had already begun to take shape and the pre-industrial labour force, with its basically self-subsistence form of organization, was rapidly disappearing in favour of a pro-

---

[1] Adam Smith, *Wealth of Nations*, vol. I, p. 83.   [2] *Ibid.* p. 83.

letarian labour force with a rising appetite for domestic manufactures and for such imported luxuries as sugar, tea and
tobacco. The cottager was being forced by enclosure into the
position of a landless agricultural labourer. The domestic
industrial worker was becoming more and more dependent on
the capitalist merchant to supply him with raw materials and
to market the finished product. The English economy was
becoming more specialized and hence more independent, and
the uses to which the working man could put his cash income
were becoming more urgent and more various. In these circumstances a backward-sloping supply curve for labour was
hardly likely to illustrate the general case.

To say that English labour was relatively 'cheap' at the end
of the eighteenth century does not imply that it was relatively
poor either in relation to labour in other countries or to past
experience in Britain. English wages were generally agreed to
be lower than American wages, for in North America labour
was scarce and land plentiful, and the fact that the potential
employee always had the choice of becoming an independent
land-owning farmer kept wages higher than they would
otherwise have been. On the other hand, English wages were
certainly above French wages. When Arthur Young travelled
in France in the 1780's, and observed the comparatively low
level of wages which prevailed there, he was no longer so
convinced as he had been when travelling in eastern England
in the 1760's of the virtues of a low-wage economy.[1] 'The vast
superiority of the English manufactures, taken in the gross, to
those of France united with this higher price of labour', he wrote
in 1789, 'is a subject of great political curiosity and importance,
for it shows clearly, that it is not the nominal cheapness of labour
that favours manufactures, which flourish most where labour
is nominally the dearest. Perhaps', he went on, 'they flourish
on this account, since labour is generally *in reality* the cheapest
where it is *nominally* the dearest; the quality of the work, the skill
and dexterity of performance... must, on an average, depend
very much on the state of ease in which the workman lives. If
he be well nourished and clothed and his constitution kept in
a state of vigour and activity he will perform his work incom-
parably better than a man whose poverty allows but a scanty
nourishment.'[2]

[1] Young, *Travels in France*, ed. Maxwell, p. 315.   [2] *Ibid.* p. 311.

Nor indeed was English labour evidently poorer than it had been in earlier decades. It was a widespread contemporary belief that there was an appreciable improvement in the real earnings of the labouring classes in the first three-quarters of the nineteenth century. Phelps Brown's estimate of the purchasing power of a building-craftsman's wages suggests that by the 1780's it was 15 per cent above what it has been in the 1680's: and that although it fell back during the war years it was 12 per cent above the level of the 1780's by the 1820's and nearly 20 per cent above by the 1830's. In 1688 Gregory King estimated that £622,000 was received by families below the poverty line to supplement their incomes, and this transfer amounted to rather less than $1\frac{1}{2}$ per cent of the national income of England and Wales. By 1800 expenditure on poor relief amounted to about 2 per cent of national income, but this went to support a much more liberal relief policy. The notorious Speenhamland system, inaugurated by a decision of the Berkshire magistrates in 1795, and ratified by Parliament in the following year, authorized outdoor relief in all parishes and drew up a scale of public assistance related to changes in the price of bread; this augmented wages with parish relief in proportion to the number of mouths to be fed.

The fact was that by becoming more dependent on the return from specific employments instead of being able to rely on several possible sources of income—earnings from domestic industry, food from cottage plot or commons pasture, as well as wages from various casual employments—the labourer became a great deal more vulnerable to harvest crises and trade depressions than he had been in the past. Given that both kinds of unforeseen disaster were frequent in the climatically unfavourable and war-torn years of the late eighteenth and early nineteenth centuries, it is difficult to see how the country could have avoided social and political upheaval without a fairly liberal policy of poor-relief. Nevertheless the traditional interpretation, stemming almost undiluted from the Poor Law Commissioners' Report of 1834, has been that the Speenhamland System was 'a bounty on indolence and vice' and a 'universal system of pauperism'.[1] Wages were permitted to sink

---

[1] For example, Mantoux, *The Industrial Revolution in the Eighteenth Century*, asserts that 'relief given to destitution was becoming a premium on improvidence and laziness' (p. 449).

below the subsistence minimum because the employer could rely on the parish to make up the difference. It was even argued that the system, being a 'bounty on bastardy' and an incentive to early marriage, was one of the causes of the increasing population. This view goes back to Malthus: 'Among the lower classes of society, where the point is of the greatest importance, the poor-laws afford a direct, constant and systematical encouragement to marriage, by removing from each individual their heavy responsibility which he would incur by the laws of nature, for bringing beings into the world which he could not support.'[1]

Recent research and analysis has tended to modify this view of the disastrous and far-reaching consequences of the old Poor Law, and even to throw some doubt on the extent of the change brought about by the 1834 Act.[2] For one thing, the Speenhamland System was by no means universal. It did not extend to industrial areas, where relief came in the form of unemployment assistance rather than in family allowances supplementing wages. Industrial wages were determined by the state of trade (which decided the demand for labour) and the size of the labour reserve in the industrial areas (which decided its supply) rather than by any consideration of the subsistence minimum permitted by access to poor relief. Malthus knew this well enough and attributed the surplus of labour in the towns to overflow from rural areas rendered fertile by the Poor Laws. But this argument depends on the assumption that in the rural areas the chain of cause and effect ran from high poor-relief payments to large families rather than the other way round. This is an unwarranted assumption. Not all the English parishes operated the Speenhamland system, even when it was at its height, and there is no evidence that population in the Speen-hamland counties, or indeed in Scotland and Ireland which never adopted the system, grew any faster than the population of the non-Speenhamland counties. Moreover the evidence collected by the Poor Law Commissioners and published by them in the appendix to their 1834 report suggests that the system had almost disappeared by then, even in the south where

[1] T. R. Malthus, *An Essay in Population* (originally published 1798), Everyman ed., vol. II (n.d.), p. 184.
[2] See, for example, M. Blaug, 'The Myth of the old Poor Law and the Making of the New', *Journal of Economic History* (June 1963), and *idem*, 'The Poor Law Report Re-examined', *ibid.* June 1964.

it had been most prevalent. Only 11 per cent of the so-called Speenhamland counties were then giving allowances in aid of wages and only 7 per cent of the non-Speenhamland counties.[1] It appears to have reached its height in the Napoleonic wars, when it was a means of allaying dangerous discontent amongst a growing rural proletariat faced by soaring food prices, and to have died out in the post-war period, except in a few parishes.

If the Speenhamland System did influence the supply of labour in the early nineteenth century it was more likely to have been through its effect, when taken in conjunction with the settlement laws, on the mobility of labour. For to be in elastic supply it is not enough for the labour force to be numerous—it must be available in the right quantities wherever it is required; and here the laws of poor relief and settlement seem to have positively hindered the free movement of labour. The old settlement law of 1662 had set up barriers to migration by enacting that all newcomers to a parish could be forcibly removed to their last parish of settlement (at that parish's expense) within 40 days of arrival if they were likely to become a burden on the parish. In 1795 this law was relaxed by the Poor Law Removal Act, which forbad the eviction of the poor until they actually became chargeable and made the parish ordering the move liable for the expense of the removal. Nevertheless a lax parish-relief system and the risks of forcible ejection from a new parish constituted a positive disincentive to migration on the part of responsible labourers and their families. Cobbett, for example, maintained that as soon as there was any serious trade depression, the industrial centres expelled their unemployed labourers by the coach-load to the parishes from which they had come.[2] Only imminent destitution would induce a labouring family to leave their home parish when scenes like this were being enacted. The consequence was that while agricultural unemployment and under-employment were acute in the stagnating areas of the south and east, there were recurrent scarcities of labour in the expanding industrial towns of the north and west.

Had it not been for the high rate of natural increase in the industrial areas of the north-west and midlands and in their immediate hinterlands, indeed, it is doubtful whether the

[1] Blaug, 'The Poor Law Report Re-examined'.
[2] Cobbett, *Political Register* (14 May 1821).

process of industrialization could have developed as rapidly as it did. For what happened was not that labour moved from the south and east where it was redundant, to the north and west where it was in demand, but that it drifted over comparatively short distances from rural areas into the nearest industrial centres. There was some relatively long-distance migration in the 1830's when the new poor-law commissioners transferred whole families under short-term contract from the southern counties to Lancashire, but for the most part migration was local in character. An examination of the 1851 census reveals that most of the immigrants to Liverpool, Manchester and Bolton, for example, came from Lancashire, Cheshire or Ireland, and most of the migrants to Leeds, Sheffield and Bradford from Yorkshire.[1]

The migration from Ireland was particularly significant. Ireland had at least as high a rate of population increase as England in the late eighteenth and early nineteenth centuries (though it was based more on the immense food productivity of the potato than on economic progress in any broader sense of the term): and Ireland had no system of poor-law relief. So when the recurrent harvest crises struck, the destitute Irish had no alternative but to starve or to migrate. Many of them migrated to Glasgow and Lancashire and swelled the labour reserve of textile towns. As Irish domestic manufactures succumbed to the competition of the technologically superior British products, Irish hand-loom weavers came in to swell the doomed ranks of the English workers in face of the inexorable competition of the power-loom. Later, when the catastrophic potato famines of 1846–7 coincided with the English railway boom, the Irish immigrants made it possible for an immense construction effort to be completed within a relatively short period of time, without starving the rest of the economy of labour. It was not only the concurrence in Ireland of a rapidly growing labour force, a stagnating domestic economy and no poor-law system that made its labour so accessible to English manufacturers. It was also a question of transport. The journey from Kent, say, to Lancashire was expensive and lengthy at least until the second half of the nineteenth century. By contrast, in the 1820's there was a regular steamship service from Ireland which brought

[1] A. Redford, *Labour Migration in England, 1800–50* (1926), p. 158.

migrants at 2s. 6d. a head; at times—in 1827 for example—the single fare fell to 4d. or 5d. per head.

It was fortunate for British industrialists that the demographic factors were operating in their favour throughout the crucial period of the industrial revolution. It was fortunate for the community that technical progress made them able to take advantage of the demographic situation. Population, as we have seen, began to grow without check in the 1740's, largely (though by no means entirely) as a consequence of a fall in the death rate, particularly the child death rate. Its growth accelerated again in the 1780's as the birth rate, inflated by the larger numbers surviving to child-bearing age, rose even faster: and it went on to reach a peak rate of natural increase in the second decade of the nineteenth century. The arrival of this flood of young children could have seriously dragged down average productivity for the nation as a whole had it not been that the new developments in industry permitted a more complete use of the labour supply. For one thing the new textile mills could use thousands of pauper children and gave regular employment opportunities to many women for whom the pre-industrial economy offered little chance of gainful employment except on a highly seasonal basis. The greatly expanded output of yarn, moreover, made it possible to give more continuous employment to adult male weavers whose looms had often lain idle for want of yarn in the days when spinning was a laborious hand-process.

It must not be imagined, however, that the pioneers of the industrial revolution found a factory labour force ready to command. The transition from agricultural or domestic industries with their seasonal routine, their variable pace, and their family-based organization, to the monotonous, machine-driven, impersonal grind of factory work did not come easily to British workers. The early water-driven factories, generally situated in remote rural areas on the banks of streams, were constantly short of labour. They could import hundreds of pauper children, but for their adult labour force they had to depend largely on a feckless, wandering reserve of migrants with a high rate of turnover and little sense of discipline. The respectable settled population regarded the factory as a kind of workhouse and long-distance migration as a kind of transportation: and while factory owners searched the workhouses for labour and invoked the full weight of the law to tie their workers by long-term contracts and to apprehend their runaways, this attitude was understandable. To expand his labour force a mill-owner had to provide housing and other services, to offer high wages and jobs for women and children in order to attract whole families to a rural backwater, and to keep most of them on his pay-roll, even when trade was bad, if they were not to drift away to other areas. The patriarchal factory villages built by men like Strutt and Arkwright in the 1780's were

a deliberate creation, without assistance from the State or local authority and with no public services. The factory, the weir, the dams, the machine shop, the houses, the roads and bridges, the inn, the truck-shop, the church and chapel, the manager's mansion—all were devised by and grew up under the owner's eye. Most of the work was done by direct labour, just as was the machine-building in the mechanics' shop. The labour had to be attracted and held.[1]

This was not cheap labour, neither was it elastic in supply.

The use of steam-power, however, completely changed the picture. When steam became the main motive power of the spinning-mills it became preferable to build the new factories in towns, where the reserve of labour was large in relation to the requirements of the factories. There the industrialist could usually rely on attracting most if not all of the labour force justified by a trade boom without having to increase its price. He could callously cast off labour when trade was slack without any fear of losing it permanently. He could leave his workers to crowd into the garrets and cellars of existing tenements and rely on private building-contractors to adjust the supply of housing accommodation to the demand for it by running up jerry-built houses to be let off at exorbitant rents. As industry became more urbanized, the paternalism that had characterized the water-power factories gave way to a more impersonal system of labour recruitment. The labour force of the individual factory became merged into a general labour force which could move easily from one employer to another and for which no particular employer need feel any special responsibility. From this second phase of the factory age emerged the true industrial proletariat, numerous, capable of united action because it was concentrated, increasingly conscious of its political grievances, and working

[1] R. S. Fitton and A. P. Wadsworth, *The Strutts and the Arkwrights, 1758–1830* (1958), p. 98.

in an environment which became steadily more unwholesome as the towns grew and as the entrepreneur became less and less involved in a personal relationship with his workers.

Through time the changes in the organization of production, associated with the enlargement in the scale of operations and dependence on expensive fixed capital equipment, entailed radical changes in the role of the industrial labour force. In particular, for example, it led to increased specialization of labour—a specialization which had two dimensions. First there was an increasing specialization by industry, or occupation, which had the effect of narrowing the range of tasks performed by the individual workman. This kind of division of labour had already been identified by Adam Smith as a crucial source of productivity growth. A worker who can spend all his time on one or a few operations is likely to become more efficient both because he does not have to waste time or energy switching from one task to another, and because he develops in technical ability by concentrating on a narrow range of operations. On the other hand, the increase in his potential productivity may in practice be partially offset by a change in his attitude to his daily work. The narrower the range of operations which an individual is obliged to perform the more monotonous his job is likely to be. Of course not all highly specialized jobs are boring, but there is no doubt that one effect of an increasing specialization of the labour force was to increase the number of purely routine tasks falling to the unskilled operators; and while there was abundant labour the employer had no incentive to mechanize these routine operations.

The other kind of specialization that stemmed from the industrial revolution was the specialization as between labour and capital involved in large-scale capitalist industry. It also entailed changes in the labourer's attitude to his work for it changed the basic terms on which the average individual earned his living. In a traditional, pre-industrial economy where the characteristic unit of production is the self-subsistent family, dependent for its livelihood on its own joint output, no clear distinction exists between the economic and social role of labour as a factor of production. The relationship of the worker to the unit's decision-taker is the relationship of a member of family to a head of family, and the rights and obligations of the worker—even the nature of his economic return—are determined by social as much as by economic factors. Above the pure subsistence level when some specialization of activity as between families is possible, economic relationships become more complex. Feudal society, for example, was a response to the needs for defence raised by tribal conflict and developed a division of labour between fighters and workers in which economic ties were subordinated to the demands of a military hierarchy. Since trade and exchange had not yet developed sufficiently at that stage to permit economic and military obligations to be matched in monetary terms, feudal society established its economic nexus in the form of a system of remuneration and taxation based on land.

As agricultural productivity grew and trade expanded, however, it was possible to extend the division of labour and to distinguish between the cultivators of the soil on the one hand and the merchants on the other. The enlargement of the money economy which development of trade involved means that there was a steadily increasing area of human relationships over which the cash nexus was of primary importance. But the typical unit of production was still the family, most heads of families were self-employed and relatively few individuals were employed for wages; most of those who were wage earners lived as members of the family group for which they worked.

When Gregory King drew up his table of incomes entering into English national income at the end of the seventeenth century, he classified them by *families* for this was the natural thing to do, though by this time he could allocate the families to a number of distinct occupational groups, showing that some division of labour had already developed.[1] Besides the soldiers and the sailors and the farmers, for example, he distinguished merchants, shopkeepers, artisans, clergymen, civil servants, lawyers and other professional persons. Subsistence producers seem to have become a rather small sector but pure wage-earners, i.e. people whose incomes came largely through employment in the service of families not their own were still in a minority. If we add together King's figures for labouring people and out-servants with common soldiers and sailors, we find ourselves with a total amounting to rather less than a third of the estimated number of families in England and Wales. Of the rest, even the civil servants and the officers in the army and navy

[1] See above, pp. 6–7.

were much more like self-employed persons than employees, for government offices and military or naval commissions were *properties* that were bought and sold: while clergymen too had 'livings' which were also more in the nature of properties than employments.

The system of production that developed in the course of the industrial revolution, however, divided producers into two main classes—in one of which were the owners (or hirers) of the nation's capital assets, viz. the entrepreneurs taking the decisions about what was to be produced and at what price, and in the other of which were the operatives by whose labour the goods were produced. The basic distinction between capitalist and worker, between employer and employee, is marked by the character of the return which each gets for his contribution to production under this system. The capitalists receive profits, i.e. a return determined by the relationship between prices, output and costs. The labourers receive wages and salaries—contractual payments settled by a process of bargaining with the employer. Of course it is possible—even in a fully industrialized economy —for one individual to figure in both classes—for a self-employed man to labour on his own account, or for an individual to get an income from employment as well as a profit from investment, i.e. from owning capital. But the distinction between employer and employee is fundamental to a capitalist industrialized economy and most producers would fall clearly into one category or the other.

This change in the social and economic role of labour in the productive process was one of the most radical of the changes involved in the industrial revolution. For the attitudes to work and leisure which characterize the self-employed individual or the family worker are very different to those motivating a worker who is a mere wage slave and gets none of the profits of his activity. 'So long as industry was carried on mainly by small masters, each employing but one or two journeymen, the period of any energetic man's service as a hired wage earner cannot normally have exceeded a few years, and the industrious apprentice might reasonably hope, if not always to marry his master's daughter, at least to set up in business for himself.'[1] In these conditions of work the journeyman labourer was apt

---

[1] S. and B. Webb, *History of Trade Unionism* (1920), p. 6.

to look at things through the same kind of spectacles as his employer and there was generally no basic division of interest between employer and employee.

As the size of the proletarian labour force grew, however, the interests of the worker seemed increasingly to diverge from that of his master, and he began accordingly to form associations with other workers in the same trade with whom he felt some community of interest. These associations constituted the origins of trade unions. They were not—as some historians have argued—a direct descendant of the medieval craft guilds, but were a response to the new conditions of work involved in an industrializing economy. Until the eighteenth century there was little evidence for the existence of trade unions in the sense of continuous associations of wage earners for maintaining or improving their working conditions, but from about the middle of the century the Journals of the House of Commons record an increasing number of complaints against each other by employers and journeymen's associations. Trade clubs or unions thus tended to appear wherever the bulk of the labour force had ceased to be independent producers.

It was the skilled craftsmen who set up most of the lasting associations of working-class men over the period 1750–1850. They combined for a variety of reasons—to protect themselves against industrial exploitation, to maintain their customary living standards and differentials, to exploit the scarcity-value of their skills and to provide some sort of mutual unemployment and sickness insurance. Their strength lay in the diversity of their objectives. Though the industrial aims of the trade clubs were illegal through the first quarter of the nineteenth century, their functions as friendly societies providing their members with benefits against sickness, unemployment, old age and other catastrophes fell into a socially respected tradition. In the event, it was scarcely possible to prevent a local benefit club from organizing its members during a trade dispute, for no distinction was made between strike pay or social benefits as uses for their funds.

The unskilled workers had neither the funds nor the education to set up continuing trade associations in defiance of the law. But in the late eighteenth and early nineteenth centuries when there was no effective police force, they were by no means helpless when roused. Their most effective weapon against an oppressive employer was what has been called the 'collective bargaining riot'. Machine-breaking riots, which were a familiar feature of the early stages of the industrial revolution, were often directed as much against the other property of the employer— raw materials, finished foods, buildings—as against machines.[1] Although the military were always available for use against the working class, local J.P.s would hesitate until they felt that law and order in general was at risk before calling in the soldiers, whose depredations might be worse than those of the rioters and who might not arrive until after the wrecking was over. A body of disgruntled workers, their faces blackened for disguise, could often do enough damage to coerce an oppressive employer before military aid could be summoned. When the Luddite riots of 1812 were at their height, they pinned down a military force larger than that taken by the Duke of Wellington to Portugal to fight the Peninsular War.

In view of the evident ease with which a rioting mob could hold a local community to ransom, it is hardly surprising that, faced with the example of the French Revolution across the Channel, Parliament passed the Combination Laws of 1799 and 1800 comprehensively prohibiting all combinations of employers or employees. The novelty of these laws was that they provided for summary trial and conviction and hence gave determined employers a means of acting instantly against individual workers who were threatening collective action. The new laws were ineffective against the employers and they did not kill the trade clubs, merely made them more secretive and cunning in their behaviour. A Select Committe of the House of Commons which reported in 1824 on the operation of the Combination Laws concluded that 'the laws have not only not been efficient to prevent combinations either of masters or workmen, but on the contrary have in the opinion of many of both parties had a tendency to produce mutual irritation and distrust and give violent character to the combinations and to render them highly dangerous to the peace of the community'.[2] The Committee also went on to advocate that 'masters and workmen should be freed from such restrictions as regards the rate of wages and hours of working, and be left at perfect liberty to make such agreements as they eventually think proper'.

The Select Committee's advocacy of a system of free collective

---

[1] E. Hobsbawm, 'The Machine-Breakers', *Past and Present* (1952).
[2] H. Pelling, *History of British Trade Unionism*, p. 30.

bargaining was more in tune with the doctrines of classical political economy than with earlier views of the relationship between employer and employee. Most of the early factory owners accepted a paternalistic role vis-à-vis their wage force and the workers expected to receive a fair day's pay for a fair day's work—looking to the J.P.s to arbitrate when there was a dispute as to what was 'fair' in a particular instance. As industry became more urbanized, however, the separate work force attached to particular factories merged into a general labour force for which no single employer felt personally responsible. The profit-maximizing criteria for entrepreneurial behaviour advocated by the new political economy, fathered by Adam Smith, involved a deliberate de-personalization of the wage bargain and members of the industrial workforce were more and more exposed to the chill winds of competition against which they were ill-equipped to defend themselves.

It had become clear by the 1820's and 1830's, even to workers who clung to the traditional ethic of fair wages and just prices that the old system in which they had rights as well as duties was disintegrating. What they did not see at all clearly was what steps they could take in their own defence. Some felt that the solution lay in political reform and that a democratically elected government would establish rules that could benefit both worker and employer. Hence the strong working class support for constitutional reform which, when disappointed by the 1832 Reform Act, generated the steam for the Chartist movement. Others, under the inspiration of idealists, such as Robert Owen, or revolutionaries such as the socialists, thought in terms of a brave new world in which moral imperatives would prevail and the labourer get a just reward for his toil.

The fact is, however, that even after the Combination Laws were repealed in 1824/5 the labour force had not yet assumed a form which would enable it to exert enough industrial power to affect the worker's share of the wage bargain. Until at least the middle of the nineteenth century, the typical industrial worker was engaged in a small workshop, or as an unskilled labourer in more or less casual employment on the streets, building sites or docks. There was a great deal of sub-contracting through skilled workers who were employers and employees at the same time. Even in factory trades, such as textiles, there were until the 1840's more people engaged as outworkers in their own homes than there were minding machines on the factory floor; and among the factory operatives was a high proportion of women, juveniles and children—none of them groups that were easily organized in a trade dispute.

That the working class was still too heterogeneous a body to unite in a common cause was demonstrated when the Grand National Consolidated Trades Union was set up in 1834 (under Robert Owen's inspiration) to organize strikes and initiate cooperative stores and manufacturing enterprises. Within a few weeks a large number of trade unionists—variously estimated as between half a million and a million—were enrolled as members of the G.N.C.T.U., though it is doubtful whether more than a few thousand rendered any dues to headquarters. Government and employers were alarmed by the apparent strength and militance of the movement. In March 1834, the authorities reacted sharply by charging six Tolpuddle labourers (who had been guilty of nothing more than organizing the traditional trade club ritual) with administering unlawful oaths for seditious purposes and turned them into martyrs of the trade union movement by sentencing them to seven years transportation. Employers acted even more effectively by organizing a series of lockouts and by forcing their workers, as a condition of employment, to sign a document promising never the threaten strike action. The G.N.C.T.U. collapsed before the end of the year, its tiny resources exhausted by demands for strike pay, and most of its constituent unions subsequently disintegrated under the employers' loosely organized but devastating counter-attack. Even skilled labourers who were capable of organizing themselves into permanent unions, and who had some degree of monopoly in their skills to use as a bargaining weapon, had not yet learned to exploit their potential industrial strength. They showed themselves more concerned to maintain a 'just' wage by customary criteria and to prevent dilution of their ranks which might endanger employment levels, than to seek higher wages by collective bargaining.

While the capitalist-entrepreneur was able so completely to dominate the terms of the wage bargain, the scope for profitable investment must have seemed limited only by the extent of the market and the cost-reducing opportunities opened up by technological progress. It is doubtful whether the transformation of the British economy to an industry state could have proceeded

as rapidly and as fully without this special stimulus to investment. It is at any rate significant that when, towards the end
of the nineteenth century, the labour force began to expand
appreciably less rapidly, and when the demand for labour
became less homogeneous with the growth of the precision and
science-based trades, this coincided with a marked deceleration
in the British rate of growth.

CHAPTER 10

THE ROLE OF CAPITAL

The other factor of production whose development was crucial
to the British industrial revolution was capital. The reason why
the citizen of an industrialized country enjoys a higher standard
of living than his counterpart in a pre-industrial country is that
he produces more goods and services for each hour of effort; and
one of the reasons why he can do this is that he typically has
the advantage of a larger stock of capital to assist him in his
productive activities. The community in which he lives possesses
more mechanical equipment, more miles of road or railway or
canal, more ships and vehicles, more buildings and more
altogether of the kind of goods that are used to produce other
goods. He can expect to enjoy a rising standard of living because
he, or some of his fellow citizens, have formed the habit of setting
aside from current consumption enough to add to the
community's stock of producers' goods. There is enough annual
saving, that is to say, not only to replace the capital equipment
which wears out in the process of production but also to acquire
additional items.

To say that a pre-industrial country has a smaller stock of
capital than an industrialized country is not to say that it
necessarily has a lower level of capital per unit of *output* than
a more advanced economy. Indeed because it has inadequate
transport or credit or storage facilities, for example, or because
it makes intermittent or unproductive use of its existing capital
resources, it may be quite highly capitalized in relation to its
level of output: or in other words it may have quite a high
average capital–output ratio. What is certain is that it requires
a substantial addition to its existing stock of capital if it is to
industrialize, and that it will have to go on adding to its stock
if its workers are to go on raising their levels of product per head
and hence their levels of living.

Achieving this increase in its capital stock, and maintaining the increase, involves a community in some quite radical changes in its mode of economic behaviour. The net effect of these changes has often been dramatized by expressing it as a sharp rise in the percentage of national income saved and invested annually. Thus Professor W. A. Lewis has suggested that a significant difference between an underdeveloped and a developed country is that the former normally saves 6 per cent of its national income and the latter 12 per cent or more; and Professor Rostow has made a change in the national rate of investment from about 5 per cent of national income to about 10 per cent a condition of the 'take-off into sustained growth'.[1]

If there were statistics of national income and investment covering the period of the Industrial Revolution we could say when the change in the rate of investment took place for this country. Unfortunately these statistics do not exist. Gregory King's calculations made in the late seventeenth century suggest that the nation was then investing about 5 per cent of its total income: and estimates of national income and investment for the nineteenth century indicate that a rate of investment of about 10 per cent per annum had been achieved by the late 1850's.[2] What the statistics do not throw any light on is the timing of the shift in relation to the Industrial Revolution. To understand this it is necessary to ask ourselves what were the underlying changes in the character of the capital stock and when they took effect. For it is evident that the process of industrialization involved significant changes not only in the volume of capital accumulation but in its content.

First of all, then, what additions were made to the nation's capital in the eighteenth century? Some of the relevant evidence has been discussed already in earlier chapters. It is clear, for example, that the enclosure movement was associated with new investment in hedging, ditching, drainage and generally in the sort of works required to bring commons and waste into permanent cultivation. Urbanization involved investment in buildings, street paving and lighting, water supply and sanitation. Improvements in communications entailed substantial capital expenditure on roads, bridges, river navigations and canals. These developments were taking place throughout the

[1] W. A. Lewis, *Theory of Economic Growth* (1955), p. 225, and Rostow, *Stages of Economic Growth*, p. 41.
[2] Based on estimates for 1856/9 made by C. H. Feinstein, *National Income, Expenditure and Output of the United Kingdom, 1855–1965* (1972), and A. H. Imlah, *Economic Elements in the Pax Britannica* (1958).

century though more intensively in the second half than in the first, and there was a marked acceleration over the last three decades in the pace of enclosures, of urbanization and of canal building. There was also a notable acceleration of investment towards the end of the century in those industries or sections of industries that were affected by technical change, particularly in the cotton and iron industries and in mining.

But if the national capital grew faster in the second half of the eighteenth century than ever before, so too did the national income and the population. The population of England and Wales increased by roughly 50 per cent between 1751 and 1801: the volume of overseas trade almost trebled: the real national income probably doubled. Hence the level of investment would have had to increase by something like 50 per cent just to keep the capital stock growing at the same rate as the labour force: it would have had to have more than doubled to have raised the rate of investment as a percentage of the national income.

Recent research has generated various estimates of the rate of British capital formation during the period of the industrial revolution—not surprisingly in view of the paucity of primary data and the inevitably tentative nature of both national income and investment calculations.[1] These researches leave no doubt that new investment was expanding faster than population and that the stock of fixed capital per member of the labour force was significantly larger in 1830 than in 1800 and also larger in 1800 than in 1770. But there is, as yet, no convincing support for the hypothesis that there was a disproportionate increase in the savings or investment component of national income or expenditure large enough to double the overall *rate* of investment within the period 1750–1850. On the other hand, the composition of the nation's stock of capital was changing markedly.

Let us consider, for example, what the national capital consisted of at the beginning of the nineteenth century. The first thing to notice is that more than half of the nation's capital seems to have been tied up in land. This is what the contemporary estimates indicate. The Reverend Henry Beeke made a calculation of the national capital for the closing years of the eighteenth century—around 1798–9—which suggested a

---

[1] See especially François Crouzet (ed.) *Capital Formation in the Industrial Revolution* for articles bearing on this theme. For the best recent estimates of capital growth in Britain over the period of the industrial revolution, see C. H. Feinstein, 'Capital Formation in Britain' in *Cambridge Economic History of Europe*, Vol. VII, ed. P. Mathias and M. M. Postan (1978).

proportion of 55 per cent attributable to land; an estimate made by Patrick Colquhoun for 1812 or thereabouts suggested a closely similar proportion, 54 per cent; and in the 1830's Pebrer calculated for 1832–3 that again about 54 per cent of the national capital was in the value of its land.[1] The figures on which these proportions are based are no more than guesses, but they are guesses made by well-informed observers, they are mutually consistent and they justify the view that the bulk of the nation's capital consisted of the value of its land.

Even if we exclude land and confine our attention to reproducible or man-made capital, less than half of the total consisted of industrial, commercial and financial capital (such as stock-in-trade, machinery, canals and foreign assets); building and public property accounted for about a third, and farmers' capital for nearly a fifth at the beginning of the nineteenth century. By the 1830's industrialists may have been ploughing back profits at a greater rate and some farmers may have been putting more savings into fertilizers, improved breeding stock and farm machinery, than into enclosure of commons and waste. But the broad structure of the national product looked much the same to Pebrer as it had done to Beeke three or four decades previously.

After the railway age, however, a very different picture emerges. Judging from Giffen's estimates of the national capital, land still represented nearly a third of the value of total national capital but it was declining rapidly in relative importance and by 1885 accounted for less than a fifth of the total. Farm capital was also relatively less important by the 1860's, and by the fourth quarter of the nineteenth century when the great flight from the land was in process, farm capital was apparently falling in *absolute* value as well as in proportion to the national total. By 1865 the reproducible or man-made capital of the nation is estimated to have reached an aggregate value of about four and a half times the national income compared with not much more than three times the national income when Pebrer was making his estimates in the early 1830's.

In sum, therefore, the evidence suggests that if there was a sharp increase in the British rate of investment as a result of the process of industrialization, it took place in the middle decades

[1] The contemporary estimates are discussed in detail in Deane and Cole, *British Economic Growth*, pp. 270–7.

of the nineteenth century. Much of it was attributable directly or indirectly to the railways. The great railway boom reached its peak in the late 1840's. But there were other sectors too in which the process of capital accumulation was suddenly accelerated in these middle decades of the century. The period of greatest investment in the cotton industry seems to have coincided with the widespread adoption of power-using machinery. In the 15 years or so spanning the 1830's and early 1840's the number of spindles practically doubled and the number of power-looms quadrupled. It was the hand-loom weaver who bore most of the burden of the industry's transformation to power. In the 15 years when the cotton capitalists' profits expanded at an unprecedented rate, the number of hand-looms fell to a quarter of the number operating in the 1820's. By the 1850's the hand-loom weaver contributed a negligible proportion of the industry's output of woven goods. For the other textile industries the period of mechanization came somewhat later than that of cotton. The worsted industry—which was technically closer to cotton than the other branches of the woollen industry—followed quite closely in its wake. For the rest of the woollen industry the peak rate of mechanization took place in the 1850's and 1860's. In the 1850's worsted factories were developing power more rapidly than the cotton factories, and in the 1860's the woollen factories proper were expanding their rate of investment in power-looms more rapidly than the other textile industries.

Investment in mines and in the iron industry seems to have been closely allied to the railway construction boom. By the 1850's twenty-seven blast-furnaces a year were being built and new fields of coal and iron ore were being rapidly opened up in Scotland in the 1830's, in the Cleveland ore-field in the 1850's, and in the Cumberland–Lancashire field in the 1860's. Investment in puddling furnaces also increased sharply in the third quarter of the century. Between 1860 and 1870—before the big shift from malleable iron to steel—the number of puddling furnaces practically doubled.

But, above all, these middle decades of the nineteenth century were dominated by the massive developments in transport. It was not only railways. The value of ships built in the United Kingdom began to rise markedly in the late 1840's when iron ships began to be built in increasing numbers. Between then and the early 1860's the value of new construction more than doubled. By the 1860's the annual value of shipping built and registered in the U.K. exceeded one per cent of the national income. This was probably its peak of relative importance, though it was not until the 1870's that the new steamship tonnages began to overtake the new sailing-ship tonnages. Investment in ships involved sympathetic investment in docks and harbours. The dock area of Liverpool was nearly doubled in the second quarter of the nineteenth century. Of nearly £10 millions spent by government on British harbours during the first three-quarters of the nineteenth century, about a half was spent between 1850 and 1870.

It is important to notice, however, that evidence for an upsurge in the rate of capital formation in the middle decades of the nineteenth century relates entirely to increments in the nation's stock of durable productive assets. This was one of the characteristics which most sharply distinguished the industry state of the late nineteenth century from the pre-industrial economy of the early eighteenth century. At the heart of the accelerated process of industrialization called the industrial revolution was a marked shift in the composition of the nation's productive capital which changed the nature of the investment decision. The productive assets in which an early eighteenth century entrepreneur—whether trader or manufacturer or (more commonly) a mixture of both—had sunk his capital were stocks of raw materials or semi-finished or finished goods on their way to the consumer. When he started up in business what he need capital for was to buy the basic stock-in-trade and to pay the workforce processing or moving it. Machinery was rarely needed. Even in the coal mines it was limited to the occasional pumping engine. Outworkers usually owned their own spinning wheels or handlooms or horses and carts as well as their own tools and other implements. Most of the buildings used in industry were primarily dwelling houses. According to Professor Sir John Hicks: 'What happened in the Industrial Revolution, the late eighteenth century Industrial Revolution, is that the range of fixed capital goods that were used in production, otherwise than in trade, began noticeably to increase.'[1] It did not happen suddenly. Even the early cotton-spinners using powered machinery typically started up in an

[1] Sir John Hicks, *A Theory of Economic History* (1969), pp. 142–3.

old barn or a warehouse or a cornmill or part of a dwelling house. For the early textile factories, or breweries, for example, it has been estimated that buildings and plant accounted for no more than one-seventh or one-eighth of the total capital sunk in the enterprise.[1] Nevertheless, it was the changes in the scale, range and variety of the fixed capital goods in which investment was increasingly embodied that ultimately changed the system of organization of productive activity for the British economy.

What it amounted to was that under the new system of production most of the industrial capitalist's funds were tied up in fixed capital assets rather than in circulating capital. The advantage of circulating capital was that it was more liquid and hence more mobile between uses. The eighteenth century investor, or the entrepreneur, could move his capital between trades and could enter or leave a given branch of industry at fairly short notice, because he did not have to sink more than a fraction of his available funds in expensive, industry-specific, buildings, plant and equipment. He could, and frequently did, operate in several branches of trade and manufacture simultaneously, or in rapid succession. Under the new system he was increasingly forced to specialize and to take greater risks in making his investment decisions. In an effort to reduce his own share of the risks of a cyclical fall in demand he shifted as much of it as he could on to his labour force. Hence the long drawn out agony of the handloom weavers who bore most of the losses of the early nineteenth century cotton trade slumps. Hence, also, the development of a sharpening conflict of interest between capital and labour.

The most impressive feature of the big leap forward in fixed capital formation which characterized the middle decades of the nineteenth century was the railway construction boom. This was a spectacular episode. Railways themselves were not new. What was new was the triumph of the steam-locomotive. For the first quarter of the nineteenth century iron-railway construction had been limited to small-scale localized railroads operated by horse-power or by stationary engines. By the end of 1825 there were between 300 and 400 miles of iron public railroad in the United Kingdom, representing a total capital investment of probably under £2 millions. The longest railway was the Stockton–Darlington; at 25 miles it was the first to be

[1] F. Crouzet (ed.), *Capital Formation in the Industrial Revolution* (1972).

designed for steam traction and for passenger traffic and its opening can be regarded as the opening of the railway age. But it still took nearly a decade for the steam-locomotive to be assured of success. Horse-drawn coaches were used for passenger traffic on the Stockton–Darlington line for some years, and even as late as 1840 there were several public lines dependent entirely on horse traction or on stationary engines. By then, however, George Stephenson's *Rapid* had proved its worth and the steam-locomotive ran on all the trunk lines so far built.

The construction of the railways proceeded in a series of booms or manias. The first railway promotion mania coincided with the boom of 1824–5 and resulted in just over 70 miles of railway being opened to traffic over the following quinquennium. The next worked up to a crescendo in 1836–7, and in the seven years 1831–7 between 400 and 500 miles of railway were opened to traffic. By the triennium 1838–40 expenditure on construction and rolling-stock was running at an average of more than £10 millions per annum, and by 1840 the value of capital invested in railways was near £50 millions, most of which represented the cost of the track and its installations. Then there was a lull and a new mania. Between 1839 and 1843 no new railway lines, other than extensions to existing lines, were opened, but between 1844 and 1847 more than 2,000 miles were opened to traffic. The great railway construction peak was in 1847 when more than a quarter of a million men were employed in constructing 6,455 miles of railways. *Total* railway expenditure (including working expenses) was then running at a level which was more than the declared value of British exports and roughly a tenth of the total national income.

In effect the first mania in the 1820's reflected the experimental beginnings. Then, once the success of the Liverpool and Manchester line was clear, railway entrepreneurs threw all their resources into the great main-line links between London and the chief provincial centres and between the two principal industrial areas—South Lancashire and West Yorkshire. The great trunk lines of England (except the Great Northern) were laid down in the mania of the 1830's. The great mania of the 1840's 'blocked out almost the whole railway system of modern Britain';[1] and by 1852 the only sizeable towns in England not yet served by a railway were Hereford, Yeovil and Weymouth.

[1] Clapham, *Economic History*, vol. i, p. 392.

In the 1850's the railways reached out into the west and south-western corners of England and into the north-east of Scotland.

The early railways were not very different in concept or purpose from the early coal railways. The Liverpool and Manchester, for example, was a short line between an inland industrial centre and its port, designed in the hope of generating something new in the way of passenger traffic and of two-way freight traffic. The hopes were justified and encouraged a further innovation—the building of lines between London and the chief urban centres of England. The innovators who created the Grand Junction Line, the London and Birmingham, the London and Southampton and the Great Western and others were putting unprecedentedly large sums of money into an enterprise whose prospects at that stage were highly speculative. How were these large sums raised?

For the early railways, as for the canals, the bulk of the capital came from local businessmen who had a special interest in the success of the projected line. Bristol Corporation, for example, took the initiative in promoting the Great Western Railway. Gradually however their success made them ready to invest in railway lines further afield. Liverpool businessmen for example were well known for their readiness to invest in railways outside their own area. Probably most of the capital for the early railways was provided by merchants, many of whom had large holdings in several companies. Nevertheless, the thing was overdone. The manifest success of some of the railways attracted savings from people who were in no position to gauge the prospects of this or that railway line. Indeed there was too much capital available for railways at this stage. 'Blind capital, seeking its 5 per cent, a totally different thing from the clear-eyed capital of the Quaker businessmen from the Midlands and the North, had accumulated for the raiders.'[1] There was some speculation too. All this led to a waste of capital. In the boom of 1836–7 many serious investors had their fingers burned and became understandably cautious. Even the Great Western had its cheques dishonoured at one point, and the London and Southampton was driven to sell its shares at half-price in a desperate bid to raise money.

The second big railway mania, which developed in the spring

---

[1] Clapham, *Economic History*, vol. I, p. 388.

of 1845, was even more spectacular and wasteful of capital. It was characterized by the large-scale appearance of *speculative* capital in the market for railway shares. The solid success of the earlier railways which had now had time to show their paces raised hopes of an enormous potential traffic, and a large number of people in all stations of life sought a share in this source of wealth. These were respectable if over-optimistic motives for railway investment. But as the mania got under way a wider circle of people than ever before began to speculate, not on the profitability of railways but on the prospective rise in share prices. 'Ladies and clergymen were tempted by the facility with which shares in newly projected companies could be bought for a deposit amounting to only a small proportion of their nominal value.'[1] Disaster was inevitable. Capital for local lines continued to come mainly from local sources in the 1840's, but most of the money which poured into the coffers of the companies during the mania, and was extracted from reluctant shareholders in the ensuing crash, came from all parts of the country. Some of it even came from the existing main-line companies. The Great Western and the North Western, for example, sponsored a number of branch lines.

In the period which stretched from the 1830's through the 1860's, then, it is evident that a vast amount of capital was made available to British industry and commerce—at times more than the economy could efficiently digest. Nor was it only British industry that attracted British capital. In the second half of the 1850's the export of capital was flowing at a rate which represented between 3 and 4 per cent of the total national product. By 1870 it is estimated that nearly £700 millions had been invested abroad, more than two-thirds of it in the two decades since 1850. The golden age of British foreign investment came later, but the outflow had begun in the 1820's. All this amounted to a very substantial increase in the volume of national investment. Except in so far as capital was diverted from non-productive uses such as the national debt, and this must have been a negligible fraction of the total, this means that a large volume of savings was made available from domestic sources. For investment and savings are merely the two sides of the same coin. A community spends its income on consumption or investment: or to put it another way, it takes up its output

[1] R. C. O. Matthews, *Study in Trade Cycle History* (1945), p. 111.

in the form of consumption goods or capital goods. If it was possible for the nation to build up new capital on the scale that it did, it was possible only because some of its citizens were willing or obliged to abstain from consuming their full incomes by a corresponding amount.

Now Britain in the 1840's was not by any means a rich country. We shall consider in a later chapter the evidence in the famous controversy about the workers' standard of living. But whatever the upshot of this controversy, no one would seek to deny that this was a period of acute social distress for large sectors of the industrial population, a period which inspired Marx and gave rise to Engels' sombre account of the conditions of the working classes in England. How was it possible for a nation as poor as this to lay down such a massive stock of capital in such a relatively short period of time?

There had certainly been some increase in thrift since the industrial revolution had gathered momentum. Government had set out to encourage habits of working-class thrift since the 1790's when Rose's Act of 1793 consolidated the law relating to friendly societies. By 1801, according to Eden's estimates, there were over 7,000 friendly clubs in England with a membership of 600,000. The first true savings bank (as opposed to a friendly society or savings club which has an insurance or a temporary savings motive) was established in 1804. It was called the Charitable Bank and indeed proved more charitable than had been its original intention, for the 5 per cent rate of interest which it paid on deposits involved a loss to its founders and the Bank had to be wound up. Gradually, however, the movement spread, and by 1817 there were 70 savings banks in operation in England. The movement gathered momentum in the boom period of the early 1820's and grew steadily through the 1830's and 1840's. By 1830 there were roughly 378,000 depositors in England and Wales with deposits of over £12 millions, an average of about £33 per head. By 1845 the number of depositors (again in England and Wales) and the volume of their deposits had more than doubled. By then, since the number of depositors had grown faster than the total of deposits, the average deposit had fallen slightly, to about £30 per depositor. The savings habit was spreading among the better-class artisans and more than four-fifths of the depositors had a deposit of under £50.

It is evident, however, that working-class personal savings of this kind were not large enough to make a substantial contribution to the capital available for industrial and commercial purposes. What were the other sources? We can begin by eliminating two possible sources of finance for capital accumulation in industry as being of negligible importance in the late eighteenth and early nineteenth centuries, namely foreign borrowing and government investment. True, the Dutch had lent a good deal of capital to eighteenth-century England, and there had been other countries with an interest in the National Debt. But the long French wars altered this situation. Amsterdam lost its dominance in the international capital market and was replaced, though not immediately, by London. England became a lending rather than a borrowing nation, and the National Debt became largely a domestic affair. Nor was government an important source of capital, even of the kind of social overhead capital that was embodied in roads, bridges and harbours. If anything government was concerned to disentangle itself from, rather than to embroil itself in, the economic system. The tendency was, for example, to develop the road system by means of turnpike trusts rather than by direct government expenditure. Railways, canals, gas companies, water-supply companies and so on were operated by private rather than by public enterprise. Indeed the State, particularly in the late eighteenth and early nineteenth century probably did more to attract savings away from productive investment than to add to the nation's stock of capital. The Usury Laws made 5 per cent the legal upper limit to the rate of interest chargeable on commercial loans, but government could, and at times did, raise loans on terms that were more attractive to lenders than this.

Another way of financing capital formation is to use inflation as a means of generating 'forced savings'. Chronic inflation has become a familiar condition in the industrializing underdeveloped countries of the present day. In an inflation associated with an inelastic labour supply prices rise faster than wages; profits grow more rapidly than either; and because they expect prices (and profits) to go on rising industrialists are glad to plough this windfall back into capital formation which will enable them to produce more and sell more at these attractive prices. The 'savers' in this situation are the wage-earners who have to pay higher prices for goods whose costs of production have not risen correspondingly; the investors are the individual entrepreneurs who are thus enabled to finance their investments by the 'forced savings' of their customers.

The thesis that something of the kind happened in England in the period of the industrial revolution was developed originally by Professor Earl Hamilton who argued that 'If prices and wages had not behaved as they did, or in similar fashion, it is doubtful that industrial progress would have been rapid, pervasive or persistent enough to appear revolutionary to succeeding generations.'[1] The argument is not only that inflation created the forced savings by putting windfall profits into the hands of potential investors, but also that by creating a presumption of continuously rising prices they created an incentive for industrialists to go on investing. In other words inflation, it is argued, provides both the means and the incentive for a higher rate of capital formation in industry.

The validity of this argument depends on establishing that the windfall profits went to the innovating industrialists. In fact, however, this is not what happened in the British industrial revolution. For inflation, both in its milder pre-war form which arose from pressure of a rising population and in its galloping wartime form, drove up the prices of agricultural products. The prices of industrial goods in the innovating industries—cotton textiles, for example, and iron products—tended to fall rather than to rise. If there was a windfall from rising prices it went to the farmer or the merchant rather than to the industrialists, and except perhaps in so far as it freed capital for the landed interest to *lend* to canal companies, for example, this windfall can hardly be said to have contributed to the increase in capital accumulation. The profits which British industrialists ploughed back into their businesses came out of the margin between their falling costs and their less-rapidly falling prices. It had nothing to do with inflation.[2] In any case, once it was past the inflationary situation of the Napoleonic wars, the English economy was characterized not by a rising but by a falling price trend, and there is some evidence for the thesis that in nineteenth-century Britain 'periods of falling or stagnant prices were, normally, the intervals when the largest increases in production occurred and the greatest decline in

[1] E. J. Hamilton, 'Prices and Progress', *Journal of Economic History* (1952).
[2] D. Felix, *Quarterly Journal of Economics* (1956), p. 457.

unemployment'.[1] In sum, therefore, it is difficult to justify the view that the capital formation of the British industrial revolution was financed by the forced savings generated by inflation.

To begin with, as we have seen, the problem of finding the capital for the industrial revolution was not so much one of raising the level of national saving, because the *rate* of national investment seems to have grown relatively little, but of redistributing funds from those who had resources to spare to those who had productive ideas for their use. It should be remembered that although the mass of the people were too poor to save and average incomes were pitifully low, there were sizeable pockets of wealth in the community. A century and more of successful overseas trading had created a mass of cumulated profits. Professor Postan has indeed argued that as early as the beginning of the eighteenth century 'there were enough rich people in the country to finance an economic effort far in excess of the modest activities of the leaders of the Industrial Revolution'.[2] Moreover there was a very elaborate system of credit through trade. So the country bankers and the city merchants were able to use the idle resources of the rural gentry or the returned Indian nabobs to finance trade, and through this to provide some of the working capital of the industrialists.

Although the shift towards increasing dependence on fixed capital was already in progress the cost of the new equipment was typically low in most branches of manufacturing industry until after the industrial revolution was well advanced. When the cotton industry was enjoying its output explosion of the period 1790–1815, a jenny cost no more than £5, a mule £30, a steam-driven mill £50, a handloom about £11, a stocking frame £15 and a powerful steam engine £500–£800.[3] Even in the relatively capital-intensive iron industry it was possible to build a blast furnace in Scotland as late as the 1830's for no more than £10,000.[4] In practice, therefore, it was often possible for an industrious man to set up in business with very little capital

[1] W. W. Rostow, *British Economy in the 19th Century* (1948), chap. 1.
[2] M. M. Postan, 'The Accumulation of Capital', *Economic History Review* (October 1935), p. 2.
[3] Crouzet, *op. cit.*, pp. 37–8.
[4] R. H. Campbell, 'Investment in the Scottish Pig-Iron Trade', 1830–1843, *Scottish Journal of Political Economy* (1954).

and to build up his own resources until they were large enough
to attract the interest of wealthier men. Robert Owen, for
example, began by borrowing £100 from his brother and going,
at the age of 18, into partnership with a mechanic who made
looms; by the time he was 30 he was in a position to bid £60,000
for a spinning establishment. James Watt borrowed in a small
way from his friend Dr Black and then went into partnership
with Boulton, who had inherited the substance of a family
business. Arkwright began by borrowing from a publican friend
and later went into partnership with Strutt, who was already
an established hosiery manufacturer. When Marshall set up a
flax-spinning mill in Leeds in the 1790's he raised the necessary
capital in three main ways: (1) by disposing of his own drapery
business, (2) by borrowing from his friends, and (3) by overdraft
from a bank whose founder was one of a family of linen
bleachers. The iron industry required heavier capital outlays
but again it was financed on a personal basis. The Darbys and
the Wilkinsons had the backing of long-standing family
businesses. The Carron Company which was set up in 1759 to
smelt iron with coke, a venture which required the relatively
large initial outlay of £12,000, was established by three partners
and their families. It was expanded first by bank overdraft, then
by turning the company's bankers and the partners' friends into
shareholders: in 1765 it was expanded again by acquiring new
partners. In each case the capital was acquired by personal
contact.

Once the new enterprise was earning a steady profit it was
usual to finance its continuance and its expansion by ploughing
back the profits or by calling again on the friends of its owners.
'The success of a business depended, to a high degree then, on
its master—upon his powers of managing and arranging his
factors of production and his capacity to attract demand and
make his own market. Hence only those who knew the borrower
and his market would loan them capital.'[1] Later, innovations
in one branch of an industry would be financed by profits earned
in another branch of the same industry. The owners of spinning
mills, for example, were the main source of capital for the
provision of power-looms in Lancashire in the 1820's and 1830's.

In effect, the salient feature of the English capital market in
the late eighteenth century and for more than the first half of

[1] Sidney J. Chapman, *The Lancashire Cotton Industry* (1904), p. 113.

the nineteenth century was that it was highly imperfect. Perhaps indeed it was more imperfect when the industrial revolution got into its stride and entrepreneurs began to specialize than it had been in the mobile unspecialized eighteenth-century economy where men, and their funds, moved freely from one industry to another. In the newly industrialized economy savings tended to be generated by the industries—even by the enterprises—which invested them. Profits earned in agriculture were generally reinvested in agriculture and profits earned in cotton generally went back into cotton (or at any rate into some related industry like textile processing). Though there was some lending of short-term funds (by overdraft for example) from rural banks, which thus provided working capital for industry, most long-term saving was made with specific investments in mind.

To some extent this imperfection of the capital market was an institutional problem. Until the Joint Stock Company Act of 1856 legalized limited liability, corporate enterprise was a rare form of organization. Incorporation required parliamentary sanction and, except in fields characterized by abnormal size of capital and relatively unspeculative nature of operations, e.g. canals, docks, water supply, bridges, roads, insurance and later gas supply and railways, it was rare for the entrepreneurs to go to the trouble and expense of securing an Act of Parliament. The characteristic unit of production was the family firm, and the characteristic saver was a member of the family or a friend of the family. Nor indeed did the small entrepreneur want to seek funds outside his own company and his own friends, for this would have involved him in undesirable obligations to strangers. Even the promoters of large-scale projects like canals were often reluctant to let shares go to individuals who had no direct interest in the project.

Nevertheless a class of savers ready to invest in channels of which they had no personal knowledge was beginning to emerge. The financial reforms of the eighteenth century had established government as a credit-worthy borrower and by the second half of the century the non-participant investor was finding a satisfactory outlet in the Funds. The National Debt of the Napoleonic wars and the subsequent flotations of loans in London by foreign governments and mining companies created new opportunities. Some of these investors were to be disappointed in the 1820's when foreign governments defaulted and mining shares proved illusory sources of wealth, but savers were learning new habits. The education of the non-participant saver took an immense stride forward in the railway age. It was as well that it did, for without this new source of funds it is doubtful whether it would have been possible to finance the substantial increase in the level of national investment which took place in this period. In the event, unprecedented sums were invested in railway companies and, in spite of manias and depressions, the bulk of these investments survived to earn a respectable return. 'By the middle of the century railway shares had been established in the study and the drawing room, and in the second half of the century newspapers began to publish as a matter of daily routine the prices of industrial stock for the benefit of their middle class readers.'[1]

To recapitulate, then. How was the capital accumulation of the industrial revolution financed? The setting up of a factory or an iron works, the fitting out of a ship, the stocking of a commercial enterprise—these were investments which required access to tens of thousands of pounds of sunk capital at the most. With reasonable trading conditions, investors could expect to begin repaying most of their initial outlay within a few years of borrowing it. A reputable inventor or entrepreneur with a small capital of his own and an innovation which met an obvious demand could hope to raise the extra funds required to put him in business by direct loans from relatives and friends, or from other businesses even, with a strong interest in the success of his enterprise. This indeed was the way in which it was generally done. With railways (as for canals or docks) it was different. They called for hundreds of thousands of pounds to be sunk immediately in assets that might not begin to yield even a modest return for several years and might (and generally did) require still more subscriptions of capital before coming into effective operation. To obtain funds on this scale the railway promoter had to be able to tap a wider reservoir of savings and to go on making fresh calls on this wider reservoir. This required corporate enterprise, and public issues of stock which was afterwards freely traded in; and this again was the way it was done. The massive social overhead capital embodied in canals, railways, street lighting and water-supply systems was possible

<hr />

[1] Postan, *Economic History Review* (1935), p. 5.

because the promoters were able to draw on the mass of often quite small personal and institutional savings which were becoming available in an economy that had already begun to industrialize and to grow. To begin with it was largely the government, the canals to some extent, and then extensively the railways that were able to tap the savings of the non-participant investor. Later, overseas governments and overseas railways were able to tap the same source, partly because the precedent had already been set and the institutions were already there.

CHAPTER 11

THE ROLE OF THE BANKS

One of the advantages with which Britain entered upon the first industrial revolution was a developed system of money and banking. It was quite highly developed in relation to the monetary systems which many twentieth-century underdeveloped countries enjoy, and indeed in relation to most of its contemporaries in Europe: though it still had a long way to go before it measured up to the standards of a modern state exercising direct and deliberate control over its own money supply. How effectively did the banking system of the later eighteenth century fulfil its task of providing the industrializing economy with the mobile financial resources required by economic change and growth?

There had already taken place in England, mainly in the first half of the eighteenth century, a series of developments in the money market, an expansion in the number, range and efficiency of English financial institutions and facilities which amounted in all to a financial revolution. The centrepiece in this reconstruction of the English financial system was the Bank of England and the new system of public borrowing which the Bank made possible. Around it developed all the other major financial institutions which grew up during the eighteenth century—e.g. the insurance offices, the partnership banks, the great chartered trading companies and the London Stock Exchange.

The Bank of England had been founded in 1694 in the course of the company-promoting boom of the 1690's, with a capital of £1·2 million, its main objective being to raise money for the government. Within a year of its charter it had taken over the tricky business of transferring foreign exchange to finance Dutch William's wars against Louis XIV. In 1700, it offered to store imported gold and soon began to make loans against such deposits. By the 1720's it was the main source of the Mint's gold and of the public's guineas.

The primary function of a bank is to act as an intermediary between borrowers and lenders, i.e. to channel funds from those who have a surplus over their expenditure needs towards those whose current expenditure plans exceed their accessible resources. In a nation at war the State is in most urgent need of immediate purchasing power. In a growing economy, it is the newly-expanding, innovating entrepreneurs whose prospects for profitable investment outrun their own funds. In either case, the role of the banks is to pool the savings of a relatively numerous body of middle-and upper-class individuals or institutions and to make them available, against interest, to the relatively few borrowers who can confidently be expected to meet the interest and repayment charges imposed on them. The higher the risk of default envisaged by the lenders the higher the interest rate they will expect to receive for parting with their surplus and the shorter the period of loan they will be prepared to contemplate. A bank which is able accurately to predict the credit-worthiness of its debtors will be able to negotiate long-term loans at a relatively low rate of interest.

This was the service which the Bank of England performed for the parliamentary government established by the Glorious Revolution of 1688. It enabled successive governments to finance their abnormal war expenditures by borrowing from the private sector at rates which became increasingly favourable. As a result of the successful collaboration between the Treasury and the Bank in managing the National Debt, there was a remarkable improvement in the credit status of the British government, reflected in a sharp fall in the rate of interest at which it could borrow long term—from 10 to 14 % in the 1690's to 3 % under Walpole and Pelham. During the war of 1739–48 it had become possible for government to borrow cheaply on terms which specified no repayment date.

The secondary effects of the Bank's financial transactions on behalf of the government stemmed from the new financial instruments which were thus created. In return for its loans to the government the private sector received paper assets ranging from short-dated bills such as Exchequer and Navy Bills at one end of the spectrum to Consols (irredeemable long-term debt) at the other end: and because the paper assets issued by a credit-worthy borrower are themselves readily saleable, the effect was further to lubricate the channels linking savings and investment by creating a large stock of negotiable paper assets which new savers could buy whenever existing lenders wanted to realize their loans. At the same time the Bank of England (and the other banks which grew up in its ambit) was attracting regular deposits which could be used as a basis for further extension of credit to the private sector. Provided that it held enough cash to meet the likely day-to-day demands of its depositors wishing to withdraw their gold and silver, a bank could issue notes (promises to pay) exceeding the value of its deposits; and the promissory notes of a trusted bank such as the Bank of England became paper money in their own right, exchanging at their face value.

The consequence of establishing an orderly market in claims to money and credit was therefore to inject into the economy a large and growing stock of liquid assets and paper money which helped to facilitate transactions in short-term trade credit. In effect, the rise of an active London market in securities in the first half of the eighteenth century solved the government's financial problem by 'making debts that were permanent for the state liquid for the individual: subject only to the risk of capital loss if market forces fell'.[1] It helped to attract a flow of foreign investment into the British economy by giving wealthy Dutch merchants a safe route for investing in British government stock. It also made it easier for savers and investors in the private sector to extend and receive short-term credit by using paper assets as collateral or as a medium of exchange of purchasing power. More important still in its ultimate consequences for the British financial system, the issue of bank cheques or bank notes on the strength of withdrawable deposits made it possible for the banking system to create paper money unbacked by real goods or services.

The essence of the financial revolution of the early eighteenth century was the development of a wide range of securities in which the new mercantile and financial companies—the chartered trading companies, partnership banks, insurance companies etc.—could flexibly and safely invest and disinvest. The strength which these new instruments and institutions gave to the London money market made it possible for the City of

[1] P. G. M. Dickson, *The Financial Revolution in England* (1967).

London to rival and eventually displace Amsterdam as the financial centre of the world, and the centre of the still incompletely integrated British financial system was the Bank of England. In the 1750's it was banker to the government and to most of its departments. Beginning as a 'speculation with an uncertain future' it had become a national institution though it was still not operating as a central bank in consciously controlling the money supply.[1]

In principle the eighteenth-century pound was based on silver—it was still the pound *sterling*. From the time of Elizabeth the English pound had been identified with a fixed quantity of silver. The value of the golden guinea was fixed in terms of a number of shillings. Actually, however, there was a relative shortage of silver in most of Europe and still more so in the Far East, where the current market price was higher than the English Mint price. It therefore paid merchants to acquire silver at the ruling English price and to ship it to continental Europe and the Far East in exchange for gold. The inevitable result was a debasement of the English silver coinage; and when in the great recoinage of 1696–8 the clipped silver pieces were replaced by full-weight coins with milled edges these gradually disappeared from circulation. Nor indeed was the Mint prepared to go on coining new silver pieces at this price. So that by the 1760's there was very little silver coin still in circulation apart from a few worn shillings and sixpences. In effect, if not as yet in law, England was on the gold standard. In the 1770's this was formally recognized (though still not yet legalized) by a reform of the coinage which replaced the light gold coin by pieces of proper weight and restricted the legal tender of silver to payments not exceeding £25. It was given statutory recognition in 1816 when gold was declared to be the sole standard and full legal tender.

In addition to coin there were other kinds of money in common use by the middle of the eighteenth century. The earliest surviving cheques date from the late seventeenth century, though it is doubtful whether they became at all common until the nineteenth century. More important were bank-notes; that is, promises to pay the bearer a specified sum on demand. The Bank of England had been issuing them to its depositors from its inception (though it was not until later in the century

[1] J. H. Clapham, *The Bank of England*, vol. 1 (1944), p. 228.

that they came to be of regular round amounts) and they were used freely as equivalent to cash, for which they could readily be exchanged, in settlement of debts between individuals. The private banks also issued notes. In London none of them had the standing of the Bank of England, and these private note issues had practically died out by the 1770's. But in Scotland there was a long tradition of private note issue and in provincial England the country banks issued bearer notes for local circulation.

The amount of money supplied to an economy is a matter of first importance to its development because it affects the level of prices and through these the level and sometimes the character of economic activity. If the supply of money does not expand in step with the expansion of trade in a given economy —that is to say, if money becomes more scarce in relation to goods—prices will tend to fall, producers will be discouraged and it will be more difficult for entrepreneurs to obtain the financial resources they need to set up or expand their businesses. Conversely, if money is issued too freely, prices will rise and investment will tend to be drawn into those branches of activity which are most immediately affected by the price increase; in some of today's underdeveloped economies, for example, inflation tends to stimulate unduly the flow of investment resources into residential building, where rising capital values offer rewards which are out of all proportion to the real productivity of the new buildings. In a pre-industrial economy where physical communications are poor and perhaps hazardous, as was the case in eighteenth-century Britain, there is the additional problem of getting the money in sufficient quantity to the regions which are expanding economically.

What were the determinants of the supply of money in the first industrial revolution, and how did this react on the level of prices and the state of trade? The volume of coin in circulation depended primarily on the supply of gold at the Bank of England, and this in its turn depended in part on the world demand for and supply of gold and in part on the British balance of trade. For if exports exceeded imports this generally implied an inflow of gold: and conversely, if imports exceeded exports the excess had to be financed by an export of gold. Gold in effect was the international currency by which outstanding debts between peoples of different nationalities had to be settled. The Bank's ability to put gold coins in circulation depended on the price which it had to pay for gold on the world market and hence on the state of the foreign exchange, for it was this that determined the gold price of the pound sterling.

The connection between the supply of gold and the circulation of gold coins is thus obvious enough. There was also a connection, though less direct and automatic, between the supply of bank-notes and the supply of gold. The complication here is that notes were issued not only by the Bank of England but also by the country banks in England and by the Scottish banks. We do not know what proportion of the total English note issue was supplied by the country banks but it is clear that their note issue was important both quantitatively and qualitatively.[1] Bank of England notes were not in common use outside London, for they were convertible in coin only in London and they were for relatively large amounts. Until the 1790's the Bank had issued no notes of lower value than £10. The problems of speedy transport between London and the regions and the danger of highway robbery made merchants unwilling to carry stocks of coin between London and the provinces. Those who wanted coin and notes in the denominations needed for everyday transactions with labourers and tradesmen found it convenient to deal with the country banks which issued smaller notes (e.g. £1 notes) payable locally and sometimes also issued larger notes (e.g. £5 or £10 notes) payable in London as well as in the region of issue. The evidence available suggests that the bearer notes payable on demand became common in the provinces in the late 1780's and that by then they may have reached a value equal to or larger than that of the Bank of England circulation. The statistics are inconclusive on this point, however. There exist returns of a stamp duty on notes from 1784 onwards but not until 1804 do they distinguish bearer notes from other forms of paper credit (such as bills of exchange), and even then they are dubious indicators of total circulation or variations in circulation because they do not take account of wastages or of notes stamped and kept in reserve. In 1808/9, which was the one year for which the total private stampings were probably quite close to the total private circulation, the evidence suggests that total private circulation may have been in the region of about £20

---

[1] The authority on the country banks in the eighteenth century is L. S. Pressnell, *Country Banking in the Industrial Revolution* (1956).

millions compared with about £17½ millions for the Bank of England. It seems reasonably certain, however, that during the last two decades of the eighteenth century and the first three decades of the nineteenth, the notes issued by the country banks were at least of the same order of importance in the national money supply as the notes issued by the Bank of England.

This greatly complicates the question of what determined the supply of money. We can assume, to begin with, that both the private banks and the Bank of England gave as much credit and hence issued as large a volume of notes as they dared. For it was on these transactions—their loans to the rest of the community —that they made their profits and justified their existence. A merchant would, for example, pay for goods delivered by means of a promise to pay at some future date—say three months hence—by which time he hoped to have sold enough of the goods (or what he made of them) to meet the debt. The seller of the goods would not have to wait three months, however, if he could persuade a bank to discount the note for him; that is, to make him an immediate payment of cash for the amount owing *less* an amount representing the interest rate plus an allowance for risk against the debtor's default. This margin was the bank's profit. If the merchant was known to be a credit-worthy person the bank would expect payment in full on the stipulated date and, in that case, the whole of the discount margin would accrue to it as profit.

When trade was booming and orders were flowing freely there would be a larger number of recipients of bills of exchange or promissory notes seeking immediate cash, either in notes or in coin, from the banks: and the banks would be anxious to accommodate these clients wherever the credit was good, subject only to the limits of prudence imposed by the need to have enough cash reserves to meet any probable demand from their own depositors. Nowadays the proportion of a bank's liabilities which it regards as a necessary reserve against a sudden demand from its depositors is fixed within fairly narrow and rigid limits. But this is a modern innovation associated with modern policies of central control of credit and money supply. Eighteenth-century bankers did not see themselves as instru-ments of monetary policy. They were purely profit-making institutions whose duties were to their shareholders and de-positors rather than to the public at large. They operated a flexible cash ratio based on their current assessment of the dangers they ran in extending credit. If trade was good, so that the risks of credit-worthy debtors getting into difficulties or of their own depositors requiring cash suddenly were slight, they could operate with a very low cash ratio. If prospects were less encouraging they would maintain a larger reserve. The Bank of England itself operated on similar principles. It too adopted a policy of discounting any commercial paper which it regarded as commercially safe and allowed its gold reserve to fluctuate quite widely. It also regarded itself as obliged to meet all government demands for credit that offered a reasonable interest rate.

In this system the limits to the extent to which credit could be extended and money issued depended on the volume of deposits and the state of confidence. Ultimately the Bank of England could not lend more than the deposits with which its depositors had endowed it; and while it maintained its promise to convert all notes into gold coin it could not lend more than its depositors, or those who held notes against these deposits, might normally want to take out in coin. Similarly, the country banks whose cash reserve consisted of bank-notes (of other banks including the Bank of England) as well as of coin or bullion, could not pay out more than they might need to meet any likely demands by their depositors. In the end the limit to the expansion of credit was set by the amount of gold in the country. That was until 1797, when cash payments were suddenly suspended and the Bank of England was freed from its obligation to convert its notes into gold.

Clearly a system of credit which depended so heavily on the state of confidence was unstable whenever anything happened to disturb that confidence: though while the system was incompletely articulated it was possible for a loss of confidence in one region to end with a few local bank failures. If the disturbance was sufficiently general, however, the main force of the strain would fall on the Bank of England, the ultimate repository of the only true cash. This was what happened in February 1797 when it was decided to lift the strain by breaking the link between gold and the money supply. What were the reasons for this decision?

The immediate first cause was the fact that gold was flowing out of the country and that there was no immediate prospect of stopping the drain. There had been outflows of gold many times before in the eighteenth century. In the crisis of 1783 for example the August balance of bullion in the Bank showed a reserve of under £600,000—lower than the level at which cash payments were to be suspended in 1797. But the crisis of 1783 was part of the aftermath of the American war. No one expected it to persist. Commercial prospects were better than they had been for some years. There was thus no reason to expect a run on the banks which went on confidently discounting good commercial paper and kept the line of credit unbroken. In the event, confidence was justified; trade expanded; gold began to flow back into the country; and in 1789 the bullion reserve rose to a level which was equivalent to more than half the Bank's total liabilities in notes and deposits; a very comfortable reserve indeed.

The credit system, as we have seen, depended on a long line of mutual trust between lenders and borrowers. While merchants and industrialists were confident of their ability to discount bills readily, they were willing to go on expanding their activities wherever these seemed likely to yield a worth-while profit. While depositors were content with paper receipts for their investments, bankers could go on extending credit and issuing new notes to anyone who was likely to earn a good profit on his activities. The moment depositors felt that banks were unable to honour their promise to redeem notes with gold they would rush to make sure of their own share. Had the Bank of England been at the centre of this credit structure, as it is today, committed to supporting any other bank facing a run on its deposits, and able to influence directly the terms on which other banks could extend credit, then the solvency of the system would have depended on the situation and policies of the Bank itself. But although the eighteenth-century Bank of England was the most important link in the chain it was only one of a number of note-issuing agencies, and a serious break in the chain of confidence occurring in a sector over which it had no influence at all could shake the whole of the credit structure. When one remembers the multitude of small note-issuing banks operating in England in the last quarter of the century it seems amazing that the collapse of confidence did not occur before. That it did not must be attributed to two main reasons. The first was the inherent strength of most of the country banks. Some of them failed altogether: but the majority were operated by substantial tradesmen who attracted deposits from their neighbours by the fact that they were known to be sound men of substance, and who made their advances to people they knew, in trades they understood, after a shrewd appraisal of the prospects of the borrowers. Of course there were risks in lending to entrepreneurs in a newly industrializing economy, but the risks were intelligently undertaken and well spread through the community. The other main reason for the relative stability of the system was the fact that the industrial revolution had already introduced a strong upward pressure on the national rate of economic growth. Commercial prospects were so good that there were always enough borrowers who could inspire warranted confidence in their ability to earn a good return on investments, and enough investors who were more intent on earning profits than on keeping their money safe.

But 1797 was different. The country was at war—a difficult and dangerous war which was very close to home and whose character and outcome were totally unpredictable. The French revolutionary war was not a remote colonial war, nor was it one of those balance-of-power minuets to which the eighteenth century was so well accustomed. It was something outside all previous experience—something much nearer the kind of 'total war' in the twentieth-century style than anything that had ever happened before. Moreover the trade and industry boom of the 1780's had already been checked. Some over-sanguine hopes were reversed in the early 1790's and in 1793 some of the country banks had had to stop payment on their notes. British overseas trade was facing the usual difficulties of war—disturbed trade-routes and overseas markets, high transport costs and uncertain prospects. The level of commercial confidence was thus unusually low at this period, and for good reason.

Apart from the general situation there were also some special circumstances which precipitated the crisis of confidence. First among these was the bad harvest of 1795. Britain's rapidly growing population could no longer feed itself when the harvest was below normal, and heavy imports of corn were required in the season 1795/6. This meant special pressure on the balance of payments: the tendency was for imports to exceed exports and so to require an outflow of gold. At the same time government war expenditure was abnormally large both at home and abroad. At home it pushed up prices. Abroad, the heavy expenditure on British fleets and armies, the subsidies to allies, the loans raised by allies on the British market, all created fresh pressures on the balance of payments, fresh reasons why payments to foreigners should exceed the value of receipts from foreigners and so have to be met by the export of gold. An additional special reason for the outflow of gold at this stage was that there was an abnormal demand in France. The French government was struggling to put the French currency—reduced to a fraction of its pre-war value by the disastrous experiment in paper money—back on to a sound footing again. So keen was the demand in Paris in late 1795 that gold fetched £4. 3s. per ounce in London and in guineas it was obtainable for £3. 17s. 10½d. 'Direct transit was of course illegal, but it happened. In one way or another the gold went... In spite of the risks and costs of transit and insurance the temptation to melt or smuggle was overwhelming.'[1] The Bank tried to reduce its liabilities to a less dangerous level by limiting its discounts; but while the country banks were ready to supply the rising demand for money created by rising prices its attempts to restrict credit merely weakened confidence without reducing the note issue. In the end the landing of a small French force at Fishguard caused a panic run on the country banks who in turn presented their Bank of England notes for repayment, and the system broke. The government, faced with the problems of organizing a major European war, dared not risk its own gold reserves. In 1797 the Bank was forbidden to make any payments in gold or silver except for the armed forces abroad, and the country banks had no option but to follow suit. Another Act authorized the issue of notes of less value than £5, and Bank of England notes became for the first time legal tender. Gold disappeared largely into hoards and the age became one of banknotes and tradesmen's tokens.

In principle, then, the limits to the expansion of credit were lifted by the suspension of cash payments. The country banks might have to make sure that they had enough Bank of England notes to meet a sudden demand for immediate cash: but the Bank itself could go on without limit. Under the circumstances it is perhaps surprising that the money supply did not expand faster than it did. No attention seems to have been paid by the

[1] Clapham, *Bank of England*, vol. 1, p. 268.

Bank's directors either to the state of the exchanges or the market price of gold, and throughout the restriction period they were ready to discount at 5 per cent any legitimate commercial bills and to print notes accordingly.

Contemporaries criticized the Bank for over-expanding credit and blamed it for the inflationary price-rise which occurred during the war period. Recent researchers have been inclined to absolve the Bank from blame on this score. During the first decade of the suspension period the price-rise could largely be attributed to bad harvests and war conditions. Indeed there was little depreciation of sterling, whose gold price fluctuated between quite narrow limits during this decade. The depreciation which occurred in the later war period (foreign gold coin was 43 per cent above the Mint price in 1812) was also a consequence of non-monetary factors, such as the difficulties which Napoleon's continental blockade put in the way of British overseas trade or commercial speculations associated with the opening up of new markets to South America. In effect, the Bank's role seems to have been largely passive, as indeed it was intended to be. It saw its role as that of supplying the needs of government and the private sector with the money needed to conduct the war and to carry on the nation's industrial and commercial activities. The rise in prices was a cause, not a consequence, of the increase in the note circulation. Whether, in the circumstances of the time, it would have been advisable for the Bank to adopt a more active role in the economy, and to follow a discount policy designed either to stabilize domestic prices or to maintain the exchange value of sterling, is dubious. By so doing it might well have hindered the expansion of the economy and so reduced its ability to support the war. In the disturbed years which followed Waterloo the Bank continued to pursue its passive role, and it took a further six years before the gap between the Mint price and the market price of gold came close enough to permit a resumption of cash payments in 1821.

In 1821, then, the wartime emergency monetary system came to an end and Britain went formally and legally on to the gold standard. English monetary institutions at the date consisted of (1) a central joint-stock bank—The Bank of England—which acted as the government's bank and custodian of the nation's gold reserve, (2) about 60 London private banks of great strength and reputation but without note issue, and (3) about 800 small private note-issuing country banks uncontrolled in all matters except the denominations of the notes issued. In this third group lay both the weakness and the strength of the English banking system of the 1820's; the weakness showed up in the first great financial crisis of the decade.

These banks had already played an important part in the first industrial revolution. One of the problems which the merchants and the industrialists of the later eighteenth century had constantly to contend with was crippling shortage of ready cash, particularly cash in denominations small enough to pay out in labourer's wages. There was an international shortage of gold and silver which drew gold and silver coin out of circulation and into the melting-pot: and there were even occasions when the price of copper rose higher than the mint price and thus induced a shortage of copper coin. According to Ashton, eighteenth-century employers spent much time 'riding about the country in search of cash with which to pay wages and in the northern and western parts of England the dearth of coin was often acute'.[1] Many employers took to paying their labour in promissory notes or tokens which were redeemable with the local tradesmen. Some, like John Wilkinson the iron-master and the copper magnate Thomas Williams, minted their own copper coins redeemable in London and Liverpool as well as in the region of the iron-works and copper-mines. It was the need to satisfy this pressing need for ready cash as well as to find outlets for the surplus capital of the well-to-do population of the provinces that inspired hundreds of little country banks to issue notes of relatively small denominations such as £1 or £2. Their numbers began to grow significantly in the 1750's and 1760's and the 'last twenty years of the eighteenth century saw a huge crop of new private banks in almost every part of the country'.[2] They continued to grow into the first and second decade of the nineteenth century.

Because they were small and because their success hinged on maintaining confidence, the country banks depended heavily on personal connections. They were prevented by law from being big. To protect the public against the growth of giant

[1] Ashton, *The Eighteenth Century*, p. 173.
[2] R. S. Sayers, *Lloyds' Bank in the History of English Banking* (1957), p. 2. See also Pressnell, *Country Banking in the Industrial Revolution*, p. 7.

banking companies whose failure might have nationally disastrous effects, eighteenth-century legislation forbade the establishment of joint-stock banks with more than six partners. This
hindered the development of specialist banking institutions, and
most of the country bankers were primarily or originally
engaged in some other kind of business for which banking was
a natural and lucrative sideline—particularly in view of the
shortage of means of payment. Bankers often originated in
industry or trade, for example, or in the legal profession. The
location of factories and foundries tended in the early days of
the industrial revolution to be determined by the proximity of
raw materials or of water-supply and hence to be in remote
districts with no existing banking facilities. So the entrepreneur
had to create his own banking service. Traders who constituted
the link between the world market and a localized region of
production or trade also had to develop their own banking
facilities. Often, too, tax-collectors became bankers or bankers
tax-collectors, taking advantage of the long delay between
collection of a tax and its receipt into the exchequer to use public
money for private profit. One of the consequences of this
heterogenous banking system was that when the pioneers of the
industrial revolution went in search of capital, they could hope
to find local bankers who had access to enough personal
knowledge about the borrower on the one hand, and enough
practical knowledge of the trade or industry concerned on the
other, to be able to take risks which a less personally involved
banker would find incalculable and therefore out of range.
Probably the English banks have never been so ready to assist
innovation or to finance long-term investment in industry as
they were in the period 1770–1830 when the industrial revolution took shape.

Of course the system had its disadvantages, particularly as
communications improved and it became more closely articulated. A 'state of confidence' is a wayward mood and it was
possible for a state of misplaced confidence to develop a
momentum of its own. The potential consequences of this
became more dangerous as the economy expanded. 'Economic
expansion involves a growth in the *scale* of the demands for
accommodation with which the banker is confronted and there
arise difficult technical questions of spreading the risk adequately as well as the liquidity of the loans granted when a set-back

occurs in economic conditions.'[1] Over the period 1809–30 there were 311 bankruptcies of country banks, of which 179 took place in two crisis triennia—1814/16 and 1824/6. In effect, the existence of hundreds of little note-issuing institutions, each operating according to its own rules and policies, not all equally efficient or honest, rendered the whole chain of credit as vulnerable as some of its weakest links. There was little that the Bank of England, for example, could do to expand or restrict credit when there were so many other sources of credit in the economy. The essential weakness of the credit structure was brought home to the nation in the mid 1820's when a speculative boom, taking its origins in the recovery and 'reflation' which began in 1823, deteriorated into a financial collapse in 1825. There was a wild burst of company promotions, heavy foreign lending on many lunatic South American mining projects, many exports that were never paid for. When the boom broke it not only bankrupted a number of country banks, it almost drove the country off the gold standard. By the end of 1825, 73 banks in England and Wales had suspended payment and there was very nearly a stoppage at the Bank of England itself.

The government took hasty action. Legislation introduced in 1826 reduced the influence of the country banks by prohibiting the issue of notes under £5, permitted the establishment of joint-stock banks with more than six partners (except within a radius of 65 miles of London) and authorized the Bank of England to set up branches of its own throughout the country. A later Act, in 1833, permitted joint-stock banks to set up within the area in and about London, provided the banks did not issue notes.

Although the legislation of 1826 and 1833 broke the Bank of England's monopoly of joint-stock banking it had the effect of greatly strengthening the Bank's position. For it gave the Bank virtual monopoly of note issue in and around London and enabled it to operate directly in the provinces. Bank of England notes, for example, became a particularly important part of the money supply in Lancashire. There was still a good deal of opposition to the Bank as arbiter of the nation's money supply, for extreme views on 'economic liberty' were popular and the Bank had many enemies among the influential country bankers. It was not until the Bank Charter Act of 1844 concentrated note

[1] T. E. Gregory, *The Westminster Bank*, vol. 1 (1936), p. 4.

issue in the Bank of England that final supremacy of the Bank as the corner-stone of the nation's credit structure was ensured. Between then and the end of the century the old country banks disappeared, their banking services being taken over by the giant London joint-stock banks, their issuing rights devolving on the Bank of England.

In the half-century or so which led up to the Bank Charter Act of 1844 the English monetary system had been through a considerable range of experience. There had been a long period of total war and a period of post-war dislocation; there had been a considerable increase in the national rate of economic growth and in the character of the demands made in the credit system; there had been a period of non-convertibility, a difficult period of trying to restore convertibility and some alarming financial crises. It was evident that the monetary system called for reform though it was by no means clear exactly what kind of reform was required. An active controversy developed among economists, bankers and all those concerned with the formulation of economic policy. This controversy took various forms at various stages in the economic experience of the period: here I shall concentrate on the forms that it took immediately before the Bank Charter Act.

Then the controversy crystallized into the opposition between two 'schools' of thought: the 'currency' school and the 'banking' school. It is convenient to see these two streams of opinion as two 'schools' of thought but it is important to remember that in so doing we over-simplify the situation. The main protagonists in the controversy cannot be neatly dropped into one pigeon-hole or the other. There was a good deal of variation between them and a good deal of common ground. When we look back on it from the vantage of the twentieth century the common ground is almost as significant as the disputed ground. What both groups took for granted was that an 'automatic' monetary system in which the value of the currency was firmly linked to gold (and hence to the money-rates and price levels of all other countries on the gold standard) was the ideal to be aimed at. This view stands in sharp contrast to the prevailing modern view that currency values ought to be controlled by government and adapted to domestic needs rather than to international standards. It was fully in accordance, however, with the economic liberalism that stemmed from Adam Smith and his contemporaries and was to become the distinguishing characteristic of the Victorian age. To the rising entrepreneurs of the early nineteenth century it was important to keep government interference with the economy to as low a level as was consistent with the maintenance of some semblance of economic order: and the economists were inclined to agree with them.

The problem was, of course, how was the economic order to be maintained—more particularly, how was the economy to be protected from the recurrent financial crises which caused such an unnecessary flood of bankruptcies and social distress, and sometimes threatened the solvency of the central bank itself? In 1825 and in 1839 the Bank of England had been as near as it could be to having to stop payments of cash: in the former crisis it had been saved, or so it seemed, only by the lucky find of a parcel of a million one-pound notes in reserve; in the latter crisis only by mobilizing a credit with the Bank of France. On both occasions it had been a very near thing and it was not reasonable to suppose that it would always be as lucky.

It became increasingly evident during the first few decades of the nineteenth century that the foreign exchanges were a vulnerable part of the system and an important source of financial crises. In the restriction period the Bank of England steadily refused to recognize the connection between the foreign exchanges and the note issue. Its directors considered that the function of the Bank was supply the 'legitimate needs of commerce' and that so long as they continued to discount sound commercial paper there would be no danger of an over-issue of notes. It was only when they lent out money for speculative purposes that the danger arose. The difficulty about this policy, however, is that it is not always easy to distinguish the 'legitimate' needs of commerce from speculative ventures. If during an excess of confidence (such as existed in the first part of the 1820's) the banks met all the reputable requests for credit, prices would rise as entrepreneurs competed for resources in short supply, demand for British exports would contract as their prices rose, and demand for imports (stimulated by rising incomes and expectations) would rise; and of course gold would begin to flow out to finance the excess of imports.

The fact that an unfavourable balance of trade could actually be caused by unduly high prices, which could only be reduced through a contraction of credit, was pointed out by Ricardo and the Bullion Committee during the controversy that raged around the depreciation of sterling during the latter part of the war period. This insistence on the closeness of the relation between the exchanges and the domestic note issue was the foundation of the currency-school theories. They argued that the only way of protecting the economy against over-issue was to make paper behave in exactly the same way as a purely metallic currency would have done. If gold flowed out, the quantity of money should be contracted, just as it would have been by an outflow of gold coin when these were the sole form of currency. To let the banks follow their profit motive in extending all the credit that reputable merchants and industrialists might demand was to run straight for a financial crisis whenever entrepreneurs' expectations proved to have been too optimistic.

The banking school, on the other hand, argued that adverse exchange rates generally arose from independent causes, such as bad harvests or an abnormal foreign demand for gold, and that it was no solution to these problems to contract domestic credit. Thus exchange fluctuations would revert to normal as soon as the special causes had worked themselves out, and the duty of the banks was to keep enough reserve of bullion to weather this kind of storm. It was when the banks contracted credit without reference to domestic needs, the banking school argued, that financial crises developed. The banking school also pointed out that notes were not the only form of money and ridiculed the currency school's obsession with the note issue as such. 'They pointed to the great volume of country notes, bills of exchange and cheque payments, and to the machinery of the bankers' clearing house, whereby immense payments were made without the passage of a negotiable instrument at all. Was it reasonable, they asked, to suppose that this enormous volume of purchasing power was sensitive to small changes in a Bank of England note issue amounting to only about £20 millions in all?'[1] It was already clear in the second and third decades of the century that the country bank-note issues could go on expanding even when the Bank of England was restricting its own issue.

In the end the currency school's views prevailed in the Bank Charter Act. They had already won the day within the Bank, whose directors had by the 1830's come to admit the connection

[1] E. V. Morgan, *Theory and Practice of Central Banking* (1943), p. 125.

between the note issue and prices and between prices and exchange rates. It was then that the so-called 'Palmer rule' was explicitly enunciated, if not put into full operation. This rule, named after Horsley Palmer, a governor of the Bank, proposed that the Bank should keep about two-thirds of its total liabilities in securities, leaving about one-third as a bullion reserve: and that it should contract or expand its note issue in response to the fluctuations in its bullion reserve; or in other words that the circulation should behave as though it was wholly metallic. What the exponents of the 'Palmer rule' were looking for was an *automatic* principle of monetary management which would free the Bank's directors from active responsibility for currency control.

It was the kind of automatic mechanism that Peel tried to set up with the Bank Charter Act of 1844. Believing that banking ought to be separated from control of the currency, because its objectives were totally different (one being to provide credit, the other being to regulate the price level) he separated the two functions. Believing that the note issue should be a paper reflection of the nation's gold reserve, he gave the custodian of the nation's bullion the ultimate rights of note issue and made all but a fixed quota of the note issue a direct function of the gold-bullion reserves. To ensure that the Bank should be seen to abide by the clearly established rules of the game he insisted on weekly publication of accounts.

The Bank Charter Act, which established the Victorian supremacy of the Bank of England and wrote *laissez-faire* principles into orthodox monetary policy, did not solve the problems of the British banking system. The next 30 years were amongst the most troubled in the history of the banks. There were three major crises, in 1847, in 1857 and in 1866, each of which produced its crop of bank failures both amongst the private banks and the joint-stock banks. In this hard school of experience the banks which survived each shock learned a new kind of caution. They began to realize the importance of being continuously liquid, and accordingly learned to avoid long-term investments which might lock up sizeable resources in a particular industry. Now that there were no longer any restrictions on their size they learned also to spread their risks over the regions by developing a national network of branches. These were years of experiment and adaptation and uncertainty. Even the Bank of England was for a number of years uncertain as to its role in the economy. It made no attempt to control or lead the market for funds or to check speculation, for example, though it did not hesitate to put bank rate up to panic levels of 10 per cent when bullion began to flow out strongly.

Nevertheless, although these were years of experiment the banks continued to play a vital and flexible role in the expanding economy. They had already built up a complex service for the overseas trade. By the early 1830's Nathan Rothschild could say in evidence to a Committee on the Bank of England Charter that 'England is the place of settlement for the whole world',[1] and London bankers were providing credit to support trade in goods which never found their way to Britain. When in the 1830's and early 1840's it appeared that there was a surplus of funds in the economy the banks helped to channel it to the railway builders and to feed the railway boom. When the railways were saturated with funds and the non-participant investor was looking around for fresh outlets for his surplus the banks were able to use their experience of overseas economies to guide his capital abroad. Throughout the first three-quarters of the nineteenth century the salient feature of the typical bank portfolio was the wide variety of investments which it contained. To the modern banker, accustomed to being able to build up a safe portfolio, with a wide spread of maturities, almost entirely out of the paper assets created by an enormous public debt, the risky character of a nineteenth-century bank's portfolio would seem quite shocking. But their nineteenth-century investments were productive investments in the sense that the national debt was not, and they made an important direct contribution to the finance of British trade and industry.

[1] *Report from the Committee of Secrecy on the Bank of England Charter* (1833), Minutes of evidence 4866.

CHAPTER 12

THE ADOPTION OF FREE TRADE

An elaborate system of tariffs designed to protect domestic industry from foreign competion is the hall-mark of a static economy where the major task of commercial policy is to maintain the *status quo*. Innovation and successful industrialization, however, provide opportunities for expansion and encourage a less restrictive commercial policy. Before the end of the eighteenth century English manufacturers had begun to realize that their interests lay less in the swaddling clothes of Protection than in an opening up of the channels of trade. The Eden Treaty which relaxed some of the tariffs on trade between Britain and France in 1786 was a measure of their growing confidence. Adam Smith's forceful arguments in favour of freer trade were having their influence on the minds of statesmen and policy makers.

The long wars which began in 1793, however, reversed the trend towards Free Trade by introducing a multitude of new uncertainties into the economic situation and by forcing the government to raise revenue-yielding tariffs in the effort to finance the war. The economic uncertainty and the search for government revenue persisted into the post-war aftermath, and although statesmen reared in the doctrines of Adam Smith paid lip-service to a more liberal commercial policy, producers had lost their nerve. 'The great expansion in agriculture and industry had brought habits and commitments attuned to high prices and profit levels. Faced with difficult and unpleasant readjustments and with reviving European competition the vested interests, new and old alike, felt that they needed stiff duties and prohibitions to keep afloat.'[1] Moreover, without the income tax, which had been jettisoned as soon as possible after the war, no government could afford to go far in the direction of free trade.

[1] A. H. Imlah, *Economic Elements in the Pax Britannica* (1958), p. 118.

In the 1820's it proved possible to take more positive action. Between 1823 and 1825 trade was expanding and manufacturers were recovering some of their confidence. In 1824 and 1825 the government was running a surplus, and Huskisson accordingly managed to get through Parliament measures reducing import duties by a total of over £4 million a year: in 1826 there were some further cuts amounting to about half a million pounds. This represented a very modest advance towards free trade. Indeed Britain was effectively more protectionist even after the reforms of the 1820's than she had been in the pre-war period. The average rate of duty on net imports was still in the region of 53 per cent in the late 1820's compared with 57 per cent in the early 1820's and under 30 per cent at the end of the eighteenth century. Huskisson was concerned not so much to abolish protection as to rationalize the tariff system. He did away with import prohibitions and prohibitive duties and export bounties, none of which were yielding any revenue. He reduced to nominal levels some of the rates which fell on the raw materials of British industry and thus inflated manufacturers' costs. For other products he aimed at a tariff ceiling of 30 per cent in order to discourage smuggling. At the same time he liberalized the Navigation Laws so as to extend rather than to restrict the trade of the colonies. In effect he reshaped the old colonial system into a new system of imperial preference. The colonies were permitted to enter the field of international trade on their own initiative and on their own terms, provided that they granted preferential duties to British goods. With foreign countries, on the other hand, he proceeded on the principle of reciprocity. From then on Britain proceeded to use its tariffs as bargaining weapons, and successfully set out to negotiate reciprocity treaties abolishing or equalizing duties on a reciprocal basis with most of its commercial rivals.

For a while this had to suffice. The worst excesses of the British tariff system had been removed and the liberal reformers of the 1830's were too preoccupied with institutional and constitutional questions to take it further. Then, in the 1840's, Peel returned to the task of rationalizing the finances of the British Government. He found the tariff much as Huskisson had left it, though the burden had lightened, largely because there had been a disproportionate increase of the volume of trade in these commodities (raw cotton and wool were outstanding examples) on which the duty was very low, so that by the late 1830's the average rate of duty on net imports had actually fallen to 31 per cent of their market value. Nevertheless there was still room for another spring-cleaning exercise—the Committee on Import Duties which reported in 1840 found 1,146 articles liable to duty, although 17 articles produced 94½ per cent of the total revenue. 'At the other end of the scale 531 articles yielded only £80,000, in many cases because the duties were so high as to reduce trade to a mere trickle.'[1]

Peel's first budget, introduced early in 1842, did not go very far in the direction of lightening the tariff burden. He put a ceiling of 5 per cent on duties on raw materials, 12 per cent on partly manufactured goods and 20 per cent on manufactured goods. The duties on spirits and wines he preferred to retain unchanged so that he could use them as bargaining weapons in reciprocity agreements. Taken in the aggregate, his reductions amounted to less than those involved in Huskisson's 1824 measures. But the significant feature of his budget lay in the reintroduction of income tax. This, by giving the government an alternative source of revenue, effectively opened the way to complete free trade. In 1845 the income tax was renewed and duties were repealed on 450 articles and lowered on many others. The introduction of the income tax, however, was no more than a permissive factor in the situation. The crucial step towards complete free trade, the most significant break with the pre-industrial past, was the repeal of the Corn Laws in 1846.

Among the structural characteristics that lie at the heart of every industrial revolution is the change in the position of agriculture. From being the dominant industry of the pre-industrial economy, agriculture shifts to the ancillary position which it takes in an industrialized economy. Nowhere did the transformation, the reduction of agriculture to a subordinate role, go farther than it did in Britain. The shift took place over a long period of time and to a large extent spontaneously. As industry and transport reduced their costs by innovating and so became more profitable, and as trade expanded, most of the annual increment in the labour force and in the capital stock moved into these more lucrative activities. The share of agriculture in the gross national product of the country (though not

---

[1] Alexander Brady, *William Huskisson and Liberal Reform* (1928), p. 94.

its absolute size) had begun to decline before the middle of the the eighteenth century. By the middle of the century it had probably fallen below a half; by the early years of the nineteenth century it was at about a third and then about a fifth by 1851.[1] It was after the middle of the nineteenth century that the rate of transformation became really rapid. By 1881, as Britain began to draw a large part of its food supplies and raw materials from overseas, the agricultural industry accounted for only about a tenth of gross national product and by 1901 its share had fallen to near 6 per cent.

In this culmination of the industrialization process the ultimate cause was the radical change in commercial policy which was symbolized by the repeal of the Corn Laws. What is particularly interesting is that it came at the end rather than at the beginning of the period of the industrial revolution proper. At the beginning of the period Britain was a grain-exporting country. In the middle of the eighteenth century England was sending out enough grain to feed a million people per annum—a surplus equivalent to the staple food supply of about a quarter of its population. In the second half of the eighteenth century, however, the picture changed completely. The growth of population, of towns, and of the non-agricultural labour force and a spate of bad harvests rapidly took up the nation's grain surplus. In the course of a series of bad harvests the exports of corn dwindled to nothing after 1765 and by the end of the century England was on balance a net importer of corn except in years of abundant harvest. By the 1840's Britain was feeding between 10 and 15 per cent of its population on foreign wheat.

For most of this period the levels of import and export were artificially lifted or depressed by legislative policy. There was no free overseas trade in corn. It was to be expected of course that a government of a pre-industrial community, with a fairly narrow margin of subsistence, would regard itself as having special legislative responsibilities in connection with the nation's staple food, and the Corn Laws have a long history in England. Adam Smith, with characteristic disapproval of government regulations, wrote scathingly on this point.

---

[1] For these estimates of the contribution of the agricultural industry to gross national product of Great Britain see Deane and Cole, *British Economic Growth*, e.g. p. 291.

The laws concerning corn may everywhere be compared to the laws concerning religion. The people feel themselves so much interested in what relates either to their subsistence in this life, or to their happiness in a life to come, that the government must yield to their prejudices, and, in order to preserve the public tranquillity, establish that system which they approve of. It is upon this account perhaps that we so seldom find a reasonable system established with regard to either of these two capital objects.[1]

Certainly in the years which preceded the repeal of the corn Laws something very like a religious movement developed, a crusade almost, that roused human passions on a scale and an intensity even greater than those roused by the anti-slavery movement.

It was in the second half of the eighteenth century that the Corn Laws became a vital policy issue. During the strong growth of corn exports which characterized the period up to the 1750's the important thing about the Corn Laws was that they provided for a bounty on exports. The fact that importation was also regulated was of very little importance in a country with a relatively stagnant population and a rising agricultural output. 'It was only when the amount paid out became so enormous that the local customs funds were inadequate and the debentures given by customs offices were not honoured by the Treasury in Westminster because of lack of funds'[2] that indignant voices were raised. But this inability of the government to pay the bounties to which it was legislatively committed was a temporary problem. As the home-market expanded, the claims for bounty diminished. In the next few decades the only revisions called for in the Corn Laws were occasional downward and upward adjustments to the price levels at which bounty was paid or duties collected—adjustments which were not intended to do more than take account of changing price levels.

It was in the 1790's that the problem of the Corn Laws began to reflect the class struggle. Bad harvests caused food riots (as they had often enough done before), particularly in the starvation years 1795/6 and 1799/1801. And in the tense atmosphere created by the excesses of the French Revolution these riots assumed a deeper significance than they might otherwise have had. 'Landowners frankly said that it was as

[1] Adam Smith, *Wealth of Nations*, vol. II, p. 42.
[2] D. G. Barnes, *History of the Corn Laws* (1930), p. 288.

important to defend their property from the mob as from Napoleon.'[1] The growing army of labourers and industrial workers became conscious, as never before, that their interests diverged from those of the landed gentry who then determined economic policy; and nowhere was this divergence so marked as in the case of the Corn Laws.

At the end of the war the agricultural interest dug itself in behind a high wall of protection. The bounty had been abolished in 1814; it was already an anachronism. In 1815 the existing sliding scale of duties which permitted the imports of corn to vary with the market price was abandoned in favour of absolute prohibition up to a certain price level (80s. per quarter in the case of wheat) and duty-free admission above that price. For the next 30 years the Corn Laws were one of the key issues in British social and economic policy, a symbol of the conflict between rich and poor, between agriculture and manufacturing industry and between free trade and protection. They kept the price of food high and so depressed real wages. But they provided a measure of protection to what was still the major British industry—agriculture.

War, as it usually does, had brought relative prosperity to agriculture. The price of food soared. Wastes and commons were put under the plough to supply an insatiable demand for food. Farmers with ready cash could afford to improve their horses and cattle, to lime and manure their land, to erect strong buildings and drain bogs. People who had to buy their food suffered a loss of real income in the country as in the town, but on balance it is reasonable to suppose that the countryman held his own better in conditions of food scarcity than his urban counterpart. The landowners enjoying rising rents took much of the burden of war taxation and the landless labourers depended heavily on poor-relief. Except in years of unusual dearth agriculture prospered.

The aftermath of war was another story. Prices collapsed, rents dwindled, profits vanished and capital in stock, land and buildings deteriorated rapidly. For nearly a quarter of a century agriculture endured unrelieved misery; the distress affected landlords, tenant-farmers and labourers together. 'Between 1813 and the accession of Queen Victoria falls one of the

[1] *Ibid.* p. 286.

blackest periods of English farming.'[1] It was this deep agricultural distress rather than the enclosure movement that drove the small yeoman farmer off the land. Unable to weather the violent fluctuations in prices and the crushing burden of poor-rates many small farmers sold up, or got out, and became applicants for pauper allowances. Agricultural labourers were thrown out of work and wages tumbled. 'Those who had saved money or bought a cottage could not be placed in the poor-book: they were obliged to strip themselves bare and become paupers, before they could get employment.'[2]

Reports and inquiries into agricultural distress were numerous and we may tend to exaggerate the extent and depth of the demoralization in the rural areas when we take our evidence from these highly coloured accounts. But the rural riots and the incendiarism that were endemic in this period confirm the view that the morale of the agricultural sector was at a desperately low ebb in the quarter of a century or so that followed Waterloo; and it is worth recalling again that, even as late as 1850, agriculture was still the major British industry. Whatever affected the level of incomes in the agricultural sector affected the standard of living of more than a third of the population of Great Britain during most of the first half of the nineteenth century.

In the circumstances it is difficult to see how any responsible government could have abandoned the Corn Laws and subjected the nation's chief industry to another burden—the chill winds of foreign competition. True, most of the classical economists, following the line set by Adam Smith, were in favour of free trade in corn, as in other commodities. Their most authoritative representative, David Ricardo, argued indeed that only the landlords, whose interest 'is always opposed to the consumer and manufacturer' were the gainers from a policy designed to maintain corn prices.[3] Manufacturers were against the Corn Laws because they regarded them as inflating industrial wages and reducing urban purchasing power for non-food products. Liberal reformers opposed them in the interests of the hungry poor and in opposition to the rich landlords. But even

[1] Ernle, *English Farming Past and Present* (1936 ed.), p. 319.
[2] Ernle, *English Farming Past and Present*, pp. 328–9.
[3] David Ricardo, *The Principles of Political Economy and Taxation*, Everyman ed., ed. Donald Winch, p. 225.

if most of the effective policy makers in parliament and the cabinet had not been members of the landed gentry and aristocracy it would have been surprising if they had wilfully chosen to add to the problems of a desperately depressed agriculture. Actually they did add to its problems by an attempt to reduce the completeness of protection in 1828. The Act of 1828 introduced a sliding-scale duty which varied with the price of wheat in the preceding six weeks. If the averages were below 67s. the rate of duty became virtually prohibitive: above this price the duty fell jerkily from 13s. at 69s. to 1s. at 73s. The effect of this was to push up the price of corn by making its importation into Britain a risky and speculative business and to discourage farmers by introducing unpredictable fluctuations into their incomes.

The debate over the Corn Laws ebbed and flowed in the 1820's and 1830's and flared up in the 'forties. In times of bad trade, merchants and manufacturers called for repeal. In times of good trade they were more concerned with some of the other vital issues of the day—currency reform, for example, or constitutional reform. In the second half of the 1830's, however, the fundamentals of the situation began to change. For one thing, agriculture seemed to be emerging from its desperate depression. It is not clear exactly when or why the improvement took place. Recovery from distress is always less well documented and less spectacular in its effects than the downward plunge. But if we cannot establish the date of the turning-point for agriculture we know that its circumstances changed for the better. In the middle decades of the nineteenth century agriculture enjoyed three to four decades of progress and prosperity. Rents and profits rose and the area under corn expanded. There was an increased use of fertilizers, a spate of improvements in agricultural implements and machinery; there was more expenditure on breeding and housing livestock, on farm buildings and roads and on drainage schemes.

Various reasons have been suggested for this improvement in the economic situation of agriculture. One helpful factor was that the new Poor Law improved its tax position by lifting the burden of the poor-rate. Expenditure on poor-relief, which exceeded £7 millions in 1832, was not much more than £4 millions in 1837. Wages had to rise of course. But it is reasonably certain that farmers lost less in higher wages than they gained from the reduced poor-rate. The Tithe Commutation Act of 1836 also gave some relief to agriculturalists by removing an irksome tax on the annual produce of the land which could be claimed in kind, was in any case highly variable as between one year and another, and was a perpetual source of litigation, and by replacing it by a corn-rent fluctuating predictably with the septennial averages of the prices of wheat, barley and oats.

The second group of reasons that is often advanced for agriculture's rise from the depths attributes it to an increase in efficiency. Farmers responded to extreme adversity, it is claimed, by introducing cost-reducing innovations. The more inefficient farmers were gradually forced out by a succession of crises from which there was never time to recover, and those that were left were, by definition, the fittest to survive. Perhaps the reduction and rationalization of the burdens of the poor-rate and the tithe also encouraged investment of capital in improved methods and hence higher productivity. The Board of Agriculture had been dissolved in 1822, but the Royal Agricultural Society of England, first established in 1838, took its place in disseminating ideas and information to farmers and was according to Ernle 'a powerful agent in restoring prosperity'.[1]

Thirdly, it is evident that the rising rate of urbanization and industrialization was bound to bring with it a reinforced demand for the products of agriculture. Between 1821 and 1841 the net increase in the population of Great Britain who lived in towns with 20,000 or more inhabitants, and hence could not have contributed directly in any appreciable way to their own food supplies, was nearly $2\frac{1}{2}$ million. However poor they were, this represented a powerful demand for the staple foods. In the late 1830's, as the railway age gathered its momentum, it involved enormous wage-payments to sectors of the population with a high propensity to spend their incomes on food and drink.

In the late 1830's a series of deficient harvests brought the Corn Laws dramatically back into the political arena. In September 1838 the Anti-Corn Law Association was set up in Manchester and the great campaign was on. Repeal did not come until 1846, when the most disastrous famine in modern British history swept Ireland and forced the situation. Nevertheless the Anti-Corn Law League had already made political history and had effectively prepared the ground for the capitu-

[1] Ernle, *English Farming Past and Present*, p. 362.

lation. If the League could not have forced repeal without the active co-operation of Sir Robert Peel and Lord John Russell it was doubtful whether Peel could have done more than suspend the duties without the propaganda efforts of the League. Indeed the League was so successful that it succeeded in converting not only a large body of contemporary opinion but also the majority of succeeding economic historians to the wisdom and justice of the case against agricultural protection.

It was essentially a middle-class organization. Control of its activities was vested in a council of substantial subscribers, each subscription carrying with it one vote. It was thus organized in full sympathy with the principles embodied in the 1832 Reform Bill, with the view that policy ought to be guided by the owners of property. Its ideology therefore contrasted strongly with that of Chartism, the other great reforming movement of the late 1830's and 1840's. This was a working-class movement which sought to achieve economic justice by means of parliamentary reform; and the six points of the People's Charter were: manhood suffrage, vote by ballot, payment of Members of Parliament, annual parliamentary elections, equal electoral districts, and the abolition of the property qualification for Members of Parliament. The Chartist revolutionaries, true representatives of the working-class proletariat, suspected the League because their enemies the manufacturers supported it, and because they believed it was part of a conspiracy to keep down money wages. But the Chartists—melodramatic, irresolute, wild leaders of hungry men—lost their fight, and the confident, moralizing respectable members of the Anti-Corn Law League won theirs. 'The attack on the Corn Laws was consciously planned on the model of the anti-slavery agitation, the Corn Laws were attacked not only as an inconvenience but as a sin, and a chorus of ministers of religion was invoked to pronounce the anathema.'[1] The movement had large funds, an efficient centralized office administration and a simple consistency of purpose. In 1841 the decision was taken to contest elections, and the League became a powerful political force, focusing the aims of economists, manufacturers, and liberals of every description; it carried with it the leaders of commercial or industrial opinion and the intelligentsia of the new *laissez-faire*

---

[1] G. Kitson Clark, *The Making of Victorian England* (1962), p. 38.

economy which commerce and industry was beginning to recognize as its true interest.

Their opponents, they claimed, were the rich landlords and the aristocrats. In fact, as Kitson Clark has shown, the strongest objections to repeal came from the small farmers who felt that their whole livelihood was at stake.[1] The gentry and the aristocracy were divided, for in practice they generally had other interests and ambitions in trade and industry and they did not find themselves wholly identified with the fortunes of agriculture. Nor was there yet a strong strategic interest involved. The British navy's control of the seas was undisputed and Britain still supplied the bulk of her own foodstuffs. There was no need to bolster up agriculture as an insurance against total war and enemy blockade.

During the first half of the 1840's the success of the League varied with the state of the harvests and of trade. There is evidence that Peel, who had already shown himself in sympathy with greater freedom of trade, was contemplating a revision of the Corn Laws in 1845. But full repeal was an unlikely prospect. In 1845 and in early 1846 the price of wheat varied between 45s. and 59s., in spite of the failure of the 1845 potato crop. It had been above 70s. in the 1830's. It was when the Irish potato harvest failed, and the British with it, and was accompanied by a general failure of the harvest throughout Europe that the situation became explosive. In 1846, faced with a difficult political situation at home and harrowed by news of mass starvation in Ireland, Peel decided that he must act. The Corn Laws were swept away, without substitute other than a token registration duty of 1s. a quarter on wheat. Cobden hailed Repeal as a victory for the middle-class but Peel's motives had been practical rather than ideological. 'I must be insane if I could have been induced by anything but a sense of public duty to undertake what I have undertaken in this session', he wrote.

The immediate result of Repeal was to break the social tension that had been building up to explosion point in the distressed decades following Waterloo. A resounding victory had been won by the forces of liberalism and reform and there was a kind of a lull in the overt conflict between rich and poor. Chartist activity revived, it is true, with the return of depression

Ibid. p. 8.

in 1846, and in 1847 and 1848 the movement grew. It is doubtful whether, even with competent leadership and a unified purpose based on common interests, Chartism could have achieved any influence in Whitehall at this stage. In the event the Chartists presented hastily compiled petitions that were doomed to be scorned, attempted strikes that were too ill-prepared to be anything but fiascos and threatened government with a force that was pathetically inadequate. There were three main groups of workers who had a real stake in Chartism: a small craftsmen group, the factory operatives of the textile districts, and the domestic outworkers who ranged from the hand-loom weavers to the nailmakers. It was extraordinarily difficult to weld this heterogeneous collection of workers into a unified political movement. All that they had in common was that they were the losers in the great redistribution of incomes that was involved in the Industrial Revolution; and when economic growth gathered momentum on the scale that the railway age made feasible, it became clear that it was not possible to put the clock back. There were too many vested interests in the new industry state, and not all of these were in the upper income groups. So the Chartist movement collapsed in the anticlimax that followed Repeal. The objective of a cheap loaf meant more to the distressed working classes than the vague Chartist aspirations to stand in the way of further economic change.

Nor did agriculture find the expected disaster after Repeal. True, there was an agricultural panic which swept through the corn growers in the years of falling prices 1848–52, but to a large extent this was a consequence of speculative activities which Protection had encouraged. There had been speculation in land, rents had risen to extravagant levels, and it was these extravagances which came to grief with Repeal. Meanwhile the British farmer was still effectively insulated from severe foreign competition by geography. It was difficult to import large quantities of corn from great distances without running up heavy transport costs and there were few cheap sources of supply outside Europe, where supplies were limited by local restrictionist policies. At home the level of demand for the products of agriculture and methods of cultivation was steadily rising. Demand went up simply because population went on growing. Between 1841 and 1851 the population of Great

Britain went up from 18½ millions to nearly 21 millions, and went on rising to over 23 millions in 1861. There was a vast migration between country and town which, when added to the high rate of natural increase of the urban areas, meant large additions to the number of non-food-producers who had to be fed. Between 1841 and 1851 over 700,000 people migrated into the towns and colliery districts of England and Wales, and between 1851 and 1861 over 600,000 more flooded into the towns. By then, moreover, British farmers had reached what seemed to be the limit of their cultivable acreage. The enclosure movement was over. There were no more wastes and commons which could be put to profitable use. On the other hand, farmers who were willing to innovate, to put capital into drainage and fertilizers, were assured of a huge and expanding market. 'The age of farming by extension of area had ended: that of farming by intension of capital had begun.'[1]

In the 1840's there were considerable advances in scientific research on agriculture. The most urgent need of the moist islands of Britain was for drainage, in striking contrast to many modern developing countries where the need is for irrigation. Drainage experiments perfected in the 1820's and 1830's led to millions of acres being improved in the 1840's. The introduction of a clay drainage-pipe in 1843 and of a pipe-making machine in 1845 provided a cheap and effective conduit. 'Within the next few years two large public loans for drainage...were taken up and treble the amount was spent by private owners or advanced by private companies.'[2] Drainage gave the clay farmers longer seasons and earlier, heavier crops; it raised their yields and lowered their costs by permitting more effective use of manures and fertilizers.

At the same time a new alliance between agriculture and science was beginning to yield results of practical use to farmers throughout the country. The German chemist Liebig published in 1840 his famous book which set out the relations between the nutrition of plants and the composition of the soil. The first cargo of Peruvian guano had been shipped to Liverpool in 1835 and six years later the import was still only 1,700 tons. But by 1847 the importation amounted to 220,000 tons. Improving farmers had begun to buy their fertilizing agents rather than

---

[1] Ernle, *English Farming Past and Present*, p. 364. [2] *Ibid.* p. 367.

to rely on farm-produced manure; and the chemists and the geologists were evolving new types of fertilizers. In 1843, for example, Lawes set up a factory to produce superphosphate of lime. A new attitude to farming grew up, not merely among the owners of the great estates as in the eighteenth century but among the mass of small farmers. A farmer who had paid good money for fertilizers was unlikely to allow them to fertilize weeds or to waste in undrained land. Whereas the old type small farmers had been content to raise enough food to feed their families and buy them the essential clothing and furniture they needed from the manufacturing sector, the new farmer was prepared to plough back part of his return into improving next year's yield.

It must not be supposed however that all this happened at once, that the results of scientific research were immediately converted into successful innovations. There were many experiments that failed, many farmers who applied unsuitable fertilizers which did more harm than good or who wasted their capital in sinking drains that were too deep. At the time of Repeal high farming was still the exception rather than the rule, and the majority of farmers made no more effort to increase the productiveness of their land or to modernize their techniques than their fathers had done before them.

Perhaps indeed it required the sharp shock of complete abandonment of agricultural protection, and the wretched years of falling prices which followed it, to put the British farmers' opportunities and limitations in their true perspective. Many tenant farmers got out in the years of depression and left their farms on the hands of their landlords. But there is evidence of a significant change in attitudes not only on the part of the individual farmer, but also on the part of the large landowners. It seems clear that those in charge of the large estates were paying close attention to the best agricultural knowledge of the day and were doing their best to pass this on to their tenants. The Royal Agricultural Society ('the heart and brain of British agriculture', according to Ernle) became a clearing house for the best scientific research in agricultural techniques. An expanding class of professional men—land-agents and solicitors —managed the great estate on modern lines.

In effect, from 1853 onwards, the prospects for British agriculture were seen to have changed radically for the better.

Fundamentally this was because of the improvement in techniques and in the conditions of demand but, there were some special circumstances in the early 1850's that set the industry off on an upward trend. Expanding trade and manufactures (stimulated by rising prices which were associated with the gold discoveries) meant a swiftly rising demand for agricultural products. The seasons were kind in the 1850's. The Crimean War closed the Baltic to Russian corn. Rents rose, farming profits rose and large sums were spent on drainage (money could be borrowed for agricultural drainage under the Act which Peel passed at the same time as the repeal of the Corn Laws) and on agricultural buildings. The general level of farming rose rapidly to the best standard of individual farmers in the Protection era and the British agricultural industry reached the all-time peak of its productive capacity. The decade 1853–62 has been called with reason 'the golden age of English agriculture' and it was not indeed until the last quarter of the nineteenth century that the industry began to feel the full effects of the abandonment of agricultural protection.

In sum, it was in the second quarter of the nineteenth century that the balance of power, economic and political, shifted finally from agriculture to manufacturing industry. In the first three decades of the century agriculture and manufacturing industry gradually changed places in relative importance, measured by the number of jobs they provided. Measured by the volume of incomes generated the mining–manufacturing–building group of industries had taken the lead in the years of agricultural distress that followed Waterloo: and in the second quarter of the century agriculture's contribution to the British national product fell from a quarter to about a fifth.

The change in the balance of economic power was reflected in and assisted by changes in the balance of political power. It was the industrious middle classes—that comfortable army of artisans, clerks, shopkeepers, merchants, bankers and industrialists—that were the chief beneficiaries of industrialization. The labouring poor in town and country, factory and farm, suffered equally from harvest failure and trade depression, and found it as difficult to keep their families fed and clothed as their fathers and grandfathers had done in the eighteenth century. It was not their day and their leaders could expect no more response to their claims than riot squads, imprisonment and transportation. But for the middle classes it was a period of political recognition and growing prestige. The aristocratic leaders of government listened earnestly to the advice of middle-class economists, and developed personal interests in business and industry that were at least as important as their interests in land and agriculture. The 1832 Reform Act did not, as is sometimes claimed, put the middle classes in power in Britain, but it did admit them to the electorate and it did formally admit their right to influence economic policy. Their supreme triumph, the result of their influence, was the repeal of the Corn Laws. It was then that the right of the agricultural industry for special treatment—a right that goes without saying in a pre-industrial economy—was formally rejected by a community which had accepted the full consequences of the industrial revolution.

Once the choice had been irrevocably made, the way was open to the great international specialization of the late nineteenth century. When the railway and the steamship made the fruitful prairies of North and South America accessible to the British consumer, the numbers engaged in British agriculture began to drop in absolute as well as in relative terms. Not until that happened did the consequences of Repeal finally work themselves out and industrialization become complete.

CHAPTER 13

THE ROLE OF GOVERNMENT

It is usual to regard the British industrial revolution as a spontaneous event, and to the extent that the outcome of the first industrial revolution was something which no government could have been expected consciously to contrive it was indeed spontaneous. But it should not be supposed therefore that government's role in the process was entirely passive. On the contrary, then—as now—the ineptitude or competence of governments was an important fact in retarding or accelerating economic growth. Changes in the conditions of supply and demand under which the different industries operated, called for, and produced, changes in economic legislation. Failure to legislate could be as important as new legislation in assisting or hindering the structural change which was essential to effective industrialization.

One of the myths that has grown up about the industrial revolution in England is that it happened in the absence of rather than because of government intervention, that government's role in the process was to efface itself as rapidly as possible in order to allow private enterprise to pursue its beneficent part in generating sustained economic growth. A famous passage by Adam Smith, in a chapter advocating free trade, provided the rationale for this legend by arguing that the maximization of private profit by individuals involves the maximization of national income.

As every individual...endeavours as much as he can both to employ his capital in the support of domestic industry and so to direct that industry that its produce may be of the greatest value; every individual necessarily labours to render the annual revenue of the society as great as he can. He generally, indeed, neither intends to promote the public interest nor knows how much he is promoting it. By preferring the support of domestic to that of foreign industry he intends only his own security: and by directing that industry in such a manner as its produce may be of the greatest value, he intends only his own gain, and he is in this, as in many other cases, led by an invisible hand to promote an end which was no part of his intention.[1]

This was the 'doctrine of the invisible hand'. Adam Smith used it to justify free trade. His followers developed further the philosophy of *laissez-faire*, the view that the business of government was to leave things alone, and adopted wholeheartedly the view that the unrestricted operation of private enterprise was the most effective way of securing the maximum rate of economic growth.

Two questions need to be considered in this connection. On the one hand, how far was it true that the doctrine of *laissez-faire* was brought into full operation in the course of the English industrial revolution? And on the other hand, was it true that the British government's main contribution to the industrial revolution was to leave things alone?

To begin with, then, did *laissez-faire* triumph? There is no question at all that between 1760 and 1850 a mass of governmental rules and restrictions on economic activity, many of them dating from medieval times, were swept out of the statute book. At the beginning of the period, for example, there was a whole network of restrictions on the mobility of labour and capital. By the Statute of Apprentices a person had to serve seven years before he could follow a trade and there were many local limitations on the number of apprentices. Adam Smith, in a bitter attack on the privileges of corporations reeled off an indignant list of them: 'In Sheffield no master cutler can have more than one apprentice at a time...In Norfolk and Norwich no master weaver can have more than two apprentices...No master hatter can have more than two apprentices anywhere in England, or in the English plantations.'[2] The wages of London tailors were subject to a legislatively prescribed maximum which could be varied by the Justices of the Peace at Quarter Sessions.

Then there were the laws which restricted the mobility and use made of capital. The Usury Laws, for example, set a limit of 5 per cent on the rate which could be charged for loans. The effect of this was to divert capital from industrial and commercial

[1] Adam Smith, *Wealth of Nations* (Cannan Edition), vol. I, p. 421.
[2] Adam Smith, *Wealth of Nations* (Cannan Edition), vol. I, p. 121.

uses, where there were risks and the interest limits were too low to compensate for the risks, to the government; for the government was not subject to any legal restriction when it made new issues, and the price of existing government paper could fall to an extent which made its effective return to a prospective investor exceed any commercial alternative. There were also the laws regulating the organization of capital and enterprise. The Bubble Act of 1720 prohibited the formation of joint-stock companies except under special dispensation granted only by Act of Parliament. 'It has often been said that the Bubble Act impeded for more than a hundred years the use of large-scale manufacturing businesses in England.'[1] Then there were the numerous regulations imposed by the Navigation Acts which prohibited imports from certain countries except in British ships, manned largely by British crews; and there were the various foreign-trade monopolies held by the chartered companies, though these were beginning to dissolve by the middle of the eighteenth century.

In addition there existed a variety of regulations which specified, often in meticulous detail, how things should be manufactured or put on sale. The object was to exert some control over their quality in the interests of the consumer at home or abroad. Woollen and linen manufacturers for example had, from time immemorial, to submit to a mass of laws concerning the length and width and weight of the cloths they made. Many of these had lapsed by the middle of the eighteenth century—cotton manufactures, being relatively unimportant until towards the end of the eighteenth century, were happily free from such restrictions. But as late as 1765 an Act was passed to control the quality of West Riding woollen cloth 'for preventing frauds in certifying the content of the cloth and for preserving the credit of the said manufacture at foreign markets'. This Act 'provided a whole hierarchy of searchers, inspectors and supervisors to certify the length and quality of the cloths, to see to it that they had not been overstretched on the tenters'.[2] But 'older than the oldest regulations which had been laid upon the manufacture of cloth, so old indeed as to be dateless—a kind of economic common law—was the Assize of Bread'.[3] This

---

[1] Ashton, *The Eighteenth Century*, p. 119.
[2] Clapham, *Economic History*, vol. I, p. 338.
[3] *Ibid.* p. 338.

prescribed the weight and price of bread and the bakers' margins, it legislated against adulteration and it prescribed that bakers should keep legal weights and measures. Finally there was the complicated system of Protection which placed a variety of restrictions on the free flow of overseas trade. There were absolute prohibitions of export (such as wool) and complete embargoes on some imports (such as printed calicoes) and high rates of duties on most others. In 1759 the standard rate of tax on imports had reached 25 per cent and, in spite of William Pitt's efforts to rationalize the tax system, the effect of the War of American Independence and of the French wars was to push up the effective level of duties.

Of course we should not fall into the trap of supposing that the existence on the statute book of a mass of medieval restrictions on economic activity meant that these restrictions were effective. Take for example the apprenticeship laws. These did not apply at all to new crafts not visualized in the original Elizabethan Act, and some of the new towns were able to escape them almost completely. Manchester, Birmingham and Wolverhampton did so, for example. Moreover, where the Statute of Apprentices was enforced it was often a source of cheap labour or premium income to the employer rather than a means of training craftsmen. William Hutton, for example, 'served his first apprenticeship in the silk mills of Derby starting when he was too small to reach the machines without the aid of wooden pattens fixed to his feet'.[1] But this was no more than child labour, for he did not learn the kind of trade that he could practise as a man.

Nor, as Ashton has pointed out, did the Bubble Act hinder the formation of joint-stock companies in industries where the scale of operations made them particularly valuable.

It was still possible to set up a joint stock by private Act: the canal companies were brought into being in this way. And the device of the equitable trust under which mutual covenants were made between subscribers and trustees nominated by them, led to a growth of what were, in effect, companies in other fields of enterprise. All these had a joint stock continuity of life and transferable shares; and late in the century some of them found it possible to limit the liability of members.[2]

[1] D. Marshall, *English People in the Eighteenth Century* (1956).
[2] Ashton, *The Eighteenth Century*, p. 119.

As for the Usury Laws, it is difficult to believe that they were not often evaded in practice and easily too, by mutual consent, wherever borrower and lender were both concerned to complete the transaction on terms that equated the supply and demand for loanable funds. In so far as a legally binding contract was necessary it was easy enough for the borrower to undertake to repay a larger sum than he had received and thus in effect to pay a higher rate of interest than was formally recorded in the the contract.

Similarly there were ways of evading the restrictions on overseas trade. The prohibition on the export of wool was regularly evaded by sending it to Holland or France via Scotland or, more often still, by smuggling it out at night in small boats to ships lying off shore. There were also ways of getting wool out of the country by making it look like something else (e.g. in bales of drapery) or in the luggage of passengers. A flourishing smuggling trade flowed in the other direction too. Valuable and relatively light commodities like tea, tobacco, wines and spirits, lace, silk and printed calicoes probably came in in larger volume in the smugglers' cargoes than they did in the declared trade. The smuggler was a respected member of the community. Adam Smith spoke of him, for example, as

a person who, though no doubt highly blameable for violating the laws of his country, is frequently incapable of violating those of natural justice, and would have been, in every respect, an excellent citizen, had not the laws of his country made that a crime which nature never intended to be so...Not many people are scrupulous about smuggling when, without perjury, they can find any easy and safe opportunity of doing so. To pretend to have any scruple about buying smuggled goods, though a manifest encouragement to the violation of the revenue laws, and to the perjury which almost always attends it, would in most countries be regarded as one of those pedantic pieces of hypocrisy which, instead of gaining credit with anybody, serve only to expose the person who affects to practice them, to the suspicion of being a greater knave than most of his fellows.[1]

How large the smuggling trade was in commodities subject to high duties may be judged from what happened when the import duty on tea was lowered from 119 per cent in 1784 to $12\frac{1}{2}$ per cent. Within a year the amount entered for home consumption had increased from under 5 million lb. to nearly

[1] Adam Smith, *Wealth of Nations*, vol. II, p. 382.

$16\frac{1}{2}$ million lb. It had quite suddenly become unprofitable to smuggle tea, which immediately began to flow through the ordinary legal channels of trade in increasing volume.

In effect, then, many of the restrictions on economic activity that were on the English statute book on the eve of the industrial revolution were more tiresome than effective. The smuggler ran the risk of forfeiture and heavy penalty, but with the rest of the community on his side he stood a good chance of outwitting the customs men. The apprenticeship and usury laws were more often broken than kept. Many of the industrial regulations would have required the apparatus of a modern police state for their enforcement and were safely ignored. When the laws regarding Yorkshire woollens were investigated by a Select Committee in 1821 one manufacturer after another cheerfully admitted to being a habitual law-breaker.

Moreover policy makers were becoming aware of the fact that over-repressive measures defeated their own ends: a mild regulation effectively enforced was more useful than a severe restriction which no one respected. In the last two or three decades of the eighteenth century, British manufacturers facing expanding overseas markets, and increasing opportunities for technical progress, had less incentive than ever before to lobby for government interference with the free flow of international trade. At the same time Pitt, anxious to improve the revenue-yielding qualities of his import duties, began to replace some of the prohibitive duties by taxes that slashed the smuggler's return and diverted trade into legal revenue-earning channels. The tax on tea was one example. By the time the French wars broke out in the 1790's, British customs rates, though still high, were generally quite moderate by contemporary standards for other countries.

The war, however, created an entirely new situation. On the one hand, the excesses of the French Revolution and the present national danger rendered the ruling classes more nervous than they would otherwise have been and the laws against workers' combinations were tightened up. On the other hand, the search for revenue to meet war expenditures reversed the trend towards a reduction in Protection. After the war the search went on, for the unpopular wartime income tax was hastily dropped and left a large gap in government revenue to be filled by indirect taxation. British customs rates accordingly soared during the war and its aftermath to reach in 1822 what must

have been an all-time peak of 64 per cent of the market value
of net imports. According to Imlah 'they became so much more
severe in weight and effect after the war that they constituted
virtually a new system'.[1] There were chronic trade-deficits
throughout this period and it is reasonable to suppose that the
heavy burden of Protectionism in post-war Britain hindered
the recovery of British industry and intensified the social distress
involved in economic change.

The traditional explanation for what happened next was that
successive governments, recognizing the error of their interventions in economic affairs, inspired by Benthamite utilitarians
on the one hand and by the exponents of Adam Smith's doctrine
of the 'invisible hand' on the other, gradually relaxed the dead
weight of legislative restrictions on private enterprise and gave
the economy free rein. By 1850, so goes the story, the triumph
of the *laissez-faire* philosophy of government was virtually complete in Britain.

What was the basis for this view? First of course, there was
the fact that a large number of restrictions on economic activity
and on the free flow of trade were reduced or removed. The
apprenticeship clauses of the Elizabethan labour law were
among the first to go in 1814. The East India Company had
lost its monopoly of the India trade in 1813, but because it
retained its monopoly of the China trade it continued to withhold
from British merchants, not only a potential market, but a key
point in a lucrative triangular trade—raw cotton and opium
from India to China and silver, silks, spices and tea from China
to Europe. This monopoly finally lapsed with the end of the
company's charter in 1834. A number of industrial regulations
were repealed in the 1820's. First the Yorkshire woollen-cloth
regulations were set aside, followed rapidly by the laws regulating the Scots linen manufacture. Then in 1824 the Acts
'relating to the use of those hides in making boots and shoes and
for the better preventing the damaging of raw hides in the
flaying thereof' were repealed. The bread regulations had a
chequered history in the post-war period; they were revived in
bad times and they decayed in good. Bread was relatively cheap
in the 1820's and the Assize was repealed in London in 1822;
it was moribund in the provinces though not finally repealed
until in 1836 an Act finally abolished the power and obligation

[1] Imlah, *Economic Elements in the Pax Britannica*, p. 115.

of the J.P.s to regulate either bakers' profits or the price of bread.

The usury laws also came up for review in the post-war years. During most of the eighteenth century the market rate of interest on well-secured loans was below rather than above the statutory maximum. But after twenty years of government borrowing to meet the needs of a major war and twenty years of the associated inflation, the market rate rose above 5 per cent. It was the mortgage market that suffered by this, for the legal formalities in a mortgage loan were of a kind that made evasion difficult. The result was to add to the difficulties of landowners, hard-pressed by the fall in corn prices. They were forced to borrow from the insurance companies in roundabout ways which meant in effect that they were subject to an interest rate of 10 per cent or more. A Select Committee reported in 1818 and Ricardo, amongst others, testified to the fact that the usury laws were generally evaded. But the market rate was already falling and in the 1820's (except in the crisis of 1826) the statutory limitation gave no real trouble to borrowers and lenders. The Bank Charter Act of 1833 permitted the Bank of England to disregard the usury laws and later the building societies were permitted the same dispensation, so that when the usury laws were finally repealed by Gladstone in 1854 they passed almost unnoticed except by the mortgage market.

In some ways too the solutions which were found to the money and banking problems of the post-war period represented a movement in the direction of *laissez-faire*. On the one hand, there was the relaxation of restrictions on joint-stock and branch banking. On the other, there was the 'automatic' principle of monetary policy which was eventually embodied in the Bank Charter Act of 1844. For what Peel, acting under the inspiration of the 'currency' school of thought, sought to do with this Act was to set up a mechanism of currency control which was as automatic as it would have been for a purely metallic currency. In principle then, by raising or lowering the Bank Rate (and hence contracting or expanding the note issue) in reponse to the demand for the pound sterling, the Bank would be freed from any active responsibility for currency control. All it had to do was to obey the rules of the game, and these said quite simply that if gold was flowing out of the country the money supply should be contracted: and if it was flowing in it should be expanded.

Some advance, too, was made in liberalizing labour relations in the post-war decades. The Combination Acts passed in 1799 and 1800, when embryonic trade unions were seen as cover for political agitation and subversive activity, were repealed in 1824, as were the eighteenth-century laws preventing the emigration of artisans and the export of tools and machinery. But the strikes that followed the repeal of the Combination Laws revived the government's anxieties and in 1825 (a year of high food prices and serious labour unrest) a new Combination Act was passed which, while it established the legality of workers' associations for purposes of collective negotiation of wages or hours of work, in effect forbade them to organize strikes.

The spectacular triumph of *laissez-faire* came, however, in the field of foreign trade. What many people have in mind when they talk of the triumph of *laissez-faire* in the nineteenth century is the retreat from Protection and the adoption of a complete free-trade policy. It was in this area of economic policy that Adam Smith and his disciples were so sure of their ground and were beginning to make headway before the end of the eighteenth century. The trouble was, however, that war checked their progress and in the aftermath of war it was not easy to pursue a liberalizing policy; though people like Robinson at the Board of Trade were aware of the fact that tariffs on imports, for example, tended to choke off exports by depriving foreigners of the purchasing power they needed to buy British goods. After the experience of wartime food shortages the Corn Laws were seen as a vital security measure and even the industrialists had lost their nerve. So that although Huskisson made some progress in the 1820's and Peel had laid the basis for a more extensive reduction in the tariff system by his income-tax plans of the early 1840's, it was not until the Irish famine forced repeal of the Corn Laws in 1846 that the retreat from Protection became an irreversible movement. In just four years Peel had cut tariffs by about 25 per cent and brought the average rate on imports down to 21 per cent—not far above the 1790 rate. The process he had started was carried on by his successors. In 1849 the Navigation Acts were repealed and in 1854 foreign ships were permitted to engage in the United Kingdom coasting trade. Steadily the duties on the necessities of life were reduced or abolished and free trade was effectively completed by the budget of 1860, which repealed the duties on 371 articles.

That the adoption of free trade was very much to the

advantage of British industry at this stage there is no doubt. By the 1850's falling costs and prices in British industry and agriculture made British producers almost invulnerable to foreign competiton except in very special and unusual cases. They were assured by their own superior efficiency of an expanding share in world markets and by rising incomes and population of an expanding domestic market. What mattered, then, was that potential customers should not be starved of purchasing power by restrictions on U.K. imports and that no possible excuse for retaliation should be offered to those who might be tempted to exclude British goods from foreign markets.

In sum, then, between 1780 and 1860 a great many restrictions on economic enterprise were done away with. Was this really due, as Arnold Toynbee would have had us believe, to the triumph of the doctrine of the 'invisible hand'? Did it reflect the deliberate self-effacement of government in favour of a policy of complete *laissez-faire*? Was the British government really a passive agent in the British industrial revolution?

When we come to consider the motives and acts of successive governments during this period the traditional interpretation of the triumph of *laissez-faire* seems to be altogether too facile. For one thing, many of the restrictions that were on the statute book were of a kind which the government of the late eighteenth and early nineteenth century was manifestly incapable of enforcing; and the first restrictions to go were often those that were least effective. A government without an effective police force or a widespread political intelligence system could not enforce regulations against combinations of employers or workers, nor could it intervene effectively in establishing standards of quality control. The cost of collecting an incoherent multitude of customs duties was immense, and in many instances must have outweighed the revenue that was extracted from an unwilling and evasive people. When the profits of smuggling were so evident and widespread it was unlikely that the scattered groups of customs and excise men stationed along the English coastline could have enforced many of the embargoes or prohibitive duties. The first thing any government had to do if it was to intervene purposefully in the conduct of economic affairs was to come to terms with its opportunities and its limitations.

It was indeed as government took a more and more positive and serious role in the economy that it began to streamline its administrative machinery, to jettison regulations that it had no hope of enforcing, to formulate a considered view on what form its interventions should take and to sharpen its powers in the areas where it wanted to exert most influence. The beginnings of a purposeful government economic policy can be traced back to Pitt the Younger. Before the French wars came to substitute a single aim of economic policy—victory—for the complex aims of peace, he started out in all seriousness to rationalize the government's finances. He experimented with a variety of new taxes, he reduced certain prohibitive duties and thus diverted the smugglers' profits into the national exchequer, he established a sinking fund for the reduction of the national debt and 'he preached as strict an economy in the public services as Gladstone was to do in the middle of the nineteenth century'.[1]

A quarter of a century of war and its aftermath, accompanied as it was by radical changes in economic and social structure and in the size and distribution of the population, transformed the economic policy problems of government. By the 1820's Britain was no longer a pre-industrial economy. It was a changing, growing industrial complex in which the old moulds of economic and social behaviour were being rapidly broken before the new moulds had begun to set. Riots in town and country spoke of increasing economic distress and an urgent need for economic and social discipline which could only be supplied by the central authority. It was no longer possible to leave such matters to the J.P.s and the parish authorities. There was need for a national economic policy evolved and applied at the national level. This could only be provided by a central authority with a clearer conception of its functions and responsibilities then had been present for most of the eighteenth century.

In effect then, the nineteenth-century government's role in promoting economic well-being for the nation at large had to be more deliberate and positive and was also more difficult than it had been in pre-industrial times. This was so for a number of reasons. First because the great war had put enormous responsibilities on the central government. It had changed the structure and purpose of the nation's economic activity and in so doing it had given government a directive role. As in the great

[1] Briggs, *Age of Improvement*, p. 118.

wars of the twentieth century, the lessons learned in the practical experience of economic planning for victory were important in conditioning the attitudes and techniques of the post-war governments. Secondly the post-war dislocation was as violent an upheaval as war itself and central government was confronted unequivocally with its responsibilities in trying to keep the economic and social fabric from disintegrating under the strains then placed upon it. Thirdly it was by now evident that industrialization brought with it acute social distress which it was government's responsibility to alleviate. Fourthly it was also evident that the regionalized economy of the eighteenth century was becoming a national economy and this put additional responsibilities on central government. The growth of cities and of factory industry meant that there were more and more people for whom a slump implied absolute destitution: the growth in the importance of international trade meant that more and more often the causes of economic instability at home were generated by conditions which might be affected by government economic policy rather than, as in the past, by climatic uncertainties and other Acts of God.

The British governments of the 1820's and 1830's were not all equally competent in dealing with the economic-policy problems with which they were confronted, but that they were aware of them there is no doubt. They tried to evolve consistent policies in the light of the teachings of the leading economists. Among the audiences who heard McCulloch give the first Ricardo memorial lectures were Huskisson, Canning, Peel and Liverpool. They did not always take the undiluted advice of the economists but they did realize more than any of their eighteenth-century predecessors that the execution of the appropriate economic policy required serious thought and positive action.

So too did some of the civil servants who were concerned with the implementation of economic policy. The personnel of the Board of Trade, for example, was being chosen more and more for its professional qualifications than for its personal and political sympathies. This was another departure from the eighteenth-century pattern where government officials had characteristically been the lackeys of the landed aristocracy. It was the beginning of a new kind of bureaucracy, an officialdom from which today's professional civil service can trace direct descent. Unlike today's bureaucracy, however, the Board of Trade in the first half of the nineteenth century saw no need to disguise its views on economic policy beneath a mask of neutralism. 'In the eighteen-twenties the Board of Trade had led the movement for commercial liberalism.'[1] Its tradition of dogmatic free trade left no doubt about where it stood in the Corn Law controversy and in the final triumph of free trade in the 1840's and 1850's. For reasons which were just as doctrinaire, the Poor Law Commissioners of the early 1830's made no attempt to be objective about their analysis of the evidence on the operations of the old Poor Law. They believed, with Malthus and the exponents of the Wages Fund doctrine that the Speenhamland system of outdoor relief perpetuated the poverty it was intended to relieve by depressing earnings and stimulating the growth of population. Instead of analysing systematically the results of the elaborate questionnaire that they sent out to the parishes, they selected the facts and opinions that supported their view 'so as to impeach the existing administration on predetermined lines...what evidence they did present consisted of little more than picturesque anecdotes of maladministration'.[2]

The fact was that as industrialization proceeded the state was intervening more deeply and more effectively in the economy than it had ever done before. There was indeed a revolution in the technique and philosophy of government that was at least as significant in shaping and accelerating the first industrial revolution as the other transformations which we have come to regard as part of it. It was of the same kind too. That is to say it was a revolution in organization and behaviour and in the personnel taking the effective policy decisions; it involved an increase in the scale of operations and in the division and specialization of labour; it was marked by a new readiness to experiment with techniques and to make practical use of developments in the natural sciences; and it developed a self-sustaining momentum. These were the distinguishing characteristics of the industrial revolution itself.

The odd thing was that a revolution in government which represented the beginnings of collectivism and of the modern

[1] Lucy Brown, *Board of Trade and the Free Trade Movement 1830–42* (1958), p. 21.
[2] Blaug, 'The Myth of the Old Poor Law and the Making of the New', *Journal of Economic History* (1963).

welfare state should have taken place in a community whose articulate political prejudices were flatly in opposition to such a development. It happened because of the existence of strong underlying pressures which proved in the end irresistible. There were, for example, the ideological pressures associated with the spread of utilitarian doctrines amongst educated people. These looked on the face of them as though they were going to weaken the power of the state, for they were in close sympathy with Adam Smith's doctrine of the 'invisible hand' and were constantly attacking the complicated and ineffective network of government regulations which characterized the traditional pre-industrial society. The real objective of the philosophical radicals, however, turned out to be not freedom from government but freedom from inefficient government; and efficiency meant effective and purposeful intervention in the economic system as opposed to ineffective and aimless intervention. The growth of humanitarianism was another factor in the situation and so too were the historical events or revelations (the epidemics, the shipwrecks, the recurrent human disasters) that shocked this humanitarian feeling into an impulse of reform. There was also the growth in scale and intensity of social problems in a rapidly changing, rapidly growing economy, and there was the growth of knowledge about possible ways of dealing with these problems together with a growth in the sense of social responsibility amongst those who had such knowledge. These were the underlying pressures which ensured that a generation reared in the doctrines of *laissez-faire* should systematically lay the foundations of modern collectivism.

The point of no return in this revolution in government seems to have been reached in the 1830's. The duty of Government to intervene in the economy on behalf of socially oppressed groups had already been accepted. Hanway's Act to protect the chimney-sweeps from exploitation went through in 1788. Sir Robert Peel's Act to control the conditions of work of pauper children was passed in 1802, and the 1803 Passenger Act laid down a system of regulations for the protection of poor emigrants. Moreover, in the decades immediately following the Napoleonic wars, the initiative in evolving economic and social legislation tended to pass from the dedicated private Member of Parliament to government and the permanent civil service. The Board of Trade was dominated by the economists who were dogmatically sure that they knew what ought to be done about overseas trade policy. The Benthamite utilitarians 'dominated royal commissions and Parliamentary committees by their superb confidence that they knew exactly and scientifically what was to be done'.[1] Such developments were the beginning of the retreat from *laissez-faire*; but they had as yet no revolutionary consequences because they were completely ineffective.

Then in the 1830's the reforming legislation began to include provision for inspection and enforcement by means of state officials with executive powers. The first of these were the factory inspectors. The 1802 Factory Act, which had achieved little to protect the 'health and morals of apprentices' because it had no enforcement machinery, was replaced by the 1833 Factory Act which set up a central authority and a subordinate local inspectorate with powers to make and enforce regulations. It was followed by a series of similar enforceable statutes (chimney-sweeps in 1840, mines in 1842, ten hours 1847–50, and so on) relating to workers' safety and education and conditions of work generally. The first emigration officer was appointed at Liverpool in 1833 to supervise the enforcement of the passenger acts and to work with the local magistrate in seeing that justice was meted out to offenders, and in 1834 six other ports accepted emigration officers appointed by the Colonial Office. These were the first of the expanding corps of government inspectors who were to do much to enforce, experiment with, and formulate social legislation in the nineteenth century.

In some spheres the developments of the 1830's went further in the direction of bureaucratization than the nation was prepared to tolerate permanently. The old poor law, for example, which had left so much to the discretion of the local authorities was replaced by a new poor law designed to liquidate the problem of poverty by administrative action. In this it did not succeed: the causes of poverty lay deeper than the Poor Law Commissioners knew. But it represented a revolution in social administration. It created a new set of local government units in the form of the parish unions and it laid down a nationally standardized policy of relief, imposed and enforced by a set of bureaucrats with no parliamentary respon-

[1] J. Bartlett Brebner, 'Laissez-faire and State Intervention in Nineteenth Century Britain', in *Essays in Economic History*, ed. Carus-Wilson, vol. III, p. 256.

sibility. Relief was administered by boards of guardians elected locally, but these were under the direct supervision of the three national Poor Law Commissioners. The Poor Law Commission lost its bureaucratic independence in 1847 when it became the Poor Law Board under a responsible minister in Parliament, but central government responsibility for preventing social destitution had been irrevocably established. A start had also been made with the business of organizing an effective national health service, for the new poor law arranged for the appointment of paid medical officers to unions or groups of unions who gave free medical care to all aged and infirm and permanently sick or disabled persons in receipt of relief. The attempt to centralize the administration of public health which was embodied in Chadwick's Public Health Act of 1848 also went further than contemporary society could digest, and in 1854 'the forces of dirt and decentralization triumphed' when Chadwick, the dictorial reformer was dismissed. But this was a problem that could be and was dealt with at the level of the big cities, which faced the problem in its most critical form. It could also be supervised and guided more delicately at the national level. The first Medical Officer of Health was appointed in Liverpool in 1847, and when the General Board of Health was abolished in 1858 its health functions were transferred to the Privy Council with Dr Simon (an equally dedicated but less overbearing reformer than Chadwick) as its adviser. In time health inspectors were appointed to Simon's staff to travel the country in order to see that the local authorities were complying with the Sanitary Acts.

Nor was it only in the social sphere that government intervention in the changing economy became direct and decisive. British railways were built by private enterprise, but they were supported and controlled by a whole panoply of state regulation embodied in acts of Parliament. If the railway promoters 'could make out their case before a private bill committee, then they were given, like the canals, that really great "interference with property", the right to buy land compulsorily, subject however always to elaborate safeguards—sworn and impartial commissioners or a jury to see that the to-be-expropriated landlord was not to be imposed upon'.[1] By the Railway Acts

---

[1] Clapham, *Economic History*, vol. I, p. 413.

of 1840 and 1842 a Railway Department of the Board of Trade was set up and three officials were appointed to inspect the operations of the railway companies and to prosecute them if they failed to conform with the law. These inspectors had freedom of access to all railway projects, the right to postpone the opening of lines until they were satisfied with them and the duty of deciding inter-company disputes about the management of through traffic.

So too the Bank Charter Act, which by creating an 'automatic' currency control system looks on the face of it like another piece of *laissez-faire* legislation, was really another sphere in which government used private enterprise as a tool but accepted ultimate responsibility itself. When the governor and deputy governor of the Bank of England, for example, were examined by the Select Committee on Commercial Distress which sat in 1847–8, they agreed that the Bank Charter Act had relieved the Bank of any responsibility for the circulation. It was their job to follow a set of mechanical rules and government's job to step in when the crisis was such that automatic adjustment failed to restore equilibrium. The responsibility, they said, lay with the law, not with the Bank. Even in the sphere of foreign trade government was ready to take decisive action. The Foreign Office, for example, accepted responsibility for the political control of trade. When the Chinese took action against opium smugglers in 1840 the British navy blockaded the Canton estuary and in 1842 the Chinese had to admit British merchants on the British government's terms. The church itself came within the sphere of government action and was duly subordinated. The exclusive privileges of the Anglican clergy were steadily whittled away and grants in aid of British education went both to Anglican and non-Anglican schools in steadily increasing amounts from 1833 onwards.

Nor was it only the central government that was strengthening its power and its will to intervene in the conduct of private enterprise. Local government, particularly the government of the large new urban concentrations, began to assume wider responsibilities in this respect. The social problems tended to appear in their most acute form at the local level. It was on the initiative of the mayor and corporation of Liverpool that the Colonial Secretary appointed the first emigration officer, for example. When the Municipal Corporation Act of 1835 reformed all existing corporations and extended the franchise to all rate-payers it began to shift the balance of power from the representatives of the pre-industrial economy to the middle-class reformers. The change was effected more rapidly in some areas than in others, but it meant that experiments in social control could sometimes be adopted more readily at the local than at the national level. This was particularly true, for example, of the kind of intervention which was called for by problems of sanitation and town improvement. It was at the local level that government first began to regulate the activities of landlords and speculative builders, who were turning the centres of the great industrial cities into insanitary slums. The Borough Police Act which Manchester Corporation promoted in 1844 imposed standards of housing and sanitation which it took a generation and more to enforce at the national level. In particular it prohibited further building of back-to-back housing. Liverpool, which had led the way by appointing the first British Medical Officer of Health in 1847, was by 1860 building houses for the working classes out of corporation funds. The City of London Sewers Act of 1851 prohibited cellar dwellings and the keeping of live cattle in courts, permitted condemnation and destruction of unwholesome property and established inspection of common lodging-houses and properties let for under 3s. 6d. per week.

In the 1830's and 1840's, therefore, and still more in the 1850's the State was steadily taking responsibility for wider and wider control of private enterprise in the interest of society as a whole. To enforce the legislation of control a new division of government was being built up, the executive arm, which ensured that State intervention in the social and economic affairs of the nation would be fully effective and which had a kind of self-reproducing effect in that the experience so gained was used to formulate new kinds of intervention and create more executive officers to support it. Dr MacDonagh, describing the development of this executive arm of government in the emigration service, for example, has shown that by the middle of the century the 'officers and commissioners not merely requested and secured, they even anticipated legislation which would award them the widest discretions and independence... There could be no doubt now that the limit of State activity was imposed, not so much by individualism, contract, free trade or any other notion, as by the paucity of the human and physical resources at the executive's disposal.'[1] So far from being triumphant by the 1850's, the *laissez-faire* movement had been finally routed by new techniques of government control of the economy which had their own built-in tendency to develop, grow and multiply.'

[1] Oliver Macdonagh, *A Pattern of Government Growth 1800–60* (1961), p. 345.

CHAPTER 14

ECONOMIC GROWTH AND ECONOMIC CYCLES

The net result of the galaxy of revolutions in the way men organized their economic life was that continuous economic change came to be part of the natural order of things and that the scale of the economy began to expand perceptibly and without limit. It was within the century 1750–1850 that the crucial transformation took place that led eventually to a sustained growth in incomes per head. It is difficult at this distance in time and with the sketchy statistical data at our disposal to calculate precisely when this sustained growth began, how much it amounted to and how rapidly it developed. But analysis and interpretation of the existing statistical series suggests a certain pattern, and this pattern is probably reliable enough even if the precise figures are questionable.

Somewhere about the middle of the eighteenth century there is evidence that total national output began to grow—perhaps not faster than it had ever done before in earlier decades, but certainly faster than it had over most of the preceding century. At this stage, however, population had also begun to grow, and it is doubtful whether output was growing any faster than population at the beginning of the period, and hence whether incomes per head were growing at all. In the last quarter of the century, however, the evidence for an improvement in incomes per head becomes much stronger, though it is still not conclusive. We know that population and prices, and certain kinds of production and incomes, and overseas trade, were growing much more strongly than ever before in the fourth quarter of the century. Our problem is to decide whether prices were growing so fast that they outweighed any improvement in incomes, or whether population was growing so fast that it outweighed any improvement in production.

If we take money-income statistics as our starting-point in trying to assess this growth and then adjust them for changes in the value of money with the aid of the existing price indices, we find little evidence of growth in real incomes per head in the last quarter of the eighteenth century and the first decade of the nineteenth century. Indeed when we apply price indices to national income or to wage data the results suggest a decline in the standard of living over this period. But the problem is that the rising price indices cannot be regarded as a reliable reflection of the fall in the value of money because they are incomplete, and moreover they are incomplete in a biased way. In particular they are heavily weighted with commodities which rose sharply in price (these of course were the prices which contemporaries were most concerned to record), and exclude many commodities whose prices fell (especially manufactured products which being non-homogeneous commodities are not in any case easily included in a price series).[1] Hence the price indices tend to exaggerate the fall in the purchasing power of incomes at this period.

If however we take output and trade statistics as our starting-point in trying to assess the national rate of economic growth and make the assumption that foreign trade (which provides us with our best continuous statistical series for the eighteenth century) was of considerable importance to the economy, we find convincing evidence not only of growth in total national product but also in national productivity and standards of living; that is, a growth in real incomes per head. In this approach we avoid having to depend on biased price statistics but, since we do not have enough production and trade statistics to cover the whole economy, we have to make certain assumptions about the relative importance in the total national output of the production and trade sectors whose growth we *can* measure. Clearly we cannot get an accurate measure of the rate of economic growth from these rough calculations but it is reasonable to suppose that we can get answers of the right order of magnitude.[2]

The results, then, are as follows. After a period of stagnation

[1] The point is that although a ton of coal or a bushel of wheat can be regarded as being much the same as between one price quotation and the next, a yard of cloth or a piece of machinery may vary considerably in content and quality, so that the quoted price of a manufactured good may reflect a change in the character of the product.

[2] The problems of making estimates of economic growth over this period and the results used here are discussed critically in Deane and Cole, *British Economic Growth*. See also N. F. R. Crafts, *Economic History Review* (1976).

in output, prices, population, incomes and standards of living in the first part of the eighteenth century, there was a noticeable upward trend in total national output dating from somewhere about or just before 1750.[1] At this stage, however, population growth had begun to outweigh part of the improvement in total national product and it is doubtful whether the improvement in standards of living was appreciable enough to be obvious to contemporaries. A considerably sharper upward trend appears in the 1780's and 1790's when total national output may have been growing at a rate of 1·8 per cent per annum (approximately twice the rate of growth in the middle of the century) and output per head at a rate of about 0·9 per cent per annum. In sum, when Adam Smith was writing he was looking back on a period in which the rate of growth in the *total* national product would imply its doubling in 70–80 years. This is not a fast rate of growth but it should have been obvious to contemporaries that the economy was in fact growing, and it is not surprising that Adam Smith was conscious of national growth. On the other hand, it is doubtful whether the improvement in standards of living—which was proceeding at a rate implying a doubling of the standard in about a century and a half—*was* very obvious to contemporaries except in those sectors which were growing fastest. But by the beginning of the nineteenth century the growth in total national output was proceeding at a rate which implied its doubling in not much more than 40 years and the growth in incomes per head at a rate which implied its doubling in 70–80 years. A significant feature of this end-of-century acceleration in the rate of growth of incomes per head is that it was accompanied by an acceleration in the rate of growth of population. This is the justification for the importance which economic historians have attached to the last two decades of the eighteenth century. It seems to have been the period within which the rate of growth in national product effectively outstripped the rate of growth of population and the spectre of Malthusian stagnation was banished.

It seems likely that the national rate of growth was retarded, though not actually checked, by the French wars, and that it accelerated again in the 1820's and 1830's. So that as between the first and the fifth decades of the nineteenth century total national product seems to have been growing at a rate of about

---

[1] See A. J. Little, *Deceleration in the Eighteenth Century British Economy* (1976), for a discussion of the evidence for the view that there was a period of retardation in the second quarter of the century.

2·9 per cent per annum (this implies a doubling in not much more than a quarter of a century) and incomes per head at about $1\frac{1}{2}$ per cent (which implies a doubling in about half a century). This was not yet the peak rate of growth achieved by the British economy—that came in the second half of the nineteenth century—but it represented sustained growth on a scale which was beyond the wildest dreams of earlier generations. The middle and upper classes certainly got a great deal more out of this improvement than the working classes; capital got a larger share than labour; some groups in the community came near to starvation levels. But, when all allowance is made for changes in the distribution of income which accompanied economic growth, it can hardly be doubted that by the middle of the nineteenth century the majority of the population were beginning to experience, though not yet to expect, a slow rise in their ordinary standard of living.

To say this is not to deny that the 1830's and the 1840's were periods of widespread social and economic distress or that the conditions of large sections of the population was at times as bad—perhaps worse—than it had ever been before. The 'hungry forties' did not owe their name simply to the accident of the Irish famine. Engels' passionate denunciation of the industrial system was based on a biased selection of information, but it was not without substance. The deplorable cases of poverty and degradation that he cites were not by any means uncommon. The fact is that economic growth was not a process of steady improvement in standards of living for the mass of the population. It was a process of economic and social change which often left certain sections of the population very much poorer in every sense than they had been in pre-industrial times, and which made larger and larger sections of the population acutely vulnerable to depressions in trade or industry or to variations in the state of the harvest. Even those whose standards of living were, on balance, improving, were subject to unpredictable periods of unemployment or short-time which would bring them face to face with destitution again. Engels recognized this clearly enough. After citing three horrible cases of London poverty he wrote:

It is not, of course, suggested that all London workers are so poverty-stricken as these three families. There can be no doubt that for every worker who is rendered utterly destitute by society there are ten who are better off. On the other hand it can be confidently asserted that thousands of decent and industrious families...live under truly deplorable conditions which are an affront to human dignity. It is equally incontestable that every working man without exception may well suffer a similar fate through no fault of his own and despite all his efforts to keep his head above water.[1]

There was one of the penalties of industrialization. At the pre-industrial stage, where manufacturing was generally organized on a domestic basis, a trade depression would mean that the average manufacturer had less money to spend, but not that he would starve, for he could still work as an agricultural labourer or cultivate his own plot of land. Similarly, when harvests fell short of the normal the agricultural family could often add to its income and so meet the higher food prices, by working harder at the spinning wheel or the loom. By contrast, in an industrial economy any state of depression, however slight, is liable to involve unemployment for some workers and hence complete destitution for them. Moreover in an integrated industrialized economy where there is a high degree of specialization, there is inevitably a high degree of interdependence between the different sectors of the community. A depression in one branch of trade is liable to be communicated at once to the ancillary and related occupations. Whereas in a traditional economy, in which each region or family is accustomed to produce a large proportion of its own subsistence requirements, a depression in one sector has only limited effects on other sectors, the reverse is true for an industrial economy. There a loss of trade or a reduction in output in one industry affects the prospects of a wide range of other industries and the chain of bankruptcies and redundancies spreads rapidly, and often with cumulative force, throughout the economy.

The fact is then that the process of economic growth is overlaid by fluctuations in economic activity of varying severity and length which have significant effects on the distribution of incomes over time and between sectors of the economy. When we try to assess rates of economic growth we deliberately look past these ups and downs in order to arrive at estimates of average rates of growth per head per annum. This gives us some sort of unique measure of the long-term changes in product and

---

[1] F. Engels, *The Condition of the Working Class in England* (1844), trans. and ed. W. O. Henderson and W. H. Chaloner (1958), p. 37.

productivity which we can readily compare with similar measures for other periods or other countries. But it is important to remember that these calculations of rates of growth represent an over-simplification of the data. We draw an imaginary straight line, as it were, through the wavy line that represents the annual changes in income or output per head for a given economy. To complete the picture it is necessary to look directly at the ups and downs and to analyse some of the cycles and swings in British economic activity over the period 1750–1850.

There are of course a wide variety of kinds of cyclical fluctuations in economic activity, ranging from the very short to the very long. Within the space of a single year one can distinguish the fluctuations which are dependent on the rotation of the seasons. In a pre-industrial economy seasonal fluctuations are generally more significant than in an industrialized economy, partly because so much of economic activity is concerned with agriculture, fishing, seafaring and building—all of which are heavily influenced by climatic conditions—and partly because one of the forms which technical progress takes is the adoption of methods and equipment which permit a more even utilization of capacity and labour and an even flow of transactions throughout the year. In mid-eighteenth-century England winter turned the roads into bogs, froze up the rivers and hemmed the ships up in their harbours. Summer robbed industry of its power by drying up the rivers and created shortages of milk and butter. Most of industry was dependent on the seasonal rhythm of agriculture, either because it processed agricultural products or depended on labour released by the slack periods in the agricultural cycle. 'The frost that killed the sprouting corn, or the heavy rain that beat down the straw, might simultaneously put a stop to the water-wheels or interfere with the delivery of materials.'[1]

The seasonal fluctuations are distinguished above all by their regularity. Except that some summers are hotter (or wetter) than others and some winters are colder (or drier) than others, it can reasonably be expected that there will be a regular alternation in climatic conditions which—give or take a few weeks in either direction—will be predictably distributed through time. Less regular, but none the less rhythmic in their

---

[1] T. S. Ashton, *Economic Fluctuations in England* (1959), p. 34.

incidence are the cycles that we call trade cycles and are characterized by a succession of recognizable phases in economic activity: revival, boom, recession, slump. Of these too one might say that the intensity of each phase, the depth or height of the fluctuation as between one cycle and the next, is variable; in addition, however, the distance between boom and boom or between upper (or lower) turning-points in the cycle also tends to be variable. An analysis of English business-cycles since 1793–1857 suggests that the average length of a cycle was just under 5 years, but there were two cycles in this period that lasted 3 years or less (1807–10 and 1829–31) and one which lasted 10 years (1837–47), so the range is quite wide.[1]

Two significant characteristics determine the outlines of a trade cycle. First there is the initiating cause which sets on foot an upward surge in economic activity or creates a crisis of confidence and a downward turn; second there is the chain of interaction which carries this disturbance from one sector to another and into the heart of the economy. The more inter-dependent the economy the longer and stronger is the chain of the interaction and the greater the impact of the initial disturbance on the total of national economic activity. It might be expected, therefore, that the more industrialized the economy became, the more significant would be the cyclical fluctuations —more significant both in that they affected a wide area of economic activity and in the range of the upward and downward fluctuations in economic activity that could be generated by a given impulse. This does indeed seem to have been the case. That is to say, the nineteenth-century English cycles are more pronounced, more continuous and more easily distinguished than the eighteenth-century cycles. But it should be remembered that we do not have *annual* indices of total economic activity for the eighteenth century and before, and hence that we cannot recognize the *shape* of the cycle: we can only identify it in terms of the crisis; that is, the upper turning-point.

Financial crises or panics reflecting the upper turning-point of a cycle can of course be traced back to the seventeenth century. Notably, for example, there was one in 1667 following the great fire of September 1666; another in 1672 caused by the

[1]   W. L. Thorp and W. C. Mitchell, *Business Annals* (1926), p. 45.

Dutch war; and another in 1696, soon after the foundation of the Bank of England, also associated with wartime difficulties. The crisis of 1708 can be traced to political difficulties, and the South Sea Bubble panic of 1720 was the culmination of a ludicrous indulgence in speculation. The result so chastened the speculators that the financial situation of the economy remained undisturbed until in 1745 Bonnie Prince Charlie invaded England, got as far as Derby, and precipitated a currency, bank and stock-exchange crisis before his expedition collapsed. In 1763 there was another crisis ending the boom which followed the Seven Years War. In 1772 the failure of an important banking house caused a severe panic. The American War brought a deep trade depression, and was followed by an excited boom which collapsed in 1783 with another financial panic.[1] The next panics took place in 1793 at the outbreak of the French wars and in 1797 on the occasion of a naval mutiny.

Contemporary economists in the late eighteenth and early nineteenth centuries were well aware of these recurrent events but they found no theoretical interest in them. Classical economists from Smith to Mill regarded business depressions and booms as being attributable to causes lying outside the range of their economic science (to speculative frenzies, for example, or to wars or to technical change) and they therefore did not attempt to analyse them in any detail.[2] Ricardo, for example, referred to the 'temporary reverses and contingencies produced by the removal of capital from one employment to another',[3] but he did not recognize the cyclical characteristics of these events. Indeed while the crises were associated so obviously with particular outside causes such as wars, technical changes, harvests, speculative manias, etc., there was no obvious need to explain them.

In effect, then 'until the regularity of the disturbances was established... their explanation was no challenge to theoretical economics'.[4] Even when their regularity was recognized, in the second half of the nineteenth century, the tendency was to explain the cycles in terms of non-economic causes. W. Stanley Jevons, for example, the first British economist to recognize the

[1] Thorp and Mitchell, *Business Annals*, p. 150.
[2] S. D. Merlin, *The Theory of Fluctuations in Contemporary Economic Thought* (1949), p. 17.
[3] D. Ricardo, *On the Principles of Political Economy and Taxation* (1951), ed. by Piero Sraffa, p. 263.
[4] S. Kuznets, *Economic Change* (1954), p. 4.

rhythmic character of prosperity and depression phases, attributed them to solar cycles. He observed that there were sixteen cycles in English trade over the period 1721 to 1878, each of which accordingly could be given an average length of 10·466 years, and he compared this with the length then assigned to the sunspot cycle which was 10·45 years. From this of course it was a short step to argue that the two were related. Since then doubt has been thrown on the length of the sunspot cycle, which seems to be more often 11 years, i.e. more than $10\frac{1}{2}$, and on the length of the business cycle, which seems to be appreciably less than 10. Nevertheless, the sunspot thesis has been revived in different forms since, though not very convincingly for the more recent (late-nineteenth-century and twentieth-century) cycles. Clearly, however, since it has been established that there are crop and weather cycles, these may well have produced sympathetic commercial cycles in pre-industrial economies, when agriculture was the chief economic activity and both trade and industry depended heavily on the fortunes of agriculture. Sir William Beveridge, for example, studying European wheat prices over a period of three centuries from 1545 to 1844, found evidence not of one or two but of many cycles in the weather. He concluded that 'Somewhere or other in the solar system there are periodic movements affecting our weather and crops, 10 or 20 or more in number, far more regular than had ever been believed, possibly approaching in some cases the regularity and persistence of free orbital motion, subject in other cases to sudden birth and death.'[1]

However sceptical they might be of solar theories of the trade cycle, however, most economic historians would agree in attaching considerable weight to theories which stress the influence of harvests on levels of economic activity, especially in periods when agriculture was the major industry; and for the whole of the period we are now considering, 1750–1850, agriculture was the premier British industry. It probably absorbed about half of the country's labour force in 1750 and more than a fifth even as late as 1850; it provided most of the nation's food: indeed in 1750 it made an important contribution to the nation's export trade, while by 1850 the state of the harvest was a major factor in the level of imports and

[1] Sir Wm Beveridge, 'Wheat Prices and Rainfall in Western Europe', *Journal of the Royal Statistical Society* (May 1922), p. 452.

hence—through its effects on the balance of trade—on the state of credit in general.

It is easy to see that abnormally good, or bad harvests could create pervasive and intricate repercussions on the economy of eighteenth-century England. Most eighteenth-century industries depended directly on agriculture for their raw materials; most eighteenth-century consumers had an inelastic demand for the large food component of their budgets and an elastic demand for manufactures. The output of starch, spirits, malt and beer, for example, tended to fluctuate with the output of certain cereals; the output of the leather, candle and soap industries was closely tied to that of the livestock industries; the profitability of the woollen or linen industries hinged on the price of raw wool or flax. When harvest conditions were such as to produce a general dearth of agricultural products the wide-ranging consequences of the event would include: (1) a rise in raw-material costs for a large number of industries; (2) high food prices and unemployment for agricultural workers and hence reduced purchasing power for industrial products; (3) budget deficits due to a decline in the output of commodities subject to excise (most of which were processed agricultural commodities) which reduced government revenue, together with a rise in the food bill of the armed forces which increased government expenditure; and (4) an unfavourable balance of trade due either to a reduction in the exports of agricultural products or to an increase in the imports of food.

Thus, indirectly or directly, a bad harvest could be expected to reduce levels of income and industrial activity and to shake business confidence in the eighteenth century.[1] Moreover, the climatic aberrations responsible for harvest failures would often be compounded by their simultaneous effects in certain non-agricultural activities—such as building, transport or mills generating water-power—all of which would be hindered by bad weather conditions.

Of course there were other reasons for the fluctuations in English economic activity in the eighteenth century, as Ashton has pointed out. War, for example, was a powerful factor in the

[1] The longer-term effects of a sequence of good or bad harvests would of course depend on what happened as a result of the associated redistribution of incomes between farmers or landlords (disadvantaged by low and benefited by high agricultural prices) and the rest of the community. See above, pp. 131–4 and 207–9 for further discussion bearing on this point.

fluctuations in overseas trade. When war seemed imminent, the tendency was for exports to rise faster as merchants hastened to get goods shifted before the expected interruption in the trade routes. Exports were stimulated for this kind of reason in 1701, 1743, 1756, 1774–5 and 1792. Once a war had broken out and the seas were infested by hostile ships, imports tended to be discouraged, though exports were often maintained by government expenditure abroad. As wars ended and normal commercial contacts were resumed, both exports and imports tended to expand.[1]

We may reasonably ask ourselves whether the eighteenth-century trade cycles, shaped largely by climatic shocks or wars, were really the same kind of phenomenon as the nineteenth-century cycles. Certainly they seem to have been less regular either in their incidence or in their pattern. Though there were some crises which seemed to have originated largely in a financial situation, such as the crises of 1720, 1763, 1772/3 and 1788 (all of which were international), there were few eighteenth-century cycles that were not conditioned more by political events than by economic events. There was little to suggest that prosperity, boom, slump and recovery would continue to succeed each other in inevitable sequence. But before we write off the eighteenth-century fluctuations, however, as being disconnected up-swings and down-swings attributable mainly to harvests or wars or political events rather than self-perpetuating cycles, it is worth remembering that our information for the eighteenth century is very scanty and that such annual series as we have cover only limited sectors of economic activity. When Sir William Beveridge wrote his classic work on unemployment he concluded that before 1858 it is impossible 'to find a cyclical fluctuation of trade in the sense in which such fluctuation is found later, as an influence dominant alike over finance and trade in the narrow sense and over industry and the whole economic life of the nation'.[2] But some years later when more data became available he compiled an index of industrial activity which suggested cyclical fluctuations that looked distinctly modern in rhythm and amplitude.

[1] Ashton, *Economic Fluctuations in England 1700–1800*, p. 64.
[2] Sir Wm Beveridge, *Unemployment: a Problem of Industry* (1912), p. 342. See also J. Parry Lewis, *Building Cycles and Britain's Growth* (1965) for the evidence for the existence of the building cycle.

For the nineteenth century, however, the analysis of business cycles has now been carried much further. The period 1790–1850 has been the subject of an exhaustive inquiry by an American trio of research workers, Gayer, Rostow and Schwartz, and the results of their researches have been published in a two-volume monograph which explores the character and causes of British trade cycles in immense detail.

The main conclusion reached by Gayer, Rostow and Schwartz was that the cycles in British business activity which can be recognized in the period 1790–1850 were dependent on two main factors on the side of demand: first the fluctuations in the demand for British exports (particularly for textile exports), and secondly fluctuations in domestic investment. These two factors were interrelated in that an expansion in domestic investment generally followed an increase in exports and when both factors were present in force they generated a major cycle. Within the period 1790–1850 these authors trace six major cycles (1797–1803, 1808–11, 1816–19, 1819–26, 1832–7 and 1842–8) and a number of minor cycles in which the expansion of exports was not great enough to stimulate an expansion of domestic investment but nevertheless produced a recognizable cycle of general business activity.

The generalized picture of expansion which emerges is of recovery begun by an increase in exports and, after a period, supplemented by large-scale domestic investment. It is probable, further, that these two sources of new orders to industry were related. The primary and secondary (multiplier) effects on total income, due to the increase in exports in the early stages of revival, helped to induce and to finance the later construction of capital equipment.[1]

In effect, they argue that an expansion of the demand for exports produced three effects, each of which encouraged new domestic investment: (1) a condition of full capacity in some sectors, (2) an expectation of continued increase in output, and (3) an increase in profits. Each of these tended to stimulate an expansion of domestic investment. Of course it was necessary, if the cycle was to have its modern form and to characterize business activity as a whole, rather than particular sectors of the economy only, that the reactions should be fairly pervasive.

[1] A. D. Gayer, W. W. Rostow and A. J. Schwartz, *The Growth and Fluctuation of the British Economy 1790–1850*, vol. II (1953), p. 534.

When the increased export demand was concentrated on a particular industry it was necessary, if a major cycle was to develop, for this to create a climate of confidence over a wider area and set cumulative effects in motion through the tendency of businessmen to assess their prospects in terms of a national rather than a parochial development. There seems little doubt that this tendency for businessmen to think and act in step—which is one of the most significant characteristics of the modern trade cycle—increased as communications improved and as the national market for both goods and capital became more integrated. It is very much in evidence in the cycles of the 'twenties, 'thirties and 'forties of the nineteenth century. Gayer, Rostow and Schwartz, for example, see conditions in the money-market as being mainly responsible for the rapid spread of business confidence or pessimism which characterized the post-1820 cycles. In the expansion phases it was relatively easy to raise money, and confidence was therefore high. 'This increase in entrepreneurial daring (both in industry and in the long-term capital market) can be traced clearly in the major cycle expansions of the last three decades of the period... Even in the relatively atomistic economy of Britain in the early nineteenth century, entrepreneurs made their judgements about the future on the basis of pervasive conditions.'[1] In sum, while we may reasonably reserve judgment, pending further research, on whether the eighteenth-century fluctuations in economic activity were cyclical in the sense of the modern trade-cycle, there seems to be good reason to regard the trade cycles which had their peaks in 1825, 1836 and 1845 respectively as being essentially modern in form.

The short-term fluctuations that we call trade cycles, however, are not the only rhythmic movements that economists have recognized in the statistical series which reflect national and international economic activity. In 1913 the Dutch economist van Gelderen claimed to have discovered the existence of 'large cycles' in economic development lasting about 60 years; and in the 1920's the Russian economist Kondratieff developed independently his theory of the long waves in economic life.[2] These long waves were apparently superimposed on the trade

[1] Gayer, Rostow and Schwartz, *Growth and Fluctuation*, vol. II, p. 558.
[2] N. D. Kondratieff, 'The Long Waves in Economic Life', *Review of Economic Statistics* (1935).

cycles in the same way as the latter were superimposed on the seasonal cycles which make up each year. Kondratieff analysed historical price and production data for a number of western countries—Britain, France, U.S.A. and Germany—and concluded that the western world had seen $2\frac{1}{2}$ 'long waves', each of 50 to 60 years in duration, since the closing years of the eighteenth century. The first he traced from its beginning in the 1780's or early 1790's through its crest in 1810–17 and down to its trough in 1844–51; the second ended in the 1890's. Kondratieff merely reported on the evidence of the statistical series. He made no attempt to explain the long waves that he found, but he did insist that they represented regular rather than random fluctuations, and he did give it as his opinion that 'the long waves arise out of causes which are inherent in the essence of the capitalistic economy'.[1]

It was left to Schumpeter to suggest an explanation for the long waves and to interpret them in a historical context. Schumpeter argued, as Kondratieff had done, that the cyclical nature of economic development was inherent in the capitalist system: and he began his argument, as Kondratieff had done, with the 1780's. Nevertheless, he also claimed to see evidence of earlier swings, though he saw these as somewhat muted by comparison with the later waves simply because the capitalistic system of economic organization was less well developed. 'The smaller the capitalist sector embedded in an otherwise precapitalist world, the less the fluctuations characteristic of the capitalist process will assert themselves and...external factors (harvests, wars, plagues, etc.) will dominate.'[2]

Briefly, Schumpeter's interpretation is based on his theory of innovations. A major innovation always stimulates a cluster of related innovations and completely changes the range of opportunities open to a certain group of industries. While entrepreneurs are taking advantage of these innovations for the first time and adapting themselves to the changed economic circumstances which they involve, the economy tends to be prosperous and expansive. Within the up-phase of the long wave there may be occasions in which entrepreneurs tend to overshoot the mark and when over-speculation causes crises and temporary recessions; the ordinary trade cycle, that is to say,

[1] A.E.A., *Readings in Business Cycle Theory*, p. 42.
[2] Schumpeter, *Business Cycles*, vol. I, pp. 224–5.

continues to operate, but it is of the essence of the upward section of a long wave that years of optimism and expansion are more frequent than years of contraction or depression. In time of course, the repercussions set up by a particular major innovation die away, prices fall faster than costs and the long wave enters into its down-phase, when years of contraction and depression are on balance more frequent than years of optimism.

The first long wave analysed by Schumpeter in these terms runs from 1787 to 1842. This was the long wave which coincided, more or less, with the Industrial Revolution. It was set off, according to Schumpeter, by the innovations in the cotton industry, supported by innovations in the iron industry and by the advent of the steam-engine. Its up-phase coincided with the period when the cotton and iron industries were growing at a spectacular rate from small beginnings. It turned downwards in the depressed aftermath of the Napoleonic wars. During the 1820's and 1830's the long wave continued down, while the cotton and iron industries, now relatively massive, grew more slowly on the strength of past innovations. It turned upwards again in the railroad boom of the 1840's when steam-power began to be used on a large scale for transport, for the weaving section of the cotton industry and for other textile industries, and as the coal and iron industries surged upwards in response to the new demands being made upon them. This second long wave, stretching from 1842–1897, was the age of steam, steel and railways.

It is clear, then, that British economic growth has developed not by a steady expansion of economic activity but in a fluctuating way. It is clear also that some of these fluctuations have a rhythmic quality and take the form of a series of cycles. I have chosen to mention only three kinds of cyclical fluctuation —the seasonal cycles completed within a single year; the trade cycles (sometimes called Juglar cycles after an economist who analysed them) generally completed within a span of under 9 years (they averaged about five in our period); and the long waves (Kondratieff cycles), which stretch over a period of 50–60 years. Statistical analysts have drawn attention to many more rhythmical regularities in the various aspects of economic activity, but all of these regularities, except the strictly seasonal, show up more clearly and intelligibly after the middle of the nineteenth century than in earlier periods. It is not merely that the statistics for the later period are more complete and reliable (though this of course is true) but also that the national economy which grew out of the industrial revolution was characteristically prone to self-generating cycles in income and output.

There were a number of reasons for this, all of them arising from the fact that an industrialized economy is more closely articulated, less atomistic, than a pre-industrial economy. The more capitalistic the economy became, the more it was subject to alternating periods of prosperity and depression as innovating entrepreneurs optimistically imitated each other in building up capacity until it outstripped demand, and then subsequently abstained from further investment, until their collective pessimism was dispelled by new opportunities to innovate in face of a demand for goods which was growing appreciably faster than supply. Specialization of industry meant the growth and ramification of highly interdependent industries. The more the economy moved away from dependence on traditional agriculture with its strong seasonal rhythm, and the more it came to depend on the fortunes of mechanized industry, the more likely it was to find the level of demand fluctuating in time with the age cycle of man-made assets in general use. When an interruption in the path of industrial growth (due, perhaps, to an exogenous cause like an invention or a war) induced a sudden increase (or decrease) in the rate of expenditure on certain machines or vehicles the probability was that the increase in capacity would discourage further investment until, at some later date, the wearing out of assets concerned concentrated a new burst of demand, and set the cycle off again.

Geographical integration of the economy also helped to generate, or at any rate to emphasize, cyclical fluctuations in economic activity. The more nationally integrated an economy became, the more likely was it that regional cycles in optimism or in opportunity would synchronize so as to produce a national rhythm that was more emphatic than any of its components. It is significant, in this context, that the 20-year building cycle which is so marked a feature of the British statistical indicators in the later nineteenth century fails to show up at all clearly in the earlier data, although it is there at the regional level. It has been observed, for example, that 'the first half of the nineteenth century was marked by regional building cycles somewhat out of phase with each other'.[1] Integration at the international level also helped to set up a more emphatic rhythm in national fluctuations of economic activity. Specialization of industries as between countries was another characteristic of nineteenth-century industrialization and as nations became more and more dependent on trade with each other they became more vulnerable to disturbances arising in each other's economies. When two or more national trade cycles fell into step they produced more emphatic fluctuations than the component cycles would have generated in isolation.

Whatever the reasons, however, the consequences of this tendency for cyclical fluctuations in output and incomes to intensify in the course of industrialization were generally unfortunate. The industrial revolution subjected a low-income community to a fluctuating type of economic growth in which the down-swings were prolonged and painful for the proletarian sectors of the population. Of course it was not only the working classes who suffered from the growing instability of the economic system. In bad years the number of bankruptcies rose to alarming levels. 'John Kennedy, himself a successful cotton spinner, remarked that at the end of the French wars not more than seven cotton mills in Manchester were under the same management as at the beginning.'[2] But whereas the landowners, the capitalists and the middle classes could usually husband enough of their abnormal earnings in the up-swings to cushion their standards of living in the down-swings, the proletariat swung helplessly between destitution and sufficiency. Until average productivity had risen high enough to lift the mass of the working classes so far above subsistence levels that even the periodic downward fluctuations in national income did not dip them below the poverty line, and until the weight of the public sector had become so powerful a factor in the economy that government could largely compensate for a decline in private demand with a rise in public demand, industrialization meant an insecure as well as a rising standard of living for the majority of the people.

[1] J. Parry Lewis, 'Indices of House Building', *Scottish Journal of Political Economy* (1961), p. 154.
[2] Donald Reed, *Press and People 1790–1850* (1961), p. 20.

CHAPTER 15

STANDARDS OF LIVING

Economic growth and economic change involve an expansion of the flow of goods and services produced in the economy and change in its composition. One way of assessing the achievements of an industrial revolution therefore is to measure its consequences in terms of their effects on standards of living. It might be expected that the process of industrial revolution, bringing with it, as it does, a great lowering in costs of production both in agriculture and industry, a perceptible reduction in the amount of human effort required to produce a given unit of output and a consequent increase in the flow of goods and services available for consumption would automatically involve a corresponding rise in the standard of living of the working man. Whether or not it does have these consequences, however, depends on a variety of circumstances, not least of which is the rate of population growth. It is rapidly becoming apparent in today's newly developing countries, for example, that even assuming a fairly brisk rate of technological progress in industry it is only too easy for the number of mouths to be fed to multiply more rapidly than productivity per person in active employment, and hence for the average standard of consumption to fall. If the rising population is due, as it frequently is, to a higher birth rate or a lower infant mortality rate it brings with it a larger *dependent* population and a smaller *proportion* of the total population in active employment. And if technical change begins, as it frequently does, in industries employing a relatively small section of the labour force rather than in, say, agriculture in which a majority of the labour force is engaged, it will have to be very rapid indeed to raise the output of goods and services fast enough to compensate for those factors which are tending to depress average consumption levels. Moreover, if there are important discontinuities in the development process such that the growth of new kinds of industry requires substantial initial expenditures on new capital assets (buildings, harbours, roads, canals, railway-lines, ships and vehicles, plant and machinery) before incomes begin to rise, current consumption may actually have to be reduced so that funds can be diverted to these capital expenditures.

In effect, the evidence suggests that some countries have experienced a period of what has been called a 'swarming' of the population in their early stages of industrialization, a period within which the numbers of the people increased faster than productivity and the flow of consumer goods *per head* actually declined for a time. It is therefore of special interest to ask ourselves whether the English experience included such a period and, if so, when it occurred.

Actually it is quite difficult to produce a conclusive answer to this question and in fact one of the most persistent controversies in the history of the industrial revolution is the argument that has raged around the workers' standard of living. Two schools of thought have grown up in connection with this topic. The pessimistic view, held by a long line of observers from contemporaries of the process to modern historians—by Engels, Marx, Toynbee, the Webbs, the Hammonds and a host of others, more recently Dr Hobsbawm—is that the early stage of industrialization in England, though it brought affluence to some, caused a net deterioration in the standard of living of the labouring poor. The optimistic view, put forward by an equally long line of observers—by McCulloch, Tooke, Giffen, Clapham, Ashton and more recently Dr Hartwell—is that although economic change left some workers displaced and distressed, the majority of them were enabled by falling prices, more regular employment and a wider range of earning opportunities to enjoy a rising standard of living.[1]

The controversy has been muddied by political prejudice and the myopic views to which prejudice so often gives rise. It is common to find left-wing writers, their sympathies strongly engaged by the sufferings of the proletariat, holding the pessimistic view; and is equally common to find right-wing writers, more confident of the blessings assured by free capitalistic enterprise, holding the optimistic view. Engels, whose *Condition*

---

[1] For a review of the issues in the debate, reprints of some of the significant articles and a useful select bibliography, see A. J. Taylor (ed.), *The Standard of Living in Britain in the Industrial Revolution* (1975).

of the Working Class in England (originally published in 1844 and
translated by Henderson and Chaloner) is one of the most vivid
and angry denunciations of the factory system, made no bones
about his political motives. In a letter written to Karl Marx he
called his book 'a bill of indictment'. 'At the bar of world
opinion', he wrote, 'I charge the English middle classes with
mass murder, wholesale robbery, and all the other crimes in the
calendar.'[1] The theory of deterioration was buttressed by a
somewhat legendary picture of the golden age that was supposed
to have preceded the industrial revolution—an England of
happy prosperous yeomen and independent domestic craftsmen
free from exploitation and care. But in fact the domestic
outworker was no less exploited by the master-manufacturer
who supplied his family with cotton to spin, or yarn to weave,
than the factory worker by the owner: and women and children
often worked as long hours at the laborious process of domestic
industry as they ever did at the factory machines.

The argument has been further complicated by the introduction of 'moral' and 'aesthetic' and other non-economic
considerations. The Hammonds, for example, inveighed against
the 'curse of Midas'.

Thus England asked for profits and received profits. Everything
turned to profit. The towns had their profitable dirt, their profitable
slums, their profitable smoke, their profitable disorder, their profitable
ignorance, their profitable despair...For the new town was not a
home where man could find beauty, happiness, leisure, learning,
religion, the influences that civilize outlook and habit, but a bare and
desolate place, without colour, air or laughter, where man, woman
and child worked, ate and slept...The new factories and the new
furnaces were like the Pyramids, telling of man's enslavement rather
than of his power, casting their long shadow over the society that took
such pride in them.[2]

There is room for a good deal more sociological research on
the social consequences of the industrial revolution, but many
of the political and moral assessments are highly subjective. The
argument has its parallel today in the modern controversy about
whether or not we should seek to bring backward village
communities, with their relatively simple scale of wants and

[1] Engels, *The Condition of the Working Class in England*, trans. and ed. W. O. Henderson
    and W. H. Chaloner, p. xxiii.
[2] J. L. and Barbara Hammond, *The Rise of Modern Industry* (1925), p. 232.

pattern of activities, into the rough impersonal competition of
a market economy. It is not at all a meaningless problem from
the social point of view, though it is not easy to discuss it
objectively. But even if we refuse to be drawn into philosophical
or moral arguments about whether the workers actually involved in the social and economic upheavals of the industrial
revolution grew happier or more civilized, there remains a
considerable area of legitimate controversy about whether their
material standard of living rose, stagnated or fell.

Here again, as with most of the problems of economic history
which are concerned with establishing the facts of growth or
decline, or the turning-points which mark their beginning or
end, the doubt arises because the historical record is incomplete;
in particular the quantitative data are too few or too scattered
or too selective to be conclusive. We are again obliged to
reconstruct a picture in which various crucial pieces of the
jigsaw are missing and to guess at what it means.

Consider, for example, the evidence for a rising standard of
living for the working population over the controversial period
1775–1850, within which we can assume that the English
industrial revolution largely took place. I have already discussed
the evidence on national income.[1] If we juxtapose the contemporary estimates by Arthur Young for 1770 and various authors
in the first two decades of the nineteenth century they actually
suggest a decline in real incomes per head up to, at any rate,
the immediate aftermath of the Napoleonic Wars. But we are
justified in regarding these estimates sceptically. They are not
strong enough to take the weight of analysis. Attempts to trace
the course of total national output on the basis of incomplete
production series are more convincing. They suggest a rise
which may perhaps date from the 1740's in overall terms and
probably accelerated in per-head terms in the last quarter of
the eighteenth century under the influence of strongly expanding
overseas markets. An index of British industrial production
which has been compiled by the German scholar Hoffmann, and
which is also of necessity heavily dependent on the foreign-trade
series, suggests a similar movement.[2] It shows a rate of growth
of total *industrial* output averaging under one per cent per

[1] See above, pp. 5–10 and pp. 238–40.
[2] W. Hoffmann, *British Industry 1700–1950*, trans. W. O. Henderson and W. H.
Chaloner (1958).

annum in the first three-quarters of the eighteenth century, rising abruptly to over 3 per cent per annum in the 1780's and early 1790's, falling back in the period 1793–1817 (probably as a consequence of the war) and recovering to levels of over 3 per cent again after 1817.

On the face of it then, we might say that since the evidence points on the whole to an increase in national output per head of population, beginning probably in the 1780's, muted by the French and Napoleonic wars and resuming strongly at the end of the second decade of the nineteenth century, it implies a rising standard of living on the average. Actually, whether it does or not depends on whether there were significant changes in the distribution of the national income. It may be that all the value of the increase in national output accrued to the upper income groups—to the mill-owners and the iron-masters, for example, rather than to the workers. Or it may be that the growth in marketed output of corn or meat, say, due to the enclosures, accrued to a small group of owner-farmers, while the cottagers were evicted from their food plots and deprived of the common pasture for cow and pig to become a distressed agricultural proletariat. It is possible for national output to rise faster than population and for the standard of living of the majority of the people to fall because a few people are monopolizing the results of the increase or because the new goods are not consumption goods but capital goods.

One might also say, of course, as many holders of the 'optimistic' view have said, that the evidence for a sharp decrease in mortality at the end of the eighteenth century points to a rise in the standard of living. If people were becoming more resistant to disease this could have been either because medical skills were improving or because they were living better. The medical historians, however, have discounted the evidence for striking medical advances which could have had this result and they fall back on the view that 'there was a general advance in the standard of living in consequence of the economic developments of the period'.[1] Here again, there is a problem of distribution to be taken into account, though in this case it is a question of distribution through time. As Hobsbawm has pointed out:

[1] T. McKeown and R. G. Brown, 'Medical Evidence', p. 141.

It should be remembered that the decrease in mortality which is probably primarily responsible for the sharp rise in population need be due not to an *increase* in per capita consumption per year but to a greater *regularity of supply*: that is, to the abolition of the periodic shortages and famines which plagued pre-industrial economies and decimated their populations. It is quite possible for the industrial citizen to be worse fed in a normal year than his predecessor, so long as he is more regularly fed.[1]

To this improvement in the temporal flow of incomes, investment in communications (better roads, canals, etc.) and regular marketing of foodstuffs may have contributed more than increased productivity in industry or increases in output per acre.

However, the most striking feature of the mortality figures, if we try to use them as an index of standards of living, is that they show the decline in the death rate to have been arrested, probably even reversed, in the period when the industrial revolution was in full swing and began notably to affect the way of life of a majority of the population. Death rates estimated from burial figures reached an average of 35·8 per 1,000 in the 1730's and then fell steadily (with an interruption in the 1770's, when there was a slight rise) to reach an average of 21·1 per 1,000 in the decade 1811–20. This was an impressive achievement. Then, however, they began to rise again to reach 23·4 in the decade 1831–40 and remained more or less constant at over 22 per 1,000 (these are the official figures based on registrations) in the 1840's, 1850's, and 1860's.[2]

The main reason for the rise in the national death rate in the early nineteenth century was the influx of people into the towns which had a high, and in some cases a rising, death rate. The average death rate of the five largest towns outside London (Birmingham, Bristol, Leeds, Liverpool and Manchester) rose from 20·7 in 1831 to 30·8 in 1841. For Liverpool parish the death rate for the decade 1841–50 averaged 39·2 per 1,000 and in Manchester it was 33·1. The fact is that the towns had been outgrowing the existing technology of urban living. 'Over half the deaths were caused by infectious diseases alone...Infant

---

[1] E. Hobsbawm, 'The British Standard of Living 1790–1850', *Economic History Review* (August 1957), p. 46.

[2] John Brownlee, 'History of the Birth Rates and Death Rates in England and Wales', *Public Health* (July 1916), p. 232.

diseases, product of dirt, ignorance, bad feeding and over-crowding swept one in two of all the children born in towns out of life before the age of five.'[1] As the towns expanded over the countryside and the population living in their centres multiplied, the existing sanitation systems became so inadequate as to be a growing menace to health. 'Street sewers were immense brick caverns, flat bottomed and flat sided, washed only by a feeble trickle of water', and cleared by excavation of the streets every 5–10 years.[2] In some cases town sewage was allowed to flow into the rivers from which the water companies were taking their water supply. It took a series of cholera epidemics and some alarming sanitary inquiries to persuade central and local authorities to take positive action to clean filth from the streets and courts, to adopt piped sanitation, and to make the private water-companies chlorinate their water supplies. Meanwhile it is fair to say that in most urban areas the human environment was deteriorating perceptibly through the first half of the nineteenth century and that it probably did not begin to improve generally until the 1870's and 1880's.

To probe more directly the question whether the standard of living of the working classes rose or fell in the course of the industrial revolution we need to look at the data on wages. What can we deduce from the way the real incomes of the workers moved over the period of early industrialization? Here the problem of interpreting the incomplete record is twofold— whose wages should we consider and how are we to allow for changes in the value of money?

First of all then, whose wages? For the data do not permit us to compile a national wage bill which might give a measure of overall average earnings from employment. All that is available is a somewhat heterogeneous mass of wage quotations for particular industries, occupations and regions which economists and economic historians may or may not have been able to combine into meaningful aggregates. In general, of course, the wages of workers in industry were higher than those in agriculture, so that as the proportion in industrial employment rose, the average money-wage probably grew. In the expanding industries wages sometimes rose spectacularly; and, conversely,

---

[1] Royston Lambert, *Sir John Simon, 1816–1904, and English Social Administration* (1963), p. 59.
[2] R. A. Lewis, *Edwin Chadwick and the Public Health Movement, 1832–1854* (1952), p. 48.

for craftsmen made redundant by mechanization they sometimes fell equally spectacularly. Take cotton, for example. Manchester cotton weavers were earning 7s. to 10s. a week when
Arthur Young toured the north of England in 1769—*before* the
spinning-jenny provided them with enough yarn to keep their
looms going constantly. By 1792, made scarce by the enormous
quantities of yarn which the spinning-machines made available,
some weavers were earning 15s. to 20s. a week. But the supply
of weavers proved highly elastic and the labour market was soon
flooded with them. The trend to 'long hours and short wages'
had set in before the end of the 1790's; by 1815/19 average piece
rates for muslin weaving at Bolton, for example, were only about
a third of the 1795/9 level.[1]

Clearly the wage data for specific occupations or industries
may shed little or no light on the movement of wages over wide
areas of the economy. And as far as the eighteenth-century wage
data are concerned there is the additional problem that there
was no really integrated national market for labour until the
very end of the century. In effect, the outstanding characteristic
of eighteenth-century wage history was the existence of wide
regional variations in both levels and trends. In Lancashire, for
example, the money wages of builders' labourers almost doubled
between the 1750's and early 1790's. In London they seem to
have risen by less than 5 per cent; and in Oxfordshire the
increase was of the order of 15 per cent. Actually there was a
marked narrowing of the regional wage differentials before the
end of the eighteenth century, and by the late 1780's Lancashire
building labourers whose earnings had been two-thirds of the
London average in the 1750's were earning about 9s. a week
compared with about 8s. 6d. in London and about 9s. 6d. in
Oxfordshire.[2]

Of course the typical wage-earner in the late eighteenth
century was not the labourer in industry but the labourer in
agriculture. Bowley's figures of agricultural earnings suggest
that the average agricultural wage increased by something like
25 per cent between the late 1760's and 1795.[3] The rise was most
marked in the Yorkshire Ridings, Lancashire, Northumberland

[1] D. Bythell, *The Handloom Weavers*, p. 99.
[2] Gilboy, *Wages in Eighteenth Century England*.
[3] A. L. Bowley, 'Statistics of Wages in the U.K. during the Last Hundred Years: Part
    I, Agricultural Wages', *Journal of the Royal Statistical Society* (December 1898).

and Staffordshire where the increase exceeded 50 per cent; but over a very large part of eastern, middle and southern England in the second half of the eighteenth century, agricultural wages seem to have been in a state of relative stagnation similar to that which characterized the London building-trades for this period. When war with France broke out in the early 1790's, however, the economy rapidly moved into a state of relatively full employment and money wages in agriculture soared. Before the end of the Napoleonic Wars a 'national' index of money wages, calculated by combining Wood's index of average money wages in towns with Bowley's index of money wages in agriculture, showed an increase of about 75 per cent.

On the other hand if money wages rose steeply over this war period 1792–1815, prices also rose fast. For this was a period of galloping wartime inflation. Which brings us to our second major problem of interpretation, the problem of allowing for changes in the value of money. In order to get some measure of the change in the standard of living we must form some view of the movement of *real* wages; that is, to adjust money wages so as to eliminate the effect of the upward movement in prices.

What I have said about the regional variations in the price of eighteenth-century labour applies also to the prices of commodities at this period—sometimes to an even greater extent. For eighteenth-century England in which it took 10–12 days to travel from London to Edinburgh (that was in the 1750's), when the price of coal could vary from 15s. a chaldron to over £3 a chaldron according to distance from the pits (this was true even in the 1790's), and when the wages of a building craftsman could vary from 2s. to 3s. a day according to the region in which he operated, there is no satisfactory way of constructing a general price index which could reflect changes in the value of money for the economy as a whole. Each region had its own price history and its own set of price relationships. Even if we knew enough about the prices of each region to construct a true national average it is doubtful what meaning we could attribute to the result.

On the other hand it is certain that there were important changes in the value of money during the latter part of the eighteenth century and these changes must have had their effect on prices. By the 1790's (probably by the 1760's) the majority of prices had developed an upward trend. Until after the

Napoleonic Wars, however—possibly until the beginning of the railway age—the movements of individual prices are so divergent and so variable that the attempt to measure the changes in the form of a general price index is a dubious procedure. Moreover in a period of violent inflation—such as that which developed in the last decade of the eighteenth century when the cumulative effects of a rapidly rising population, a succession of poor harvests and an expensive war drove up the price of many foodstuffs—price indices based on weights relevant to a less disturbed period do not adequately reflect changes in the value of money. This is because they do not take account of the fact that consumers look for substitutes for goods whose prices have soared. They substitute goods which are less vulnerable to harvest and war crises and their standard of living does not fall to the extent that it would have done if they had obstinately persisted in their old patterns of consumption.

So far I have been considering the conceptual difficulties of constructing price indices that might enable one to allow for changes in the purchasing power of money and so to convert money wages to 'real' wages. But it goes without saying that there are formidable data problems too. Most of the prices that are regularly available for the period of the industrial revolution relate to commodities which tended to be particularly vulnerable to trade dislocations and harvest crises. In particular they seldom cover the prices of manufactured goods (many of which were reduced by the falling costs associated with industrialization) or of rent, which seems to have remained fairly steady. And they are rich in the prices of foodstuffs and imported goods, which tended to rise sharply when harvest failure or war made them temporarily scarce. To some extent this bias is inevitable, for it was the vulnerable prices which contemporaries chose to collect and publish regularly and which are accordingly still on record. But it means, of course, that indices based on these selective quotations tend to exaggerate the movements in the general price level and become difficult to use as indications of changes in the value of money during periods of inflation.[1]

The result is that when we try to take out from the wage data the effects of the price rises due to harvest crises and war

[1] See M. Flinn, 'Trends in Real Wages, 1750–1850', *Economic History Review* (1974), and G. N. von Tunzelmann, 'Trends in Real Wages, 1750–1850, Revisited', *Economic History Review* (1979), for a critical examination of the wage and price estimates currently available.

shortages we completely wipe out any improvement in money wages and it then looks as though average real wages were declining over the period 1782 to 1815. Perhaps indeed they were. When we also bear in mind the burden of war—the British people paid heavy subsidies to their continental allies, one in ten of the labour force was absorbed in the unproductive employment of the armed forces and the growth of industries producing for peacetime markets slackened perceptibly—it is not difficult to believe that consumption standards were actually falling. On the other hand when one takes into account the fact that total war involved full employment of adult males, while the spread of the factory system and the expansion of agricultural acreages widened the employment opportunities for women and children, it seems likely that the decline in the standard of living of the typical working-class family—if decline there was—was less drastic than the wage–price data might lead one to believe.

After the war, however, inflation turned to deflation and the picture changes. Average money-wages declined and so did prices. Within ten years (i.e. between 1816 and 1824, again using the Bowley–Wood indices of agricultural and urban earnings combined into a national average) money wages had fallen by more than 10 per cent: by the 1840's the fall was 15 per cent. Prices, however, fell faster and at first glance we might deduce that the purchasing power of the worker's wage rose. For the longer period, up to about mid nineteenth century, this certainly seems to be the most plausible interpretation of the data. But for the distressed years of the immediate post-war aftermath when the demobilized soldiers and seamen flooded the labour market and the industries which had thrived in war were facing a slump in demand, it is likely that higher real wages earned by those who were lucky enough to be in regular employment were insufficient to compensate for the loss of earnings experienced by the unemployed or the under-employed. In the tense years between Waterloo in 1815 and the massacre of Peterloo in 1819 it has been said that England was nearer to social revolution than at any other time in her history.[1] It seems probable that the real earnings of the average working-class family were lower in these years than they had been in the 1780's.

Thereafter the evidence for a rise in the average real wage

---

[1] Briggs, *Age of Improvement*, p. 208.

becomes more convincing. It does not become absolutely conclusive because we do not know the incidence of unemployment. In years, in regions or in sectors of the economy where there was trade depression the evidence of acute poverty is overwhelming. But there are three strong presumptions in favour of a rising standard of living, on the whole, dating from the 1820's: (1) that as industrialization gathered momentum in the 1820's employment became more rather than less regular than it had been in pre-war years; (2) that the goods that tended to be omitted from the price indices, being largely manufactured goods, were more likely to be falling in price than the goods (largely raw materials) that were included—and hence of course that the price indices understate the post-war price fall; and (3) that the falling weight of taxation would, in a period when most taxes were indirect and hence regressive, give perceptible relief to the working classes.

Actually the conviction of the 'optimists' grows stronger for years towards the end of the controversial period than for periods towards the beginning. Professor Ashton for example is most confident about the period after 1820. 'Let me confess, therefore, at the start', he says, 'that I am of those who believe that all in all, conditions of labour were becoming better, *at least after 1820*, and that the spread of the factory played a not inconsiderable part in the improvement.'[1] Most observers agree that the 1790's, with war, harvest failures and a rapidly increasing population, was a tragic period for English labour. Clapham, another of the optimists, calls 1795, the year when the Speenhamland system was introduced to augment men's wages out of the rates, 'the blackest year', and goes on to conclude that,

whereas on the average the potential standard of comfort of an English...rural labouring family in 1824 was probably a trifle better than it had been in 1794, assuming equal regularity of work, there were important areas in which it was definitely worse, others in which it was probably worse, and many in which the change either way was imperceptible. In the bad areas the rates were drawn upon for the deficit.[2]

[1] T. S. Ashton, 'The Standard of Life of Workers in England 1790–1830', *Journal of Economic History*, Supplement IX (1949), p. 19. My italics.
[2] Clapham, *Economic History*, vol. I, p. 131.

Not even the most convinced 'optimists' have claimed that working-class standards of living improved perceptibly during the French wars or their immediate aftermath, though full employment financed by income-tax may well have involved some transfer of incomes from rich to poor. On the other hand even the pessimists will allow that perceptible improvements in working-class standards of living set in the 1840's.

In effect then we can narrow down the area of fiercest controversy to the 1820's and 1830's. Here the data on wage-rates and prices suggest a rising real wage, though not a very great improvement. Between 1820 and 1840, for example, the Bowley–Wood wage data suggest a fall of 10 per cent in money wages: and the Gayer–Rostow–Schwartz price index suggests a fall of about 12 per cent in prices. Professor Phelps Brown's index of builders' wage rates, expressed in terms of the basket of consumers' goods they might buy, suggests an improvement of about 5 per cent over the same period. Now if we assume, as the pessimists do, that 'the period 1811–1842 saw abnormal problems and abnormal unemployment',[1] then the irregularity of work could easily have outweighed these rather feeble improvements in real incomes suggested by the wage/price data. On the other hand if we assume, as the optimists do, that the price indices understate the price fall (and hence the rise in purchasing power of wages) because they omit the commodities whose prices were influenced most strongly by the cost reductions of the industrial revolution, then we would argue that the wage/price data are only a pale reflection of the true rise in the standard of living. Without a great deal more research in the areas of doubt—the incidence of unemployment for example and the rise in the value of money—it is impossible to resolve this problem, though on the whole the evidence for an improvement in standards seems stronger than the evidence for a fall at this period.

Nor indeed can we say much about standards of consumption more directly. Figures of imports of tea, sugar and tobacco for example show very little rise (in some cases there are declines) over the controversial period, and the current pessimists' case rests a good deal on this negative evidence. Unfortunately these imported commodities were not consumed in large quantities

[1] Hobsbawm, 'The British Standard of Living 1790–1850', *op. cit.* p. 56.

by the average family and were subject to import duties which made important differences to the rate of consumption. For sugar there is evidence of a stagnant, even a falling consumption: from 29½ lb. per head in 1811 to 15 lb. per head in 1840. For tea there is evidence of a rise from about 1 lb. per head in 1811 (when, however, the duty paid was 4s. per head) to about 1½ lb. in 1841 (when the duty had fallen to under 3s. per head). Consumption of tobacco, on the other hand, went down from 19 oz. per head in 1811 to about 14½ in 1841, but the duty had gone up and no one knows how much tobacco was smuggled in. These consumption figures are inconclusive in their implications therefore, and we have no reliable estimates of the consumption of more important items of working-class expenditure, of bread for example, of milk or meat or butter or eggs. True there are figures of beasts slaughtered at Smithfield market but these are for numbers only, they make no allowance for changes in average weight and they are incomplete even as an index of London consumption, for we have no information on the trade in other London meat-markets.

To sum up, then, what conclusions can we draw from all this? The first is that there is no firm evidence for an overall improvement in working-class standards of living between about 1780 and about 1820. Indeed, if we take into account the harvest failures, growing population, the privations of a major war and the distress of the post-war economic dislocation, we may reasonably conclude that on balance average standards of living tended to fall rather than to rise.

For the period from about 1820 to about 1840 it is difficult to be as definite. Certainly there is no evidence for a substantial rise in real incomes and what rise we can deduce from the statistics is not strong enough to compensate for the wide margins of error in the data. On the other hand the evidence for a fall in standards of living rests *either* on presumptions that we cannot empirically check with the information now accessible to us—like the incidence of unemployment, for example—*or* on data on actual consumption per head of certain not very important commodities whose consumption could as well be attributed to changes in tastes or the weight of duties as to a fall in real incomes. Perhaps on balance the optimists can make out a more convincing case for an improvement in the standard of living than the pessimists can for a fall. But either case is based largely on circumstantial evidence and there is one thing that we can take as reasonably certain—and that is that whichever way it went, the net change was relatively slight.

Finally, beginning in the 1840's we find much stronger evidence of an improvement in the average real incomes of the working class, evidence that has been strong enough to convince even some of the remaining pessimists. It does not rest however on a perceptible increase in real wage rates. Habakkuk, for example, observes that 'The inconclusive nature of the current debate about living standards in this period is perhaps a warrant for supposing that a substantial and general and demonstrable rise in the real wages of industrial workers did not occur until the 1850's and 1860's: it was not until about 1870 that real wages in agriculture began to rise and a steady rise was apparent only in the 1880's.'[1] The argument for an improvement in the average standard of living in the middle of the century rests largely on a change in the composition of the labour force. To quote Hobsbawm, the most recent of the advocates of the pessimistic interpretation of the industrial revolution:

Little as we know about the period before the middle forties, most students would agree that the real sense of improvement among the labouring classes thereafter was due less to a rise in wage-rates, which often remained surprisingly stable for years, or to an improvement in social conditions, but to the upgrading of labourers from very poorly to less poorly paid jobs, and above all to a decline in unemployment or to a greater regularity of employment.[2]

This shift in the distribution of the labour force from the traditional highly seasonal occupations characteristic of a pre-industrial economy to the modern sector with its mechanical aids to labour, its disciplined working habits and its continuous intensive use of capital equipment in day and night shifts is the true spirit and essence of an industrial revolution. Agricultural labourers, for example, normally earn less per week than factory workers of equivalent skill; hand-loom weavers earn less than power-loom weavers; canal bargemen less than locomotive drivers. Thus a shift in the composition of the labour force—a fall in the *proportion* of workers engaged in the low earning

[1] H. J. Habakkuk, *American and British Technology in the 19th Century* (1964), p. 139.
[2] Hobsbawm, 'The British Standard of Living 1790–1850', *op. cit.* p. 52.

categories and a corresponding rise in the proportion of those in the high earning categories—would raise the average level of earnings per worker even if wage-rates in each occupation remained unchanged. This is the process that seems to have gathered momentum in the 1840's and to have brought with it perceptible improvements in material standards of life for the working classes. It may indeed have begun earlier, but it is not until the 1840's that we can be reasonably certain of its positive effects.

So much for the wage data. What about the national-income estimates? These suggest that between 1801 and 1851 national product per head at constant prices almost doubled. As between the pre-war period (say 1791) and 1851 the improvement was probably somewhat less, for 1801 was already a year of heavy inflation. In the controversial period between 1821 and 1841, however, there was an improvement, it seems, of over a third. Whether this meant a corresponding increase in the average real incomes of the working classes, however, would have depended on the way the increase in the national product was distributed. If the increase in incomes was entirely absorbed by the property-owning classes in the form of profits and rent, and if the increased output of goods and services took the form either of capital goods or of goods and services that were outside the normal budget of the wage-earners, then it is fair to presume that the employed population gained nothing from the process of early industrialization.

The evidence available certainly indicates that there was a shift in the distribution of incomes in favour of profits and rent and a change in the composition of output in favour of capital goods, exports and goods and services for upper-class consumption. But it is manifest that this is not the whole story. The new factories were not producing entirely for the export or the luxury trade or for producers, and the fact that prices of manufactured consumer-goods fell substantially meant that the working classes gained as consumers where they did not gain as wage-earners. So that while on balance the evidence is strongly in favour of the view that working-class standards of living improved by less than the increase in national income per head would suggest over the first half of the nineteenth century; and while there is no doubt that certain sectors of the labouring poor suffered a serious deterioration in their earning-power because they were made redundant by technical progress, nevertheless it would be difficult to credit an overall decline in real incomes per wage-earning family in a period when aggregate real incomes for the nation as a whole were growing appreciably faster than population. In effect, the sustained growth of national product to which industrialization gave rise tended to exert an upward pressure on working-class standards of living in three main ways, none of which implied a rise in the price of labour; (1) by creating more regular employment opportunities for all members of the family—this meant high earnings per year and per family even without a rise in wages per man-hour worked; (2) by creating more opportunities for labour specialization and hence for the higher earnings that semi-skilled or skilled labour can command: here again the average earnings can rise without an increase in the wage rate because the composition of the labour force changes in favour of the higher earning group; and (3) the upward pressure on the workers' standard of living also operated through the reductions in the prices of consumer goods and the widening of the range of commodities which came within the budget of the working classes. Finally of course, to the extent that it raised real purchasing power for the masses, industrialization expanded the market for manufactured goods and so justified further increases in investment and output and labour productivity.

CHAPTER 16

THE ACHIEVEMENT

By 1851, the year of the great Crystal Palace Exhibition, Britain had clearly passed the point of no return in the process of industrialization. This much was obvious to contemporaries and has been accepted since by economic historians, though the latter interpret it in different ways. According to Clapham, 'the course was set towards the "industry state" but the voyage was not half over'.[1] According to the Rostow 'stages of growth' model this was approximately the date at which Britain reached 'maturity', and had, by definition,

mastered and extended over virtually the whole range of its resources all that the then modern science and technology had to offer an economy with the resources and the population-resource balance of mid-nineteenth century Britain...Less then seventy years from the launching of the canal and cotton textile boom of the 1780's when the industrial revolution may be said to have begun, Britain had wholeheartedly transformed itself into an industrial nation—its commitment confirmed by the Repeal of the Corn Laws.[2]

It is generally agreed, then, that Britain had been through an industrial revolution by the middle of the nineteenth century, though the revolution had by no means worked itself out. What did this imply? What were the significant changes that had taken place in the economy since the middle of the nineteenth century? How far had it got on the route to today's modern industrial economy? How, essentially, did it differ from the pre-industrial economy that existed roughly a century before on the threshold of the industrial revolution?

There are three main ways in which an economy which has experienced an industrial revolution differs from its pre-industrial counterpart. It differs (1) in industrial and social

---

[1] Clapham, *Economic History*, vol. II, p. 22.
[2] Rostow, *Stages of Economic Growth*, pp. 60–1.

structure, (2) in productivity and in the standards of living associated with higher productivity, and (3) in its rates of economic growth.

I. INDUSTRIAL AND SOCIAL STRUCTURE

To begin with, then, let us consider the occupational structure of the economy. What, in the first place, did its people do?

By 1850 Britain was certainly industrialized in that more of its people were engaged in manufacturing industry than in agriculture. Nearly $3\frac{1}{4}$ millions of its labour force were manufacturers, compared with rather more than 2 million who were agriculturalists. Moreover the agricultural industry was distinguished at this stage by the fact that its landless labourers constituted a relatively large proportion of its labour force. It had moved a very long way, that is to say, from the peasant economy. In 1851 more than three-quarters of the numbers engaged in the agricultural industry of England and Wales were paid employees. This was probably a larger proportion than ever before or since. After the great exodus from agriculture in the course of the following half-century the proportion of paid employees fell below 60 per cent.

It should be remembered, however, first that the term 'manufacturer' or 'manufacturing industry' covers a wide variety of activities, from the craftsman cobbler to the factory worker; and second that the factory worker was not yet the representative manufacturer. The kind of domestic industry in which manufacturing activity was an off-season employment for agriculturalists was of negligible importance by the middle of the nineteenth century. But small-scale manufacturing at the traditional family level of operations was far from dead. There were more than a quarter of a million shoemakers recorded at the 1851 census of occupations, and about half a million tailors, dressmakers and milliners. There were more blacksmiths than workers in the iron foundries and furnaces. More people were working either in their own homes as self-employed craftsmen or outworkers, or in small workshops, than in large-scale factory industry. More people, actually more than one out of every seven members of the labour force, were engaged in domestic or personal service than in the textile factories. Industrialization or no industrialization, the army of domestic servants, the host of housemaids which served the Victorian middle-class home, was still growing faster than the labour force, until towards the end of the nineteenth century it reached its peak and accounted for between 15 and 16 per cent of the occupied population of Great Britain.

The other major occupational group in 1850 was the heterogeneous group engaged in commercial occupations—the shopkeepers and their clerks, the dealers, the pedlars, the seamen and the insurance agents. There were more than a million workers in the trade and commerce group of industries and in addition about half a million in each of the following: building, public and professional services, transport and mining and quarrying. Of these, only the railway workers were in an industry which was characteristically 'modern', in that it had been revolutionized by the technological developments of the past century. Even so, 'more men were employed about horses on the roads than in all the work of the railway system'.[1] Seamen were still literally sailors, who travelled for the most part in wooden sailing-ships. Recruitment to the civil service was still dependent on patronage. 'Sometimes the patronage was exercised by a minister, sometimes by the local M.P., sometimes by the departmental authorities. Often no doubt the patronage was administered disinterestedly: but the fact remained that those who entered the Civil Service under this system owed something to somebody's influence.'[2] Even in the coal-mines, although there was mechanical lifting and pumping-gear, the men who worked on the seams still used their muscles and a pick to get the raw material on which (more than any other) British industry depended.

What changes had taken place in the pattern of occupations since the beginning of the industrial revolution? It is difficult to make an exact comparison because we have no general census of occupations for any date preceding 1841, and indeed not even a population count preceding the 1801 census. We can be reasonably certain that the population primarily engaged in agriculture was a good deal higher in, say 1770, when probably well over half of the labour force was so engaged, compared with

[1] Clapham, *Economic History*, vol. II, p. 25.
[2] Sir E. Bridges in *The Civil Service in Britain and France*, ed. W. A. Robson (1956), p. 27. Written examinations for junior posts were introduced in 1855 but these were merely elementary entrance tests. The first competitive examination was held in 1859 (for the Indian Civil Service) and in 1872 recruitment to the First Division began to be based on a competitive examination of university degree standard.

about a fifth in 1850. Probably less than a quarter of the occupied population was primarily engaged in manufacturing in 1770, and of these relatively few were employed outside their own homes.

But probably the most significant difference in the labour force of 1850 as compared with the mid eighteenth century was that it was a more specialized labour force. In pre-industrial times the vast majority of those engaged in manufacturing were part-time workers in an industry whose principal economic activity was agricultural or commercial. Even as late as the 1830's and 1840's it was difficult for those endeavouring to take censuses of occupations to distinguish between the craftsman-tradesman and the manufacturer. In 1831, for example, when a census of occupations of adult males was taken as part of the population census, those engaged in 'retail trade and handi-crafts' were grouped together in a special category which included (besides building and road transport and some cate-gories of wholesale trade) a number of occupations which were classified with manufacturing in later censuses. Probably the deciding factor which determined whether an individual should be enumerated with the retail trade and handicraft group of occupations rather than with the manufacturing group was (besides his skill) the fact that the former was a self-employed person dealing with a purchaser of final products, rather than a factory employee or an outworker. By 1850 the self-employed artisan was becoming less predominant and the distinction between manufacturer and shopkeeper was less fuzzy at the edges. But retail trade was still generally a skilled occupation.

In effect, the distribution industry was one of the last major strongholds of the traditional pre-industrial economy and continued so until well into the nineteenth century. Of course it had to adapt in some ways to the new shape of the industrialized economy. In the mid eighteenth century many of the things people consumed were made within the family or bought at markets direct from producers in the same area. Goods bought from more distant areas were usually sold at periodic fairs which then constituted the most important wholesale and retail outlet. As the towns expanded, however, and as road, river, canal and later railway communications between them improved, there was a decline in family or local self-sufficiency and a corresponding increase in the importance of fixed shop retailing. At the same time specialization in trade tended to widen the gap between producer and consumer and to multiply the number of wholesale and other kinds of intermediaries.

But these changes and developments in the distributive structure and techniques between the middle 18th and middle 19th centuries would appear to be mainly ones of degree, of modification and of shift of emphasis rather than of transformation and reorganization. The basic structure and character of the distributive trades, the emphasis on skill and experience in retailing, the higgling as to price and the important role played by open markets had not changed fundamentally.[1]

Thus even by the mid nineteenth century many people still made the bulk of their everyday purchases in markets, market-halls or fairs or from pedlars and travelling salesmen: and even the urban upper classes still bought largely from craftsmen-producers direct. The shop had begun to supplant the pedlar or the itinerant tradesman of the fairs before the end of the eighteenth century, but the fixed retail shops with window display and a wide range of goods which are today's characteristic retail outlets were still confined to the larger towns. Most retailers played an important role in the preparation and processing of the goods they sold and standards of quality were therefore individual to each retailer. Working-class consumers with a limited choice of shop, still more those who got part of their wages in kind and were thus forced to buy in 'truck shops', had to put up with adulteration of their purchases. Neither price nor quality tended to be uniform as between different retailers. In the better-class shops, for example, it was considered bad taste to price-mark the wares—as it is indeed today in some luxury establishments. Except where his choice of shop was limited, however, the mid-nineteenth-century customer could expect to influence the price he paid by bargaining with the shopkeeper. 'There was an enormous growth of shops between the 1820's and the 1850's, and much of this growth was dominated by the small general shop which tended to be operated by men and women of a similar social background to the urban poor.'[2]

What had happened however by 1850, as compared with say 1750, was that the range of goods regularly available to the

[1] James B. Jefferys, *Retail Trading in Britain 1850–1950* (1954), p. 5.
[2] David Alexander, *Retailing in England during the Industrial Revolution* (1970), p. 234.

average purchaser had widened and that the chain of inter-mediaries between producer and consumer had lengthened. To a large extent this was a consequence of the improved system to communications. 'The trade in fresh dairy produce, for example, had formerly been strictly localized, with little room for intermediaries. The steamboat now brought fresh Irish butter regularly to Liverpool and fresh West country butter to London.'[1] London's milk supplies were also affected by quicker transport facilities. Cows were still being milked on the doorsteps of suburban houses in the 1830's but country dairies 20–25 miles out were already sending milk to London dealers in closed containers in spring carts which sped rapidly over the improved radius of roads stretching out from the metropolis. The railways eventually revolutionized the market for milk though not as rapidly as had been expected, and until the railway companies learned to handle milk in such a way as to keep it cool (i.e. until the 1870's) the rail-borne milk went mainly to the poor. Vegetables were more easily transported and an elaborate organization grew up at Covent Garden to deal with a trade which as a consequence of the new coastal steamers of the 1820's and 1830's had begun to reach into the farming areas of eastern Scotland. On the other hand, the line of stations which had grown up to serve the drovers on their long trek from the grazing areas to the main towns lost their function when livestock began to travel by railway truck, and when the speedy transport of deadstock became possible on a large scale.

The fact is that, although a substantial proportion of the inhabitants of mid-Victorian England were pursuing traditional occupations with traditional techniques and methods of organi-zation, there were few of them whose way of life had not been changed radically by the industrial revolution and its associated developments—by the great growth of population and its redistribution from country to town and from south to north, by the vastly improved transport system which widened the domestic market for many commodities which had hitherto been sold only at the local level, and by the expansion of overseas trade which widened the range of goods on the British market and created an unprecedented degree of dependence on the world market. The process of change created problems of its own.

[1] Clapham, *Economic History*, vol. I, p. 227.

The demographic changes, for example, raised a variety of social problems. The great growth of population meant that people crowded into urban areas whose amenities were designed for sparser settlements. In 1770 the population of England and Wales had begun to grow but was probably not much more than 7 millions. By 1851 it was near 18 million. In the mid eighteenth century the proportion of the population living in concentrations of even as little as 5,000 or more was probably not more than 16 per cent: by 1841 the proportion was in the region of 60 per cent; and between 1841 and 1851 a further 1,800,000 people (more than the total town population of the 1760's or 1770's) were squeezed into the large towns.

More significant indeed than the absolute numbers living in urban areas in the mid nineteenth century was the rate at which these numbers were being added to by natural increase or migration. It was this that created many of the social problems, widened the gulf between rich and poor, made human labour dirt-cheap, and created a squalid environment for so many people. Composed as they were so largely of uprooted people, the towns became a breeding ground for vice and crime. Out of about $3\frac{1}{2}$ million people living in London and the main English and Welsh towns in 1851, only about a third had been born where they were then living. These early Victorian towns, impersonal, unwholesome and harshly competitive, were growing faster than the ability of the municipalities to cope with the sheer physical and social problems of urbanization. In every spare corner of the towns another house was squeezed. With largely unpaved streets and open sewers the living conditions of the poorer, most overcrowded sections of the main townships were appalling: epidemics of cholera or typhoid were uncomfortably frequent. Nor were they confined to the poor. Albert the Prince Consort died of typhoid fever in 1861. But poverty was the crime which mid-Victorian society visited with its most savage penalties. Chadwick, the crusader for public health, reported in the 1840's that the people living in the wynds of Edinburgh and Glasgow or in the cellars of Liverpool, Manchester or Leeds lived in conditions worse than in the prisons.

If standards of health were put under pressure by an expanding, increasingly concentrated, population so too were standards of education. In the pre-industrial economy of the early eighteenth century the poor got their education mainly through an increasing number of charity schools. The Society for the Promotion of Christian Knowledge, for example, had been founded in 1699 to organize charity schools 'for those whom nature or family had determined to the plough, the oar and other handicrafts' and within 35 years had set up or taken under its wing 1,500 schools designed as 'little garrisons against Popery'—thus goading Catholics and other non-Conformists to set up rival establishments. But the driving force behind the Charity School Movement had lost its momentum by the second half of the eighteenth century. Two factors brought the nation's educational system under increasing strain in the later eighteenth century—one was the bulge in the population of school age associated with the rising birth rate and falling child mortality rate; the other was the rising demand for child labour. The only area of free education which expanded in the late eighteenth century was the Sunday School movement which had the advantage of not encroaching on the pupil's working week. It may have had some effect on the gradual improvement in the proportion of women able to sign the marriage register but it is unlikely to have been effective in raising substantially the educational standards of the labouring poor.

There were of course the factory schools. In some of the early factory villages the more enlightened employers (e.g. Richard Arkwright) provided basic instruction in the three Rs for their child employees, euphemistically called 'apprentices'; and Peel's Health and Morals of Apprentices Act (1802) provided that for the first four years apprentices were to be instructed by a 'discreet and proper person'. But the Act was ineffective and it was not until the 1833 Factory Act established a factory inspectorate that schooling for child workers became at all common. Even then the provision made was often minimal especially in the early stages. Leonard Horner, one of the first of the factory inspectors for example, recorded a case where the factory 'school' was conducted by the fireman 'at intervals between his feeding and stirring the fire of the engine boiler'.

More generally, it would appear that although national educational standards may have slightly improved, due perhaps to the increasing economic opportunities open to literate individuals, in some regions and occupations there was a marked deterioration during the late eighteenth and early nineteenth centuries. The evidence on illiteracy (measured by the crude index of ability to sign the marriage register) suggests that a majority of English males were literate by 1750 and of females by the 1840's. By 1840 probably less than a third of English males were unable to sign the marriage register.[1] For Lancashire however there is evidence that literacy levels were actually declining from the late 1790's to the early 1830's: and that, even when an improvement set in in the late 1830's, there was no corresponding increase in the job opportunities for those with higher educational qualifications. The fact is that the factory workforce often required less rather than more education than the domestic outworker: it has been estimated, for example, that powerloom weavers possessed less than a third of the literacy level of the male weavers they replaced.[2]

An industrial revolution entails profound social as well as economic changes, and the first industrial revolution found society unprepared for the problems that emerged during the upheaval. The Victorians of the mid nineteenth century were acutely conscious of living in an age of transition. They were always talking about it as such. Mill described the distinguishing feature of modern life as the fact 'that human beings are no longer born to their place in life...but are free to employ their faculties and such favourable chances as offer, to achieve the lot which may appear to them most desirable'.[3] Even those who criticized the horrors of industrialism took an optimistic view of the transition. They were immensely impressed by the sheer magnitude of their achievement—bigger populations, longer lines of railway, more tons of coal, more blast-furnaces, more exports, etc. It was an industrial achievement which compared favourably with that of any other nation in the contemporary world and it is perhaps not surprising that they overrated the significance of their material progress. Some of them saw the railways as an instrument of moral and intellectual progress, and associated industrial progress with the end of war. The Prince Consort saw in the Great Exhibition concrete evidence of 'a period of most wonderful transition, which tends rapidly

---

[1] R. S. Schofield, 'Dimensions of Illiteracy, 1750–1850', *Explorations in Economic History* (1973).

[2] Michael Sanderson, 'Literacy and Social Mobility in the Industrial Revolution', *Past and Present* (1972), p. 90.

[3] J. S. Mill, *The Subjection of Women* (1869), p. 31.

to accomplish that great end to which indeed all history points—the realization of the unity of mankind'.[1]

No doubt the Victorians were inclined to let their imagination run away with them on this score, but the material achievements which stimulated these moral flights of fancy were real enough. Moreover, as far as the industrial revolution had gone by 1850, they were achievements which were evidently the work of practical men of business rather than men of education or theoretical scholarship. The great inventors adopted an empirical approach to the technological problems which interested them and reached their solutions by experiment rather than theory. Businessmen put them into practice in a hardheaded way with profits as their sole criterion. It is not surprising that anti-intellectualism became so marked a characteristic of Victorian thinking. According to Huxley

practical men still believed that the idol whom they worship—rule of thumb—has been the source of the past prosperity and will suffice for the future welfare of the arts and manufacturers. They were of the opinion that science is speculative rubbish: that theory and practice have nothing to do with one another: and that the scientific habit of mind is an impediment rather than an aid in the conduct of ordinary affairs.[2]

Before the new technologies spread to other countries on a scale sufficient to create foreign competition, there seemed nothing wrong with this homespun philosophy. Judging by the success with which British captains of industry took the lion's share of world markets and cut their costs and raised their profits, they knew how to conduct the nation's business. But when foreigners began not only to imitate, but to develop the new techniques, and when the course of technical change began to depend more on progress in pure science—with the growth of industries like the chemical industry and electrical engineering and the changes in the iron and steel industry—the English entrepreneur began to lag behind his continental competitors.

The top people, the men who took the crucial decisions, had perhaps changed least of all under the impact of the Industrial Revolution. According to Kitson Clark

[1] Quoted W. E. Houghton, *The Victorian Frame of Mind 1830–70* (1957), p. 43.
[2] T. H. Huxley, *Science and Culture and other Essays* (1881), pp. 3–4.

the eighteenth century lingered at the top of society as obstinately and as self-confidently as it did anywhere in the social pattern of Victorian England. A wanderer from the 1750's would have found much to wonder at and not a little to fear in the England of the 1850's, the machines, the factories and their masters, the busy crowds, the newspapers...all these things he might well find strange and disturbing. But when he reached those who might be considered to be at the head of society he might feel himself to be reasonably at home. Many of them would be the grandchildren of men he had known, nor would many of their thoughts and habits be altogether strange to him.[1]

The middle classes were represented and considered in the reformed Parliament but they did not control the policy decisions. Bagehot writing in 1859 noted that 'the series of Cabinet Ministers presents a nearly unbroken rank of persons who are themselves large landowners or are connected closely by birth or intermarriage with large landowners'.[2] In the 1847 House of Commons there were still more than eighty members who owed their seat to patronage. Even where democracy seemed to prevail it took some curious forms. 'In a proprietary borough like Malton, with a scot-and-lot franchise, many of the poorer tenements occupied by labourers avowedly existed only because votes were attached to them, and their votes were cast not out of tenurial attachment to Earl Fitzwilliam but because he footed the bill for bribing them.'[3] Until the Ballot Act made voting secret in 1872, landlords and employers could confidently rely on the votes of men who depended on them for their livelihood and much later than this, of course, the traditions of a deferential society ensured that the local aristocracy exerted a powerful influence in local elections. The fact that bribery was possible meant that the effective political power never became completely reserved to a closed caste. But there was nothing new about this. Namier in discussing the eighteenth-century unreformed Parliament remarked on the corruption of the popular boroughs and interpreted it as 'a mark of English freedom and independence, for no one bribes where he can bully'.[4]

It remains true, however, that in 1850 national economic

[1] Kitson Clark, *The Making of Victorian England*, p. 206.
[2] W. Bagehot, *Essays on Parliamentary Reform* (1883), p. 209.
[3] F. M. L. Thompson, *English Landed Society in the Nineteenth Century* (1963), p. 205.
[4] Lewis Namier, *England in the Age of the American Revolution* (1930), p. 4.

policy decisions were still taken largely by people who, if they were not themselves members of the nobility and gentry owed their political power to the hereditary owners of the large estates. These were not numerous. An inquiry into the holding of land in England in 1871 showed that about half the land was owned by 7,400 people. At this stage, in the golden age of English agriculture, it is safe to assumed that these were the richest men in the kingdom. Even those who made their fortunes in industry and commerce normally consolidated their economic and social position in the community by buying estates 'so that as the century went forward, among the landed proprietors could be found the Peels, the Arkwrights, the Barings, the Strutts and other families who had made their fortunes before they bought their land, many of whom became assimilated or partly assimilated to the old social system'.[1] What Namier said of the mid eighteenth century could equally well be said of the mid nineteenth century: 'wealth amassed in trade (or industry) was laid out in landed estates and used to secure seats in the House of Commons, for both helped to lift their holders into a higher social sphere'.[2] The fact moreover that investments in land were not dependent solely on the fortunes of agriculture, but owed a good deal of their return to the process of industrialization—through the royalties on coal mines, for example, or to rising land values due to railway construction or urbanization—meant that it was to the interest of many of the landed gentry to promote the process of industralization, to hasten the industrial revolution on to completion. It was this more than the growing influence of the loquacious middle classes that set the course of the new industry state by shaping economic policy at the national level. On the other hand, to the extent that the ultimate ambition of British manufacturers was to become landed proprietors, the most able entrepreneurs were likely to retire before they had reached the fullest potential of their industrial empires. James Nasmyth, for example, retired when he was only 48. Sir John Guest retained his works 'but acquired estates and a London house and diverted funds from reinvestment to maintaining a position in society'.[3]

At the micro-economic level, however, it was the middle

[1] Kitson Clark, *The Making of Victorian England*, p. 215.
[2] Namier, *England in the Age of the American Revolution*, p. 10.
[3] Habakkuk, *American and British Technology in the 19th Century*, p. 178.

classes who took most of the economic decisions. It was their enterprises that expanded the national product; it was their improving standards of living that created much of the demand for domestic manufactures; it was their savings that financed the railways and much of the growing volume of overseas investment; it was their anti-intellectualism, their puritanical moral code which shaped the attitudes of mind which we tend to regard as characteristic of Victorianism. In view then of the acknowledged importance of this group in the community it is worth while trying to form a precise view of who they were and how large a section of the community they constituted around 1850.

In an estimate based on the returns of the 1851 census Dr Erickson has calculated that the number of adult males who fell within this category was rather less than $1\frac{1}{4}$ million, which amounted to about 18 per cent of the occupied labour force.[1] About half of them were engaged in commercial occupations of various kinds—they were the merchants, the bankers, the dealers, the shopkeepers and the army of underpaid clerks and shop assistants who held down the white-collar jobs in nineteenth-century England. About a quarter of them were farmers; and the remaining quarter were members of the professional, administrative and employing classes in commerce or industry. It was this last group, the professional administrative and employing classes outside agriculture, who took the major economic decisions at the micro-economic level. It was this group from which most of the innovators and the risk-takers were drawn. It numbered not many more than 300,000 people.

The middle class was literate for the most part. Most of the top 300,000 were educated in local schools, though by 1850 the railway system was making it easier for them to send their sons to the public schools. An inquiry into the social origins of the steel manufacturers showed that in 1865 only 10 per cent of the leading steel manufacturers had been to public schools.[2] In 1850 the proportion would have been negligible. A century later one out of three of the top managers had been to public school. Few of the leading businessmen in the mid nineteenth century continued their sons' education to what might be called a secondary-school level. What it amounted to was that the

---

[1] C. Erickson, *British Industrialists, Steel and Hoisery 1850–1950* (1959), p. 234.
[2] C. Erickson, *British Industrialists*, p. 34.

managers of British industry in the nineteenth century had generally had their education on the job. In the steel and engineering industries a seven-year term of apprenticeship, beginning at the age of thirteen or fourteen, was common. In the textile trades apprenticeship for future managers consisted generally of a commercial training. This was where the sons of businessmen began their education for managerial positions. British industry was becoming inbred, highly specialized, by the middle of the nineteenth century, in striking contrast to the situation a century before when one entrepreneur might actively engage in several different types of manufacture, in agriculture and in commerce at one and the same time. In spite of the legend perpetuated and to some extent created by Samuel Smiles with his best-selling volume of biographies entitled *Self-Help* (published in 1859), the chances of a man rising from the ranks to managerial level, the chances even of a man rising to wealth on the basis of his technical skill, were severely limited. The successful British manufacturer was distinguished more by his commercial experience than by his technical skill. This was partly because successful innovation was a practical rather than a scientific art in the first industrial revolution, and partly because it was the profits earned in successful trading operations that gave a man the kind of staying-power that was necessary to enable him to ride out the cyclical depressions in demand that characterized the industrial economy.

2. STANDARDS OF LIVING AND PRODUCTIVITY

Over the century that ended in the 1850's product per head is estimated to have multiplied nearly $2\frac{1}{2}$ times in Britain, and this brought with it more than a doubling of the national standard of living.[1] Not all industries nor all members of the community shared in this improvement. In industries like transport, textiles and iron manufacture, output per worker increased beyond all previous experience, though wages per worker rose quite modestly, and prices, particularly the prices of exports, fell steeply. In some of the service industries that expanded their employment in the large towns, productivity probably fell as the population trying to earn a living in them grew faster than their sales. Thousands of people are estimated to have been subsisting

[1] Based on estimates of national product per head at constant prices made by Deane and Cole, *British Economic Growth*.

on the sale of foodstuffs in the streets of London, for example, and a few days of rain brought many of them near to starvation. Many others found a precarious living by searching the rivers and the sewers and the gutters for rubbish that might have a market value if salvaged, for cigar ends that could be made up again for resale—these were the mudlarks, the scavengers, the wool-gatherers and the gutter-snipes. The large towns with their wide range of opportunities for gainful employment attracted a larger population than they could maintain in full-time employment and the unlucky ones clutched at the chance to sell their services on any terms at all.

The large mass of labourers with nothing but their muscles for income-earning assets were no doubt better off in the up-phases of trade cycles than their fathers or grandfathers had ever hoped to be; but many of them were a great deal worse off than their ancestors when trade depression brought unemployment and destitution in the harsh shadow of the new poor-law; and the spectre of unemployment was a real threat even to those who kept their jobs. Those who stayed in employment (and most of the time they did in this expanding economy) consumed more material things and a wider range of goods than their forefathers had done, but the difference was not at all spectacular. Professor Phelps Brown's calculations of the real wages of building craftsmen, for example, indicate that in the 1850's the builder's real wage was only 20 per cent higher than his counterpart's in the 1750's.[1] And in 1848 J. S. Mill wrote gloomily in his *Principles* that 'Hitherto it is questionable if all the mechanical inventions yet made have lightened the day's toil of any human being'.[2] Perhaps this was an exaggeration. 'It was easier to mind a completely self-acting mule than to push about the carriage of the old hand-mule. The power-loom shed was noisy and its looms had been speeded up: but work in it was certainly lighter, day for day, than the bowed, endless, insanitary monotony of that lower-grade handloom weaving of the thirties and forties.'[3]

On the other hand it is doubtful whether many pre-industrial workers spent quite so many hours per day and per week, week after week, on the job as was common in the mid nineteenth

[1] Phelps Brown and Hopkins, 'Seven Centuries of Building Wages'.
[2] *Principles*, book II, ch. v.
[3] Clapham, *op. cit.* vol. II, p. 447.

century. The Ten Hours Act of 1847 had made the first real impact on hours of work in the textile factories, where the normal working day lasted from 12 to $12\frac{1}{2}$ hours even in the best-regulated factories in the 1820's and 1830's. But the 1847 Act was not fully effective because the limits of the legal day exceeded 10 hours and it was thus easy to evade the Act, since workers operated in relays. The 1850 Factory Act stopped up the loopholes in the 1847 legislation by introducing a 60-hour legal week for women in the textile trades; and it was the beginning of the English week-end for it ordered a stoppage of work on Saturdays at 2 p.m. But the textile trades, so long the location of the worst abuses of the factory system, were by then better regulated than most, for the shorter hours which were enforced for women and children could not help but affect the conditions of the men who worked in association with them. The builders worked 52–64 hours a week according to season; a London compositor worked 63 hours a week all the year round, as did the engineer and the iron-founder. 'There were trades with longer regular hours; outwork of all kinds in which inclination or necessity determined the working day; continuous processes with 12-hour shifts; and all sorts of emergency arrangements'[1] History does not record the hours worked in the sweated unregulated workshops, but there 70 hours a week and more was common enough when trade was good, and workers were cast off entirely when it was bad. In general, however, in most of the mechanized or heavy industries a working day of 10 or $10\frac{1}{2}$ hours was usual; and 10 hours a day at the beck and call of a machine, or at the controls of a locomotive, or at the difficult and often dangerous tasks of gas-works, chemical shops, engineering works or steel furnaces, must have involved more strain on the individual operative than much longer hours at the pre-industrial processes, the pace of which the worker could adjust to his own mood or inclination. Where legislation to restrict hours was effective, employers often responded by speeding up machinery and thus intensifying the toil of the machine-minders. There was a loss of leisure and a building up of tension involved in this acceleration of the pace of economic life. Perhaps it is not surprising that the suicide rate went up as the nineteenth century wore on. A writer in the 1851

[1] *Ibid.* p. 448.

Edinburgh Review observed that the struggle for existence was 'by no means confined to the lower orders. Throughout the whole community we are all called to labour too early and compelled to labour too severely and too long. We live sadly too fast.'[1] Even the city offices, to quote Clapham, 'even so capitalistic an institution as Lloyds', were open on Saturday afternoons.

It seems then that if the working classes earned more and spent more in 1850 than the labouring poor of the pre-industrial times, they paid for it in intensified toil. The industrial revolution gave them a chance to earn more by working harder. It had not yet given them anything for nothing by 1850. If we were to set against the welfare represented by higher money incomes and lower prices for manufactures (though not for food) the disutility of longer, harder working hours, it is doubtful whether the balance would be tipped in their favour. For many of them life on these terms was only acceptable if heavily laced with strong liquor; and drunkenness, together with the degradation and cruelty to which it gives rise, was one of the characteristic features of the English scene in the mid nineteenth century—as it had been of course a hundred years or so before, in the gin age. Strong drink caused endless trouble to the employers of labour, as the railway builders frequently complained, and it had an important influence on the outcome of parliamentary elections. It drew a firm line between the classes of society, between the respectable and the disreputable, between the two nations of rich and poor, in a way that was not nearly so evident in the eighteenth century.

Compared with what it had been a century before then, the standard of living of the British people in 1850 was higher on the average and a great deal more varied. It was also, for a larger number of people (if a smaller proportion of the population) more vulnerable and more squalid. For many more still, it was achieved at the cost of more labouring effort. The workers in a pre-industrial society have their hours of work dictated by the seasons, by the weather, by the hours of daylight and darkness and by the limited number of opportunities for gainful employment open to the weaker members of the community (the women and children for example). Their leisure is not always of their own choosing, though it is not therefore valueless. In

---

[1] W. R. Grey, 'England as it is', *Edinburgh Review* (1851), p. 325.

an industrial society work can go on throughout the year and through the night, so long as the output can find a market, and there are many gainful tasks for unskilled and relatively feeble hands. But, given a rising, urbanizing population and an ill-informed, unorganized workforce, the supply of unskilled, casual labour at the disposal of the typical industrial entrepreneur was normally in excess of his demand. So in times of boom most workers could be forced either to work intolerably long hours, or to cope with dangerously accelerated production processes and machines. In times of slump, they were at high risk of unemployment, protected from destitution only by an inadequate and often savagely-administered system of poor relief.

Compared with their contemporaries in other countries, the British people enjoyed a richer and more varied standard of living as a result of industrialization. Estimates of average national income per head suggest that they were then the most affluent people in the world. On the other hand, there were many of them, living in overcrowded insanitary urban conditions, whose real standard of life was much less desirable than that currently enjoyed by their North American or Australian contemporaries with somewhat lower money wages. In terms of national product per head it was apparently not until the last quarter of the nineteenth century that the level for the United States taken as a whole overtook that of the United Kingdom, though in New England and the Middle Atlantic States the Americans had probably drawn ahead by the 1850's. Moreover, American labour, because it was scarce, often found it easier to establish a claim to better working conditions. 'Immigrants' letters sometimes refer not so much to the effect of machinery in maintaining higher wages as to its use to ease the burden of the worker.'[1]

3. RATES OF GROWTH

The third respect in which the industrialized economy differed from the pre-industrial economy was in the extent to which it was growing and changing. Population, national output and incomes per head were all growing faster than they had done in the pre-industrial era and they were growing continuously.

[1] Habakkuk, *American and British Technology in the Nineteenth Century*, p. 110.

Nevertheless growth was not a uniform process, and by the 1850's there were already some areas in which retardation had set in. Population grew at a decadal rate of between 11 and 14 per cent for most of the nineteenth century but it had reached its peak rate in the second decade. For industrial production the peak rate of growth was reached in the 1820's and 1830's. For exports the peak rate came in the period 1848-56, when the volume of British domestic exports more than doubled in less than a decade.

The rate of growth of real national product was given by two factors: the momentum achieved in the sectors that were modernizing and the rate at which resources were shifted from low-productivity low-growth sectors to high-productivity high-growth sectors. So, for gross national product as a whole, the peak rate of growth was not reached until the second half of the nineteenth century when industrial output was already showing a retarded rate of growth, but when the growing weight of the industrial sector, which was associated with the great exodus of labour from agriculture, altered the balance of the economy. Until the 1850's the shift from agriculture to industry, from country to town, had been a relative shift. The labour force in agriculture was still expanding, the population in the rural areas was still growing. It was as though the old pre-industrial economy continued to exist more or less intact beside the industrializing economy which drew its numbers and its strength from the surplus generated by an expanding population. Then in the second half of the nineteenth century the pre-industrial sector began to disintegrate. The numbers engaged in agriculture and those living in the rural areas began to dwindle in absolute terms. Thenceforth the progress towards the complete industrial state was rapid and unchecked and by the end of the century the pre-industrial pockets left in the economy were rarities.

Before the middle of the nineteenth century, however, probably before the end of the first quarter, the process of industrialization had gone far enough to give the British economy a built-in tendency to continuous economic growth. The volume of capital at the disposal of the labour force was growing rather faster than the labour force itself and the long-term trend was definitely set towards a continuous increase in the productivity of the worker. But if growth was by then continuous it was neither steady nor fast. Compared with countries which have industrialized since—compared even with the countries like the United States and Germany which had gone into their industrialization before the end of the nineteenth century—the British rate of growth was a slow process. It is doubtful, for example, whether the long-term rate of growth ever went much above 3 per cent per annum, even in the second half of the nineteenth century when capital and labour resources were shifting rapidly from the low-income agricultural sector towards higher-income sectors like industry or transport. Over most of the nineteenth century the British economy seems to have been growing at an annual rate of between 2 and 3 per cent per annum. In the United States, by contrast, the rate of growth of total output for the period 1839–1913 was between 4 and 5 per cent per annum.

In part, of course, the slowness of the British rate of growth was an inevitable consequence of the fact that this was the first industrial revolution. Trail-blazing is often slow and the economies which followed in the path of the pioneer had the advantage of having some of the uncertainties removed from their path. The later a country began to industrialize the larger was the body of technological knowledge that was open to it to adopt, and the less was the cost in time, or in abortive experiment, that it had to incur in order to reach the levels of productivity achieved by its predecessors. On the other hand there are advantages as well as disadvantages in being first in the field, and the first country to industrialize must have found it easier, in the virtual absence of all competition, to open up new markets.

There are basically three main factors on which the rate of growth of an economy depends: the rate of growth of (and improvement in) the labour force, the rate of capital accumulation and the rate of technological change. In all these respects the British economy seems to have developed relatively slowly by comparison with the later countries to industrialize. The population increase reached its peak in the decades of 1811–31 when it was at the rate of about $1\frac{1}{2}$ per cent per annum, but for the rest of the nineteenth century the annual rate of change was under $1\frac{1}{4}$ per cent. In most other countries which have industrialized since the first industrial revolution annual rates of increase of over 2 per cent have been reached and sustained; and in regions where, as in North and South America, there was a strong immigration operating in conjunction with a high rate of natural increase the labour force has often expanded at long-term rates of over $2\frac{1}{2}$ per cent per annum.

Nor was the British economy distinguished by a high propensity to invest, so that its aggregate capital stock did not expand rapidly. It is probable that the nation's stock of capital grew somewhat faster than its total income in the period 1780–1830 and distinctly faster in the railway age, particularly in the period 1830–1860. But at no stage in this process of industrialization did capital formation grow to be a high proportion of the national income, and it is doubtful whether net new investment was running at an average rate which represented more than 10 per cent of net national product by the 1850's. Moreover, by the 1850's an increasing proportion of the new investments made out of the British national income were going abroad: and these foreign investments, though they created incomes for British investors and helped to create markets for British exports, did not add directly to the national wage bill or to the physical stock of capital in British industries, to the extent that investment at home would have done.

Technical progress also proceeded at a leisurely pace in the British industrial revolution by comparison with later industrializations. The transition from hand spinning-wheel to powered spinning-machines and from charcoal-fired furnaces to coal-fired furnaces took place quite rapidly after the crucial inventions in the last quarter of the eighteenth century, and the mainline railways were laid down within a couple of decades after their economic justification had been established in the early 1830's. Nevertheless these were not typical instances. In many respects British industry was distinguished more by the slowness with which it modernized its methods than by its readiness to change. Cartwright introduced his power-loom in the 1780's, but it took another 60 years before it effectively replaced the hand-loom in the cotton industry and longer still to come into general use in the other textile industries. As late as 1850 the steam-horsepower in use in the textile factories was only about 108,000: it had been nearly 75,000 in 1839. This represented, at both dates, a total of between five and six workers for every unit of steam-horsepower generated in the British textile factories. It was not until the late 1850's and the 1860's that the textile factories began to turn over to steam-horsepower on any scale, and even in 1871 there were still roughly two workers to every unit of steam-horsepower in the textile factories. Moreover, outside the textile factories and the mines, iron-works and railways, steam-power was still a rarity in the mid nineteenth century, half a century after Watt's patent had lapsed and left the way open for any British producer to adopt and adapt the steam-engine.

On the other hand, American inventiveness had begun to be apparent to contemporaries even before American manufacturers began to compete with British manufactures on world markets. By the time of the Great Exhibition of 1851 'the well-informed knew that an American was more likely than an Englishman to get tiresome and expensive handicraft operations done for him by machinery'.[1] The Americans, with their shortage of labour and with the enterprising attitudes characteristic of an immigrant community, were exceptionally receptive to labour-saving improvements. 'A number of inventions in the textile industry in the nineteenth century were made in Britain but practically applied and developed principally in the U.S.A.'[2]

By 1859, less than a decade after the introduction of the sewing machine, there were five times as many in operation in the United States, as in Britain with its extensive clothing industry. The Americans proved proved readier to mechanize because they had stronger incentives to adopt labour-saving methods and because they were relatively free from the ingrained conservatism that stems from a long industrial tradition. The Germans proved readier to develop new technologies because Prussian educational policy had given them the corps of research scientists required by the new industries emerging in the second half of the nineteenth century—the chemical and electrical industries for example. When in 1856 Perkin, a young British chemist, discovered, literally by accident, a method of making dyes (which Britain needed in great quantities for its textile industry) out of coal (a natural resource which Britain had in accessible abundance), it was the Germans who created a new industry out of the discovery and by 1879 they were producing four times the British output.[3]

The corollary of a modest rate of technical progress is a slow

[1] Clapham, *Economic History*, vol. II, p. 12.
[2] Habakkuk, *American and British Technology in the Nineteenth Century*, p. 120.
[3] The story is told by D. S. L. Cardwell, *The Organization of Science in England* (1957), pp. 79 and 105.

rate of growth in the productivity of the economy. If total national product grew between 2 and 3 per cent per annum over most of the nineteenth century, product per head grew by only about $1\frac{1}{2}$ per cent in the first half of the century and by less than $2\frac{1}{2}$ per cent for most of the second half. A growth rate of $1\frac{1}{2}$ per cent per annum implies a doubling in productivity in a little under half a century, which is not a revolutionary rate of progress, and even at $2\frac{1}{2}$ per cent per annum it would take almost a generation to double its level. The fact is that there was still a large area of British economic life that had been untouched by the industrial revolution. The number of individuals engaged in personal and domestic service, for example, continued to grow in absolute terms until the First World War; and the fact that one out of every six or seven members of the labour force was so engaged reflected the relative abundance of labour which was reducing entrepreneurial incentive either to innovate or to add to the community's capital equipment.

Finally it is worth noticing another distinctive and significant dimension of the growth record of the British economy over the period of the industrial revolution: that is the extent to which it was dependent on the international economy both for material inputs and for final demand. Between 1750 and 1800 both real gross national product and the volume of domestic exports roughly doubled, while the volume of retained imports roughly trebled. Between 1800 and 1850 gross national product and imports both increased some three and a half times in real terms; while domestic exports increased by a factor of nearly six and a half times in real terms, and somewhat less in money terms because increasing productivity was permitting a fall in the prices of British manufactured exports. The link with the international economy was a major reason why the first industrial revolution was able to develop spontaneously in a country with a relatively small population and a relatively narrow basis of natural resources. The increasing strength of that link may also have contributed to the characteristically low propensity to invest and to innovate which seems to have distinguished British industrial entrepreneurs in the late nineteenth century from their rivals in other industrializing countries. For heavy dependence on an international market increases the uncertainty of economic predictions and hence the risks of investment in new fixed capital equipment and technological change.

In sum then, endowed as it was with abundant labour, a limited and exhaustible heritage of land and other natural resources, a modest propensity to save and invest and a government which preferred to leave economic development to the free play of private enterprise, the British economy came through its industrial revolution with a relatively low growth-potential by comparison with most of the countries which industrialized later. Several decades of easy success encouraged its entrepreneurs to believe they could avoid rapid changes. At the time of the 1851 Exhibition British manufactures and British machinery were technologically superior, except in a few special cases, to those of any other country. But it was no more than a matter of time before faster-growing rivals with a clear trail to follow and stronger incentive to invest and innovate would begin to outstrip her in their readiness to reduce costs and thus to threaten her virtual monopoly in world markets. When these rivals found governments which were ready actively to assist the industrialization process—even if it was only to the extent of using tariff policy in the interest of domestic producers—the end of British industrial supremacy was definitely in sight.

GUIDE TO FURTHER READING

This bibliography does not provide an exhaustive list of publications dealing with the first industrial revolution, but is intended to introduce students to further reading on topics raised in this volume, and is biased towards collections of articles and critical surveys of current controversies. Most of the readings are listed in relation to particular chapters, but there is a preliminary general section which contains items relating to all or several chapters. The entries in the general section are not repeated in the lists relating to particular chapters.

GENERAL WORKS

1. *National studies and readings*

Ashton, T. S. *The Industrial Revolution, 1760–1830* (rev. ed. 1968).
—— *The Eighteenth Century* (1955).
Brown, M. 'Towards an endogenous explanation of industrialization', *Social Research* (1966).
Clapham, J. H. *An Economic History of Modern Britain*, vol. 1 (1939).
Deane, Phyllis, and Cole, W. A. *British Economic Growth 1688–1959* (1962).
Flinn, M. W. *Origins of the Industrial Revolution* (1966).
Hartwell, R. M. (ed.). *The Causes of the Industrial Revolution in England* (1967).
Hobsbawm, E. J. *Industry and Empire: an Economic History of Britain since 1750* (1968).
Landes, D. *The Unbound Prometheus: Technological Change and Industrial Development in Western Europe from 1750* (1969), p. 277.
Mantoux, P. *The Industrial Revolution in the Eighteenth Century* (12th edition 1961), with introduction by T. S. Ashton.
Mathias, P. *The First Industrial Nation* (1969).
Perkin, H. J. *The Origins of Modern English Society 1780–1880* (1969).
Pressnell, L. S. (ed.). *Studies in the Industrial Revolution* (1960).
Thompson, A. *The Dynamics of the Industrial Revolution* (1973).

2. *Regional studies*

Barker, T. C. and Harris, J. R. *A Merseyside Town in the Industrial Revolution: St Helens* (1954).

Chambers, J. D. *Nottinghamshire in the Industrial Revolution* (1932).
—— 'The Vale of Trent 1760–1800', *Economic History Review Supplement*, no. 3 (1957).
Court, W. H. B. *The Rise of the Midland Industries 1600–1838* (1938).
Dodd, A. H. *The Industrial Revolution in North Wales* (1933).
Hamilton, H. *The Industrial Revolution in Scotland* (1932).
—— *Economic History of Scotland in the Eighteenth Century* (1963).
John, A. H. *Industrial Development of South Wales 1750–1850* (1950).
Marshall, J. *Furness in the Industrial Revolution* (1958).
Rowe, J. *Cornwall in the Age of the Industrial Revolution* (1953).

3. Industry studies

(Other than those listed for chapters dealing with specific industries such as cotton, iron, transport, agriculture)

Ashton, T. S. and Sykes, J. *The Coal Industry of the Eighteenth Century* (1959).
Coleman, D. C. *The British Paper Industry 1495–1860* (1958).
Crump, W. B. *The Leeds Woollen Industry 1780–1820* (1931).
Clow, A. and N. L. *The Chemical Revolution* (1952).
Haber, L. F. *The Chemical Industry during the Nineteenth Century* (1958).
Hamilton, H. *English Brass and Copper Industries to 1800* (1926).
Heaton, H. *The Yorkshire Woollen and Worsted Industries from the Earliest Times to the Industrial Revolution* (1920).
Lipson, E. *History of the Woollen and Worsted Industries* (1921).
Mathias, P. *The Brewing Industry in England 1700–1830* (1959).

CHAPTER 1. THE STARTING-POINT

Alexander, R. M. 'Economic Growth in England before the Industrial Revolution', *Journal of Economic History* (1969).
Ashton, T. S. *An Eighteenth Century Industrialist* (1939).
Briggs, A. *The Age of Improvement* (1959).
Brown, E. H. Phelps, and Hopkins, Sheila V. 'Builders' Wage-rates, Prices and Population', *Economica* (1959).
Clark, P. and Slack, P. (eds.). *Crisis and Order in English Towns 1500–1700* (1972).
Coleman, D. C. 'Industrial Growth and Industrial Revolutions', *Economica* (1956).
Deane, Phyllis. 'The Long Term Trends in World Economic Growth', *Malayan Economic Review* (1961).
Habakkuk, H. J. 'The Historical Experience in the Basic Conditions of Economic Progress', in *Economic Progress*, ed. L. Dupriez (1955).
Hicks, Sir J. *A Theory of Economic History* (1969).
John, A. H. 'Aspects of English Economic Growth in the First Half of the Eighteenth Century', *Economica*, vol. XXVIII (1961), p. 19.

King, Gregory. *Two Tracts*, ed. George E. Barnett (Baltimore, 1936).

Laslett, P. *The World We Have Lost* (1965).

Lewis, W. A. *Theory of Economic Growth* (1955).

Marshall, Dorothy. *English People in the Eighteenth Century* (1956).

Mathias, P. 'The Social Structure in the Eighteenth Century: a Calculation by Joseph Massie', *Economic History Review* (1957).

Mendels, F. F. 'Proto-industrialization, The First Phase of the Industrialization Process', *Journal of Economic History* (1972).

Nef, J. 'The Progress of Technology and the Growth of Large-scale Industry in Great Britain 1540–1640', reprinted in *Essays in Economic History*, ed. E. M. Carus-Wilson, vol. 1 (1954).

—— 'The Industrial Revolution Reconsidered', *Journal of Economic History* (1943).

Rostow, W. W. *The Stages of Economic Growth* (Rev. ed. 1969).

Smith, Adam. *The Wealth of Nations* (1776).

Supple, B. A. 'Economic History and Economic Underdevelopment', *Canadian Journal of Economics and Political Science* (1961).

Young, Arthur, *Travels in France*, ed. Maxwell (1929).

—— *Political Arithmetic* (1774).

CHAPTER 2. THE DEMOGRAPHIC REVOLUTION

Chambers, J. D. 'Population Change in Nottingham, 1700–1800' in *Studies in the Industrial Revolution* ed. L. Pressnell (1956).

Flinn, M. W. *British Population Growth 1700–1850* (1970).

—— (ed.). *Scottish Population History* (1977).

Glass, D. V. and Eversley, D. E. C. (ed.). *Population in History* (1965).

Habakkuk, H. J. *Population Growth and Economic Development since 1750* (1971).

Helleiner, K. 'The Population of Europe from the Black Death to the Eve of the Vital Revolution' in *Cambridge Economic History of Europe*, IV (1967).

Hollingsworth, T. H. 'The Demography of the British Peerage', supplement to *Population Studies* (1964).

Jones, E. L. and Mingay, G. E. (eds.). *Land, Labour and Population in the Industrial Revolution* (1967).

McKeown, T. C. and Brown, R. G. 'Medical Evidence Related to English Population Changes in the Eighteenth Century', *Population Studies* (1955).

McKeown, T. C., Brown, R. G. and Record, R. G. 'An Interpretation of the Modern Rise of Population in Europe', *Population Studies* (1972).

Shrewsbury, J. F. D. *A History of Bubonic Plague in the British Isles* (1970).

Wrigley, E. A. 'Family Limitation in Pre-industrial England', *Economic History Review* (1966).
—— *Population and History* (1969).

CHAPTER 3. THE AGRICULTURAL REVOLUTION

Chaloner, W. G. 'The Agricultural Activities of John Wilkinson, Ironmaster', *Agricultural History Review* (1957).
Chambers, J. D. 'Enclosure and the Small Landowner', *Economic History Review*, vol. v (1953).
Chambers, J. D. and Mingay, G. E. *The Agricultural Revolution 1750–1880* (1966).
Collins, E. J. T. 'Harvest Technology and Labour Supply in Britain, 1790–1870', *Economic History Review* (1969).
Drummond, J. and Wilbraham, A. *The Englishman's Food* (1957).
Ernle, Lord. *English Farming Past and Present* (1961 ed. with introductions by G. E. Fussell and O. R. Macgregor).
W. G. Hoskins, *The Midland Peasant* (1957).
Hunt, H. G. 'Landownership and Enclosure 1750–1850', *Economic History Review*, vol. xi (1959).
Jones, E. L. (ed.). *Agriculture and Economic Growth in England 1650–1815* (1967).
Kerridge, E. *The Agricultural Revolution* (1967).
Mingay, G. E. *English Landed Society in the Eighteenth Century* (1963).
—— *Enclosure and the Small Farmer in the Age of the Industrial Revolution* (1967).
O'Brien, P. K. 'Agriculture and the Industrial Revolution', *Economic History Review* (1977).
Parker, R. A. C. 'Coke of Norfolk and the Agrarian Revolution', *Economic History Review*, vol. viii (1955).
Payne, F. G. 'The British Plough: Some Stages in its Development', *Agricultural History Review* (1957).
Salaman, R. N. *History and Social Influence of the Potato* (1949).
Slater, Gilbert. *The English Peasantry and the Enclosure of the Common Fields* (1907).
Thirsk, J. *English Peasant Farming* (1957).
Trow-Smith, R. *A History of British Livestock Husbandry 1700–1900* (1959).

CHAPTER 4. THE COMMERCIAL REVOLUTION

Ashton, T. S. *Economic Fluctuations in England 1700–1800* (1959).
Berrill, K. E. 'International Trade and the Rate of Economic Growth', *Economic History Review*, vol. xii (1960).
Clark, G. N. *Guide to English Commercial Statistics 1696–1782* (1938).
Cole, W. A. 'Trends in Eighteenth Century Smuggling', *Economic History Review*, vol. x (1958).

Davis, Ralph. 'English Foreign Trade, 1770–1774', *Economic History Review*, vol. xv (1962).

Heckscher, E. *Mercantilism* (2nd ed. 1955).

Imlah, A. H. *Economic Elements in the Pax Britannica* (1958).

Jenks, L. H. *The Migration of British Capital to 1875* (1927).

Letiche, J. M. *Balance of Payments and Economic Growth* (1959).

Minchinton, W. E. (ed.). *The Growth of English Overseas Trade in the Seventeenth and Eighteenth Centuries* (1969).

Ramsay, G. D. *English Overseas Trade during the Centuries of Emergence* (1957).

Redford, A. *Manchester Merchants and Foreign Trade* (1934).

Schumpeter, E. B. *English Overseas Trade Statistics 1697–1808*, edited with an introduction by T. S. Ashton (1960).

CHAPTER 5. THE TRANSPORT REVOLUTION

Albert, W. *The Turnpike Road System in England, 1663–1840* (1972).

Bagwell, P. S. *The Transport Revolution from 1770* (1974).

Davis, R. 'Earnings of Capital in the English Shipping Industry 1670–1730', *Journal of Economic History* (1957).

Hadfield, Charles. *British Canals* (1959).

Jackman, W. T. *The Development of Transportation in Modern England* (1916).

Simmons, J. *The Railways of Britain. An Historical Introduction* (1961).

Singer. C., Holmyard, E. J., Hall, A. R. and Williams, Trevor. *History of Technology*, vol. iv (1946).

Swan, D. 'The Pace and Progress of Port Investment in England 1660–1830', *Yorkshire Bulletin of Economic and Social Research* (1960).

Webb, S. and B. *English Local Government : the Story of the King's Highway* (1913).

Willan, T. S. *The English Coasting Trade 1600–1750* (1938).

CHAPTER 6. THE COTTON INDUSTRY

Baines, Edward. *History of the Cotton Manufacture in Great Britain* (1835).

Blaug, M. 'Productivity of Capital in the Lancashire Cotton Industry during the Nineteenth Century', *Economic History Review*, vol. xiii (1961).

Bythell, Duncan. *The Handloom Weavers* (1969).

Chapman, S. J. *The Lancashire Cotton Industry* (1904).

Chapman, S. D. *The Cotton Industry in the Industrial Revolution* (1972).

Collier, F. *The Family Economy of the Workers in the Cotton Industry, 1784–1833* (1964).

Daniels, George W. *The Early English Cotton Trade* (1920).

Edwards, M. M. *The British Cotton Trade, 1780–1815* (1967).

Ellison, Thomas. *The Cotton Trade of Great Britain* (1886).

Lee, C. H. *A Cotton Enterprise, 1795–1840: A History of McConnel and Kennedy, Fine Cotton Spinners* (1972).

Rodgers, H. B. 'The Lancashire Cotton Industry in 1840', *Transactions of the Institute of British Geographers* (1960).

Smelser, N. J. *Social Change in the Industrial Revolution 1770–1840* (1959).

Taylor, A. J. 'Concentration and Specialization in the Lancashire Cotton Industry', *Economic History Review* (1949).

Wadsworth, Alfred P. and Mann, Julia de Lacy. *The Cotton Trade and Industrial Lancashire 1600–1780* (1931).

CHAPTER 7. THE IRON INDUSTRY

Ashton, T. S. *Iron and Steel in the Industrial Revolution* (1924).

Campbell, R. H. *The Carron Company* (1961).

Flinn, M. W. 'Abraham Darby and the Coke Smelting Process', *Economica* (1959).

—— *Men of Iron: the Crowleys in the Early Iron Industry* (1962).

Hammersley, G. 'The Charcoal Industry and its Fuel', *Economic History Review* (1973).

Hyde, C. K. *Technological Change in the British Iron Industry 1700–1870* (1977).

Raistrick, A. *A Dynasty of Iron Founders* (1951).

Riden, P. 'The Output of the British Iron Industry before 1870', *Economic History Review* (1977).

Roepke, H. G. 'Movements of the British Iron and Steel Industry, 1720–1951', *Illinois Studies in the Social Sciences* (1956).

Schubert, H. R. *History of the British Iron and Steel Industry from c. 450 B.C. to A.D. 1775* (1957).

Scrivenor, H. *History of the Iron Trade* (1854).

CHAPTER 8. THE SOURCES OF INNOVATION

Bernal, J. D. *Science in History* (1954).

Caird, J. *English Agriculture* (1851).

Chaloner, T. E. *People and Industries* (1963).

Coleman, D. C. 'Technology and Economic History 1500–1750', *Economic History Review*, vol. XI (1959).

Derry, T. K. and T. I. Williams. *A Short History of Technology* (1960).

Dickinson, H. W. and Jenkins, Rhys. *James Watt and the Steam Engine* (1927).

Habakkuk, H. J. *American and British Technology in the Nineteenth Century* (1964).

Hall, A. R. *The Scientific Revolution 1500–1800* (1954).

Hills, R. L. *Power in the Industrial Revolution* (1970).

Musson, A. E. (ed.). *Science, Technology and Economic Growth in the Industrial Revolution* (1972).

—— and Robinson, E. *Science and Technology in the Industrial Revolution* (1969).

Pollard, S. *The Genesis of Modern Management. A Study of the Industrial Revolution in Great Britain* (1965).

Singer, C., Holmyard, E. J., Hall, A. R. and Williams, Trevor. *History of Technology*, vols. III and IV (1946).

Tarn, J. 'Fuel Saving in the Process Industries during the Industrial Revolution: a Study in Technological Diffusion', *Business History* (1973).

Usher, A. P. *A History of Mechanical Inventions* (1929).

von Tunzelmann, G. N. *Steampower and British Industrialization to 1860* (1978).

Wilson, Charles, and Reader, William. *Men and Machines* (1958).

Wrigley, E. A. 'The Supply of Raw Materials in the Industrial Revolution', *Economic History Review*, vol. XV (1962).

CHAPTER 9. THE ROLE OF LABOUR

Ashton, T. S. 'The Coal Miners of the 18th Century', *Economic History*, vol. I (1928).

Blaug, M. 'The Myth of the Old Poor Law and the Making of the New', *Journal of Economic History* (1963).

—— 'The Poor Law Report Re-examined', *Journal of Economic History* (1964).

Briggs, A. and Saville, J. (eds.). *Essays in Labour History* (1967).

Chambers, J. D. 'Enclosure and Labour Supply in the Industrial Revolution', *Economic History Review*, vol. XI (1958).

Coats, A. W. 'Changing Attitudes to Labour in the Mid-Eighteenth Century', *Economic History Review*, vol. XI (1958).

Cole, G. D. H. *A Short History of the British Working Class Movement 1789–1947* (1948).

Collier, F. 'Workers in a Lancashire Factory at the Beginning of the Nineteenth Century', *Manchester School of Social and Economic Studies* (1936).

Fitton, R. I. and Wadsworth, A. P. *The Strutts and the Arkwrights 1758–1830* (1958).

Gilboy, Elizabeth. *Wages in Eighteenth Century England* (1934).

Jones, E. L. 'The Agricultural Labour Market in England 1793–1872', *Economic History Review*, vol. XVII (1964).

Pinchbeck, I. *Women Workers in the Industrial Revolution 1750–1850* (1930).

Pollard, S. 'Factory Discipline in the Industrial Revolution', *Economic History Review*, vol. XVI (1963).

—— 'Labour in Great Britain', *Cambridge Economic History of Europe*, vol. VII, ed. P. Mathias and M. M. Postan (1978).

Redford, A. *Labour Migration in England, 1800–50* (1926).

Rudé, G. *English Hunger and Industrial Disorders: A Study of Social Conflict in the First Decade of George III's Reign* (1973).

Thompson, Edward. *The Making of the English Working Class* (rev. ed. 1968).

Thompson, E. P. 'The Moral Economy of the English Crowd', *Past and Present* (1971).

Webb, S. and B. *History of Trade Unionism* (1922).

CHAPTER 10. THE ROLE OF CAPITAL

Campbell, R. H. 'The Financing of the Carron Company', *Business History* (1958).

Chapman, S. D. 'Fixed Capital Formation in the British Cotton Industry, 1770–1815', *Economic History Review* (1970).

Crouzet, F. (ed.). *Capital Formation in the Industrial Revolution* (1972).

Deane, Phyllis. 'Capital Formation in Britain before the Railway Age', *Economic Development and Cultural Change* (1961).

Dubois, A. B. *The English Business Company after the Bubble Act* (1938).

Evans, G. H. *British Corporation Finance 1775–1850* (1936).

Feinstein, C. H. 'Capital Formation in Great Britain', *Cambridge Economic History of Europe*, vol. VII, ed. P. Mathias and M. M. Postan (1978).

Felix, D. 'Profit Inflation and Industrial Growth: the Historic Record and Contemporary Analogies', *Quarterly Journal of Economics* (1956).

Hamilton, E. J. 'Prices and Progress', *Journal of Economic History* (1952).

Hoselitz, B. F. 'Entrepreneurship and Capital Formation in France and Britain since 1700', in National Bureau of Economic Research, *Capital Formation and Economic Growth* (1955).

Hunt, B. C. *The Development of the Business Corporation in England, 1800–1867* (1936).

Jenks, L. H. *Migration of British Capital to 1875* (1927).

Mathias, P. 'Capital, Credit and Enterprise in the Industrial Revolution', *Journal of European Economic History* (1973).

Pollard, S. 'Investment, Consumption and the Industrial Revolution', *Economic History Review*, vol. XI (1958).

—— 'Capital Accounting in the Industrial Revolution', *Yorkshire Bulletin of Social and Economic Research* (1963).

—— 'The Factory Village in the Industrial Revolution', *English Historical Review*, vol. LXXIX (1964).

Postan, M. 'The Accumulation of Capital', *Economic History Review*, vol. VI (1935).

Shapiro, S. *Capital and the Cotton Industry in the Industrial Revolution* (1968).

Ward, J. R. *The Finance of Canal Building in Eighteenth Century England* (1974).

CHAPTER 11. THE ROLE OF THE BANKS

Clapham, J. H. *The Bank of England*, 2 vols. (1944).

Cramp, A. B. *Opinion on the Bank Rate 1822–60* (1902).

Dickson, P. G. M. *The Financial Revolution. A Study in the Development of Public Credit, 1688–1756* (1967).

Eagly, R. V. and Smith, V. K. 'Domestic and International Integration of the London Money Market, 1731–1789', *Journal of Economic History* (1976).

Feaveryear, A. E. *The Pound Sterling* (1931).

Fetter, F. W. *Development of British Monetary Orthodoxy* (1965).

Gregory, T. E. *The Westminster Bank* (1936).

Hawtrey, R. G. *A Century of Bank Rate* (1938).

Joslin, D. M. 'London Bankers in Wartime 1739–84', in *Studies in the Industrial Revolution*, ed. L. S. Pressnell (1956).

Morgan, E. V. *The Theory and Practice of Central Banking* (1943).

Pressnell, L. S. *Country Banking in the Industrial Revolution* (1956).

Sayers, R. S. *Lloyds Bank in the History of English Banking* (1957).

CHAPTER 12. THE ADOPTION OF FREE TRADE

Barnes, D. G. *The History of the Corn Laws* (1934).

Brady, Alexander. *William Huskisson and Liberal Reform* (1928).

Briggs, Asa. *The Age of Improvement* (1959).

Brown, Lucy. *The Board of Trade and the Free Trade Movement, 1830–42* (1958).

Clapham, J. H. 'The Last Years of the Navigation Acts', *English Historical Review*, vol. xxv (1910).

Clark, G. Kitson. *The Making of Victorian England* (1962).

Cole, G. D. H. *Chartist Portraits* (1965 edition with an introduction by Asa Briggs).

Fairlie, S. 'The Corn Laws and British Wheat Production, 1829–76', *Economic History Review* (1969).

Fay, C. R. *The Corn Laws and Social England* (1932).

Imlah, A. H. *Economic Elements in the Pax Britannica* (1958).

McCord, N. *The Anti Corn League 1838–1846* (1958).

Thompson, Edward. *The Making of the English Working Class* (1963).

Woodham-Smith, C. *The Great Hunger* (1962).

CHAPTER 13. THE ROLE OF GOVERNMENT
(See also references listed as relating to chapter 12 above)

Blaug, M. 'The Myth of the Old Poor Law and the Making of the New', *Journal of Economic History* (1963).

—— 'The Poor Law Report Re-examined', *Journal of Economic History* (1964).

Brebner, J. Bartlett. 'Laissez-faire and State Intervention in Nineteenth Century Britain', reprinted in *Essays in Economic History*, ed. E. Carus-Wilson, vol. III (1962).

Cooney, E. W. 'Public Opinion and Government Policy in Nineteenth-century British Economic History: A Review and a Study of the Building Industry', *Yorkshire Bulletin of Economic and Social Research* (1969).

Hart, J. 'Nineteenth-century Social Reform: A Tory Interpretation of History', *Past and Present* (1965).

MacDonagh, O. 'The Nineteenth Century Revolution in Government: a Reappraisal', *Historical Journal* (1958).

—— *A Pattern of Government Growth 1800–60* (1961).

Marshall, Dorothy. 'The Old Poor Law 1662–1795', reprinted in *Essays in Economic History*, ed. E. M. Carus-Wilson, vol. I (1954).

Marshall, J. D. *The Old Poor Law 1795–1834* (1968).

Parris, H. *Government and the Railways in Nineteenth Century Britain* (1965).

Prouty, R. *The Transformation of the Board of Trade 1830–1855* (1957).

Roberts, D. *Victorian Origins of the British Welfare State* (1960).

Rose, R. B. 'Eighteenth Century Price Riots and Public Policy in England', *International Review of Social History* (1961).

Taylor, A. J. *Laissez-faire and State Intervention in Nineteenth-century Britain* (1972).

Veverka, J. 'Growth of Government Expenditure in the United Kingdom since 1790', *Scottish Journal of Political Economy* (1963).

CHAPTER 14. ECONOMIC GROWTH AND ECONOMIC CYCLES

Ashton, T. S. *Economic Fluctuations in England* (1959).

Beveridge, Sir William. 'Wheat Prices and Rainfall in Western Europe', *Journal of the Royal Statistical Society* (1922).

—— 'The Trade Cycle in Britain before 1850', *Oxford Economic Papers* (1940).

Cairncross, A. K. and Weber, B. 'Fluctuations in Building in Great Britain 1785–1849', *Economic History Review* (1956).

Gayer, A. D., Rostow, W. W. and Schwartz, A. J. *The Growth and Fluctuation of the British Economy 1790–1850*, 2 vols. (1953).

Gould, J. D. 'Agricultural Fluctuations and the English Economy in the Eighteenth Century', *Journal of Economic History*, vol. XXII.

Kondratieff, N. D. 'The Long Waves in Economic Life', *Review of Economic Statistics* (1935).

Lewis, J. P. *Building Cycles and Britain's Growth* (1965).

Matthews, R. C. O. *A Study in Trade-Cycle History* (1954).

Rostow, W. W. *British Economy of the Nineteenth Century* (1948).

Schumpeter, J. *Business Cycles*, vol. I (1939).

Silberling, N. J. 'British Prices and Business Cycles 1779–1850', *Review of Economic Statistics* (1923).

Smart, W. *Economic Annals of the Nineteenth Century 1801–30*, 2 vols. (1910–17).

Thorp, W. L. and Mitchell, W. C. *Business Annals* (1926).

CHAPTER 15. STANDARDS OF LIVING

Briggs, A. *The Age of Improvement* (1959).

Brown, E. H. Phelps and Hopkins, S. V. 'Seven Centuries of the Price of Consumables, Compared with Builders' Wage Rates', *Economica*, vol. XXIII (1956).

Engels, F. *The Condition of the Working Class in England* (1844), translated and edited by W. O. Henderson and W. H. Chaloner (1958).

Flinn, M. 'Trends in Real Wages 1750–1850', *Economic History Review* (1974).

George, M. D. *London Life in the Eighteenth Century* (1930).

Hammond, J. L. and B. *The Rise of Modern Industry* (1925).

—— *The Village Labourer, 1760–1832* (1911).

—— *The Town Labourer, 1760–1832* (1920).

—— *The Skilled Labourer, 1760–1832* (1919).

Hartwell, R. M. *The Industrial Revolution and Economic Growth* (1971).

Hobsbawm, E. J. 'The Standard of Living in the Industrial Revolution', *Economic History Review* (1963).

Institute of Economic Affairs, *The Long Debate on Poverty* (2nd ed. 1974).

Lambert, Royston. *Sir John Simon 1816–1904 and English Social Administration* (1963).

Lewis, R. A. *Edwin Chadwick and the Public Health Movement 1832–1854* (1952).

Pollard, S. 'Investment, Consumption and the Industrial Revolution', *Economic History Review*, vol. XI (1958).

Taylor, A. J. 'Progress and Poverty in Britain 1780–1850: A Reappraisal,' *History* (1960).

—— (ed.). *The Standard of Living in the Industrial Revolution* (1972).

Thompson, E. *The Making of the English Working Class* (1963).

Ward, J. T. *The Factory Movement 1830–1855* (1962).

Williams, J. E. 'The British Standard of Living 1750–1850', *Economic History Review* (1966).

Wood, G. 'The Course of Average Wages between 1790 and 1860', *Economic Journal* (1899).

Woodruff, W. 'Capitalism and the Historian: a Contribution to the Discussion on the Industrial Revolution in England', *Journal of Economic History*, vol. XVI (1956).

CHAPTER 16. THE ACHIEVEMENT

Burn, W. L. *The Age of Equipoise* (1964).

Cardwell, D. S. L. *The Organization of Science in England* (1957).

Chambers, J. D. *The Workshop of the World* (1961).

Clark, G. Kitson. *The Making of Victorian England* (1962).

Erickson, Charlotte. *British Industrialists; Steel and Hosiery 1850–1950* (1959).

Ferguson, T. 'Public Health in the Nineteenth Century', *Population Studies* (1964).

Habakkuk, H. J. *American and British Technology in the Nineteenth Century* (1962).

Houghton, W. E. *The Victorian Frame of Mind 1830–1870* (1957).

Jefferys, James B. *Retail Trading in Britain 1850–1950* (1954).

Porter, G. R. *The Progress of the Nation* (1847 ed.).

Sanderson, M. 'Literacy and Social Mobility in the Industrial Revolution in England', *Past and Present* (1972).

Schofield, R. S. 'Dimensions of Illiteracy, 1750–1850', *Explorations in Entrepreneurial History* (1973).

Stone, L. 'Literacy and Education in England, 1640–1900', *Past and Present* (1969).

Thompson, F. M. L. *English Landed Society in the Nineteenth Century* (1963).

West, E. G. *Education and the Industrial Revolution* (1975).

Woolf, Michael. 'Victorian Study: an Interdisciplinary Essay', *Victorian Studies* (1964).

SUBJECT INDEX

INDEX OF AUTHORS CITED